BIG BROTHER

BIG BROTHER

THE DEREK FERGUSON STORY

DEREK FERGUSON WITH BILL LECKIE

MAINSTREAM
PUBLISHING

EDINBURGH AND LONDON

First published in Great Britain in 2006 by
MAINSTREAM PUBLISHING COMPANY (EDINBURGH) LTD
7 Albany Street
Edinburgh EH1 3UG

ISBN 1 84596 162 5

A catalogue record for this book is available from the British Library

Typeset in Baskerville and Gill Sans

Printed and bound in Great Britain by
William Clowes Ltd, Beccles, Suffolk

For the brightest star in Heaven

CONTENTS

ONE

LIVE FAST, DIE YOUNG

A life of two halves. That pretty much sums it up.

From boyhood until about 26, zooming along without a care in the world. Never stopping to think about what you did or who it had an impact on. Then from 27 to now, plotting every step you make like it's all one big minefield. Feeling like you've stepped back and are watching everyone else being the way you used to be.

The year in between?

A half-time interval I wouldn't wish on my worst enemy.

In football, the break ends with a rap on the door from the ref or a buzzer sounding in the corridor. For me, the signal was finding myself standing in the middle of a road in Sunderland at dead of night, realising my head was so screwed up I'd nearly wrecked half a dozen lives. The fact that my own was one of them was the least of the problem.

Looking back, I realise how embarrassing it felt to have walked out of that car without a scratch when I was the only one who deserved to be hurt. Or at least, that's where my head was then. Because in August 1993, I was officially away with the fairies.

My wife Carol and I had been thrilled to bits when little Lauren was born six months earlier. But at just seven weeks, we'd lost her. It was a heart defect, spotted too late for the doctors to be able to save her.

The feelings that the death of a child leave you with are indescribable. There's terrible sadness, despair, hopelessness. And then comes the guilt. Could we have spotted something? Was there more we could have done? You never stop questioning yourself, and you never get over it, not even when you've been blessed with three happy, healthy boys since.

Back then, though, it was destroying us. I was at Hearts and things were OK on the pitch, but in all honesty all I used football for was an escape from reality. Every day I'd go to training and focus on the job, push all the other stuff to the back of my mind for a couple of hours. I was too selfish to even think that poor Carol had nowhere to go, had nothing to occupy her. She must have struggled so much while I was looking after myself.

I would just disappear. I wouldn't even ask her. Yet she was suffering more than me, and she'd have had every right to leave me. In the end, the only clean break we made was to get away from the house, the town, the country where all the heartache had happened. Terry Butcher had taken over as Sunderland manager, and when he came in for me in the summer, I jumped at the chance.

They put Carol and me up at the Royal County Hotel in Durham along with other new signings Phil Gray, Andy Melville and Ian Rogerson. Carol thought she was pregnant again, and our emotions were constantly going round like a tumble dryer. So maybe it was wanting to get back to her side that night that caused the crash. Or maybe it was – or more likely *I* was – just an accident waiting to happen.

Whatever the reasons, the facts are all still frighteningly clear in my mind.

We'd played Middlesbrough in a pre-season game, the bus dropped us back at Roker Park, and I was driving the four of us to the hotel. Bottom line? I hammered it from the minute we left the car park, and when you're tired and confused and don't know the roads, well, it's all a recipe for disaster. When I look back, the other boys must have been terrified at how fast I was going. In their shoes, I would have been.

So we're bombing along the seafront road and I cut out at speed to overtake somebody – and next thing I'm flying round a bend and being confronted with this massive concrete roundabout. Which I'm about to go round the wrong way.

Three options now:

Hit the roundabout.

Hit a lamp post.

Hit an oncoming Ford that's just stopped on the other side of the roundabout.

I've slammed the brakes on but too late to avoid hitting the other car. My Astra's gone up and come back down sideways on the pavement. For a second that feels like eternity, there's this eerie silence. Then I look round and realise Ian's screaming in agony and holding his shoulder. I look to my left and Phil's got blood pouring from a cut eye. I look in the rear-view and Andy's just sitting there, staring in shock. I kick the door open, clamber free and get Andy out first, then Ian and Phil. After that, I run across to the other car to see if they're OK. They scream abuse at me, which is totally fair, but I still give them a few F-words back.

Then I stagger back to our car, just in time to see Andy faint. That's when it hit me right between the eyes.

My stupidity could have ruined three careers – or far, far worse, people could have died. Other parents could have been grieving

11

for their children the way Carol and I still were for Lauren. The fallout didn't bear thinking about.

The cops turned up, I was breathalysed – I hadn't touched a drop – and taken to the station until big Terry came and got me. It was a nightmare. The police said I'd been a hell of a lucky boy, because the way we hit the other car the engine should have come in through the footwell and crushed my legs from the knees down. But the scary thing is that I didn't give a damn if something happened to me.

That's how much of a mess I was in.

After Lauren died, I thought nothing else could hurt me, yet I was daring life to come ahead and try. I believed I could have walked in front of a car and felt no pain. Yet all the while it was whirling round in my head: how did her little heart get damaged? Was it because I drank? Had my lifestyle poisoned the baby I adored? I even blamed the piles of anti-inflammatory tablets you take to get through games when you're not fully fit.

We were both constantly looking for answers when we didn't even understand the question. We were desperate for something that would make sense of it all. In the end, we knew we were simply just feeling sorry for ourselves.

You think no one else in the world is suffering the way you are, but if you could look in from the outside, you'd realise you're only a speck. So many people are worse off, but not realising that sends you into a cocoon and stops you giving all you have to anything that matters.

I went from being this guy who was full of beans, up for everything, to someone who didn't enjoy life. Even on the pitch, my one escape, that little uncoachable bit extra that I'd built my career on wasn't there. Terry definitely didn't get the player he thought he'd signed. Neither did the first couple of managers I played under when I went back home two years later.

The black cloud lifted, of course. Darren being born healthy was the first silver lining, then Ross, then Lewis. We settled in a lovely family home in God's country – that's Hamilton, to the uninitiated – and moved on. My football career moved downwards in terms of glamour and wages, but the thrill never wavered, not even when injuries hit.

Today, I'm a contented man. But not the same man I was before half-time.

And here's something bizarre – when I was piecing all this together, there was a moment when I suddenly wasn't picturing myself in a flash Astra but an old green Hillman Hunter. It too was heading for a roundabout. Its driver was also going too fast. Except this wasn't in Sunderland but the outskirts of Glasgow.

I was back in my primary school days, reliving something that hadn't crossed my mind in many years.

It was a Thursday night, and after Dad finished work he came to pick me and Mum up from Granny Fergie's in Barlanark and run us home to Hamilton. Mum was pregnant with Barry, and we were all sitting in the front, no seat belts on. We were heading for the big spaghetti junction at Baillieston to go onto the motorway and I remember they were arguing because Mum was unhappy at the speed he was doing.

He really was hammering it, too, and I was pretty scared. Mum was shouting at him to slow down; he was shouting back for her to give him peace. Next thing, he came round a bend and smashed into the side of this other car; as he did, our front axle ripped away and we veered off into the side of the road. When we stopped, there was that same weird stillness I'd experience again as a messed-up adult.

Then I realised the windscreen had come in and my face was cut. Mum was clearly in pain. As for Dad, it had been his fault without doubt, but he went leaping out and ran across to try and pull the other guy out of *his* motor. He's a calm guy most of the time, Dad, yet the roofers he worked with used to call him Schizo because he could lose it if he thought someone was taking advantage of him. But that night? I think it was probably part guilt, part panic.

Next thing, the ambulances were rolling up, and Mum and I were whipped to hospital. They told me I'd be scarred for life, but the worse news was that Mum might lose the baby. It was touch and go for a while before she got the all-clear.

But you know the strange thing? My dad changed that night.

On Fridays, when he got paid, he always used to go for a beer. After the crash, that all stopped. That anger inside him didn't come out any more. His whole temperament changed; he was so much more mellow. Something went missing from his whole make-up.

Twenty-seven years on, the only obvious reminder I have of that brush with fate is a little nick on my left cheek. It's only the mental scars that haven't healed.

That night in Sunderland, fate saved me from being crippled. Just as it stopped my dad coming in at the slightly different angle that could have wiped out our whole family and not only robbed my brother of life but also robbed Rangers and Scotland of a future captain.

Maybe one day he'll look back and realise his whole world changed before he even drew breath.

TWO

WEE BROTHER

Tuesday, 6 December 2005

There's a little boy on the screen, smile beaming, excitement oozing from every pore.

He's 14, and he's just won a big game for his boys' club team, Mill United.

I'm so proud of him I could burst.

Of course, that boy's not who the rest of the viewing public are watching. It's not even who the rest of the people in the room are watching.

They see the 27-year-old Barry Ferguson, captain of Rangers and Scotland, as he savours the draw with Inter Milan that's just put his club into the knockout stages of the Champions League. I see my wee brother.

I've shared his life with him as he's grown from a skinny wee kid to a strong, confident man. A father. A hero. A millionaire. But at times like these, he's still the kid. Football still makes him feel the same as it did when he was playing for little plastic medals, not £40,000 bonuses and worldwide fame.

He still carries himself exactly the same way as he did when he first stood and kicked a ball. Back straight, head up, one arm out for balance as he plays the pass. Some invisible force-field around him, keeping opponents at bay. He never used to rush around the pitch with all the other ten year olds, chasing the ball this way and that. He knew where to be. He knew where the ball was going next, and once he got it, no one could get it off him. He'd watch it coming, take a touch, open himself up and play it out the other side. Always kept the game moving, was always in control.

Barry's always needed good players around him to make him tick, always been at his best when guys are on the same wavelength as he is, have the same standards as he's set himself. Standards I tried so hard to drum into him from childhood that he ended up hating my guts.

Standards that still make him better than most.

Where he is now is where I always believed he could be. Yet no matter how many times I see him lead Rangers out of the tunnel with the Champions League music booming, it never gets any less surreal.

The stadium's rocking with 50,000 inside, it's the biggest game in Britain that night. And he's up there tossing a coin. My wee brother. The wee man from Mill United. I'm chuffed for him, I'm proud of him – and always, always unbelievably nervous for him.

I always watch him as my brother, not just another player. If I'm there in the flesh, I won't follow the game, I'll follow Barry. Where he is in relation to the ball, making sure his positioning's just right. More often than not, I needn't worry. He has that radar. That's why it frustrates me when I see that arm go out for balance and he makes the shape for the pass he wants to play, but no one wants it. In the run-up to that game with Inter, it had been happening a lot, and that's so frustrating for a playmaker, when the team's doing badly and some guys decide the best way out is to hide. Sure, they *look* as if they're interested, because their legs are moving. But in truth they can be tucking themselves into places where you couldn't pick them out with a Smart Bomb.

And what happens then? The playmaker, the guy with nowhere to hide, gets caught on the ball and gets pelters from the crowd.

It looks so easy from the stands, but out there on the pitch with all the noise, all the pressure? That's when the real operators come out to play. They try and get a mental picture of the pass before the ball even comes, because good players always have their head up to see where everyone is, to fix that picture in their minds.

Ray Wilkins had the best first touch of anyone I ever played with, but Barry's isn't too far behind. He sees the big picture all the time, the way he did as a kid, still gets the ball out of his feet and pops it off before the rest see it coming.

He's always one step ahead, our Barry.

That's where I wanted to be at Rangers, at Hearts, at Sunderland and right through another eight clubs to my days with Raith. Right up until the end, I still had the same faith in my ability to make things happen with a ball. Only the body ever let me down.

At Rangers, it was my shoulders. At Falkirk and Dunfermline, the right knee. At Hamilton, the left knee went and so did my guts.

Then, a couple of weeks before Barry's date with the Italians and destiny, I went in for what I thought would be a routine clean-up on my left knee and came out to hear the news that I might never play again. The news hit me harder than Kenny Brannigan in a 50–50. And as you'll find out later, the shockwaves from the Big Man clattering you can last a long time.

* * *

So there's our Barry tonight, heading for the Champions League draw with the Real Madrids and Barcas, the Chelseas and Man Uniteds. While here am I, sitting on the couch, crutches propped up next to me. A 38 and a half year old with his left knee in bits and his career not far behind.

My wee brother's on the thick end of £30,000 a week at Ibrox. My last playing wage was £150 a week from Second Division part-timers Raith Rovers.

A ton and a half? Barry would drop that getting out of his Bentley.

I don't think he understands why I put myself through it for so long, the 120-mile round trip to train twice a week on windswept pitches, the slogs to Peterhead and Gretna, all the young gunslingers wanting to have a pop at the old warhorse. But hopefully he will one day. Hopefully one day, even though he won't need the money, he'll even fancy playing down the divisions for the sheer love of it. So why did I do it for so long? Mostly because playing football's all I ever wanted to do, and even if things haven't worked out the way I planned them back at the start, I'm still playing it and being paid for the privilege.

But then there's the other reason. The one so many other pros reading this will know only too well and have said all too often.

I keep going because I don't know anything else.

At Rangers, I used to go and pick up Hugh Burns for training. He was a lazy git in the mornings, and you'd hear his mum shouting to him to get up or he'd be late for his work. That always made me laugh. Work? It's not work. I've never done a day's work in my life. Yes, I've run and sweated and lifted weights, I've ploughed through tackles that have gashed my skin open; I've been under the knife more than a Hollywood wife scared stiff of age and gravity.

But it's not work. It's football. It's the greatest life any man can have. You only have to look at my wee brother's face on that screen to know that.

He's not beaming because he's just remembered what the cash incentive was. He's not excited because his name's going to be in all the papers next morning. He's simply thrilled to bits because all his dreams have just come true.

The way he is up on that screen is the way football should make you feel. It's how the punters felt as they left Ibrox that night, how Celtic fans feel when their team wins, how it feels at Stark's Park when Raith win, at Stenhousemuir and Forfar and everywhere that the game is played when results go your way.

It makes me feel great to know I've helped give a lot of people that level of enjoyment over the years, because nothing in life makes me happier than seeing those around me happy. And yet, I've known a lot of players who just don't get that, who don't see their role the same as I do. Too many think it's just about themselves and the 'me, me, me' attitude has done football no favours.

We watched the Inter game round at the outlaws' place: me, Carol's dad Danny and my boys, eleven-year-old Darren, nine-year-old Ross and Lewis, who's six. Danny's a Celtic fanatic, so he tries to kid on he doesn't care when Peter Lovenkrands scores the equaliser and the other four of us are jumping up and down like headcases.

The boys love their uncle Barry. They love watching him play, and they love going to his house. Then they ask how come if I played for Rangers we don't have a big mansion with a swimming pool and a cinema room. I tell them that when I was at Ibrox there wasn't much money going about, which is true.

But it's hard for them to get their heads round that when they see what Barry has – and to be honest, it was a hard enough job just getting them to believe I really *did* play for Rangers in the first place. Honestly, I had to get the old videos out, blow the dust off and press Play on the evidence before they believed me.

Not long ago, Ross had some English homework and had to make up a sentence with the word 'international' in it. He was toiling, so Carol said: 'Why not make it something like: "My dad played international football for Scotland"?'

So the wee man says: 'Yeah, but only twice.'

I laughed at that, but Carol was annoyed that it didn't seem to mean much. Maybe they're too used to seeing Uncle Barry being a fixture for his country.

Every time they've seen me play, they've been right in there criticising me on the way home, which I think is brilliant. The last time they were there, when Raith played Thistle, I picked the ball up and ran across the box but passed instead of shooting. Back in the car, the three of them gave me pelters for not having a dig, and they had me bang to rights. Always was my biggest fault.

I think it's been great for the boys to have their dad take them in behind the scenes at football grounds, just as I did with Barry. If anything, it's maybe even better for them, because they're seeing football in the raw.

From when Barry was very young, I really wanted him to be a star and I'm so thrilled that he's made it up there. For my wee brother to be captain of Rangers and Scotland is a dream come true. But as I've got older and produced kids of my own, my attitude has changed. Yes, I always want them to play football, but if they don't make it as full-time pros, I hope they have a crack at the part-time game or the juniors, or just even enjoy themselves with a Sunday-morning amateur team.

See, there are so many fantastic things about being a full-time professional footballer. But what's not in the brochure is the fact that you can actually be looked after *too* well. The club tell you where to be, when to be there and what to wear. They look after your passport, give you money when you're on trips, make your meals for you, book your rooms for you, even lay out your underpants every morning.

It's only once you step out into the real world that you realise how hopeless you are at so many things 99 per cent of people take for granted.

When I set about writing this, the publishers sent me a questionnaire to find out a few personal details, a little bit about my background and my aims for the book. First thing I did? Hand it to Carol.

I'll bet you any money that almost every full-time footballer would do exactly the same with their own wife.

God alone knows how I'd have coped with all the agent stuff and the property portfolios and the offshore investment funds that are so much a part of Barry's life. He's right into it all, knows every penny that comes in and where it all goes. Me? If I've enough left over from paying the bills to have a holiday once a year, I'm sorted.

John Greig signed me as a 16 year old at Rangers on £150 a week, then Jock Wallace hiked it up to £300 and Graeme Souness to £700. I don't remember what the bonuses were for league games, because I've always believed in winning first and thinking about the money later. Never once in my career did I ever see the team sheet on the wall without my name on it and think: 'Shit, that's X hundreds of pounds I'm down.'

My first and only reaction has always been: *'Shit, I'm not playing.'*

I do remember we were on about £7,000 a man to win cup finals at Rangers, but the advice I'd been given was to lump any extra I had into my pension and give myself a wage when I finished up. By 29, I wasn't earning enough to keep paying into the fund, but even then they said when it matured at 35 it should do me a decent turn.

And a decent turn's all I ever wanted. Money was never my driving force and the fortunes to be made in the game today don't faze me, not even when I see guys I don't particularly rate turning themselves into very wealthy young men by their mid-20s.

Because when I was on £300 at Rangers as a 19 year old, there must have been former players raging that the most the club ever paid them was £50. And they, in turn, will have had even older guys bitter that they never earned above the maximum wage of £20, and so on and so on.

Every generation of footballers misses out on the relative wealth that the next enjoys. Sign a four-year deal with Rangers today and look after your dosh and it's pretty nailed-on you'll be sorted for life, yet I'm pretty sure that one day Barry will look at some kid running round the midfield for Rangers and wonder how the hell he managed to negotiate himself £200,000 a week.

What makes me laugh is when people reckon that because someone of my generation played for Rangers and had a decent move down south, they're also sorted for life – and that even if you've blown your fortune, having a multimillionaire for a wee brother helps keep the wolf from the door.

Hope the reality doesn't disappoint them too much.

As a teenager, I had this idea that I'd stay at Rangers into my 30s then have a year or two in my home town with the Accies before retiring and moving smoothly into coaching and management. Mortgage? Long gone.

Oh, and I'd still be single.

As it went, I did pretty well at Ibrox, won a couple of league titles and a couple of cups, then fell out with the manager, moved on – and kept moving on from then until now. Picked up injuries. Got sidetracked by personal problems. Then 35 came,

I went to cash in the pension and found that the fund I thought had £400,000 in it was only worth half that much.

Half of *that* got invested in a shop Carol and I hoped would provide us with a regular income – nothing mega, maybe £400 a week – on top of whatever I was still getting from football. But guess what? Business hasn't been great, and we've spent a lot of time wondering if the long-term lease we took on the property is going to hang around our necks like a ten-ton medallion.

The monthly sum I take from the pension's enough to run our two small cars, and there really isn't enough left over from what the two of us bring in to fritter anything away. We have a lovely house, and the kids want for nothing, but there are times when we're toiling, no doubt about that.

Mortgage? Still needs to be paid every month, I'm afraid.

It bugs me, course it does, but no more than it bugs people in every walk of life who have to juggle the bills. See, this isn't a hard-luck story. It's simply the story of a guy who played football at a time when there weren't millions to be made, when agents weren't the norm and when if someone advised you to put your cash into something solid, you assumed they meant a nice big oak wardrobe.

My wee brother, on the other hand, became a star right slap-bang in the middle of the era of player power. He gets free stuff thrown at him. He's got more sponsorship deals than the average Formula 1 car. He's had media training. He owns houses and flats around the world. His is a different football world from the one I was brought up in. In fact, his is a different world, full stop. He's never had to want for anything, never had to worry about money, can go anywhere he likes and do anything he likes.

And you know what? I don't envy him one little bit.

Money's nice. But would all the money in the world have bought Carol and I back the most precious thing we ever had and lost? Not a chance.

Playing football for me has always been about doing the thing I love best and was best at. Being paid was a bonus – and that's no lie. But after Lauren died, it all became less about what I could make than ever before.

Yes, as I head for 40 I'm left nursing the frustration of ambitions unfulfilled. But how out of touch with reality would I be if I sat here writing about how unfair the game had been to me? When my dad's still clambering over roofs in his late 50s, when my mates would have handed over every penny they have in return for just one afternoon running out in front of a full house at Ibrox or Parkhead or Hampden?

I'm one of the lucky few. Millions dream of becoming a professional footballer but I actually had that dream come true. I heard my teachers tell me it would never happen, that I should get my exams and get a real job. I ignored Mr Dull and worked harder than ever to make it on my own terms.

I got to sign for a senior club – and not just any club, but the club I supported – and went on to make the first team.

The fact that I'm not still with that club and didn't achieve everything I wanted to with them doesn't matter. Neither does the fact that at the age of 38 I found myself travelling on a battered minibus every Tuesday and Thursday night to train with Second Division part-timers Raith Rovers.

A lot of guys I know would rather quit than put themselves through the slog of the lower leagues. For them, that would be a comedown. For me, it was simply a way to keep playing football. That's all I ever wanted to do with my life, and it's all I know. If that sounds sad, it's not meant to.

I'd feel a lot sadder if all I knew in life was a job I never wanted to do in the first place.

THREE

BRUFEN SANDWICHES

Arthur Numan sees me hobbling into the Scottish Television studios on crutches and flashes me a look that says: *I told you so.*

A few weeks earlier, we'd been together on Rangers TV and I'd asked him about why he packed the game in so young.

What was he? Thirty-three? Still cruising up and down the left flank for Rangers, still not a pick on him. What a waste.

'Nah,' he told me, 'it was the right time. I decided to hang up the boots when I started getting a few aches and pains. It wasn't worth it.

'Plus, I was taking the odd anti-inflammatory tablet and that wasn't a good road to go down.'

I burst out laughing. The *odd* anti-inflammatory? Scots boys live on the bloody things . . .

'Darlin', what's on my sandwiches today?'

'Brufen, your favourite.'

'Full strength?'

'Of course – nothin' but the best for you, honey. And there's a wee packet of Coproximol for afters.'

'Magic . . . '

That's the difference between our culture and theirs, I suppose. We'll do anything it takes to play football. Foreigners will do whatever it takes to have a life after it.

I'd half-jokingly told Arthur about this knee problem I'd be playing through, and he warned me to be careful, said it wasn't worth it. We agreed to disagree. Then the next time he sees me, I'm knackered.

Nothing worse than a smug Dutchman with two good legs.

But if he was expecting me to tell him he was right and I was wrong and that I wished he'd given me all that great advice years earlier, he'd better have brought a flask and a sleeping bag and a good book. Because I wouldn't go back and do a damn thing differently.

Sure, a lot of people would look at him and look at me and decide in an instant which one had the right idea about looking after himself. I'd guess most of them, though, would be people who'd never been in football. Never needed the game the way junkies need a fix. Never realised that it's your job, it's what you do.

Being a footballer at a time when the money didn't flow like water from a tap wasn't really much different from being a carpet fitter or a miner or a docker. You didn't quit just because your shift gave you aches and pain.

Christ, you couldn't *afford* to quit.

When Arthur came to Ibrox, the deal probably made him for life – and he'd already had good earning years at PSV Eindhoven. Financial comfort made it a whole lot easier for him to hang up the boots when he did. Yet even if I had a million in the bank, no mortgage and fewer worries, it would have taken so much more than the odd twinge to make me turn my back on the game.

The biggest single difference between when I started out and when Barry started out is that we saw football as a brilliant job and his generation see it as a way to make money. I find it hard to get my head round it, but there are plenty of guys around who'd rather polish pound coins than medals.

Hold out over a contract for more than five minutes and they'll give you the family silver. Lose your place and they'll need to shell out a bucketload of dosh to get shot of you. Everything's weighted towards the player at the top end of the scale.

The whole Bosman thing was meant to free us from the shackles of the old retention system, where clubs could put you out of the game if they wanted to by refusing to release your registration. But sometimes you worry that it's all gone too far the other way, that it's created a comfort zone for guys who want one. There are plenty examples of big names signing big, big deals then collecting fortunes for barely kicking a ball.

But even great pros like Arthur baffle me when they decide overnight that they don't fancy it any more. Why did they play? Just to get enough security behind them so they could stop? Was it all really that cut and dried to them? Didn't they have that desire inside them to keep going and going as long as they were wanted?

It's not only the foreigners, either. I've known Scots boys who've played at a high level then packed it in rather than drop down a peg or two so they can keep kicking a ball. They don't want to get hurt. Some guys decide to pack it in the first time they get out of bed and can't get going. But surely that's when you should get the most satisfaction out of your fitness, when you push through the pain?

The feeling of standing under a hot shower after a really tough session on a morning when you couldn't be bothered is indescribable. You feel truly *alive*. I'm not having a go at anyone who doesn't get that, I just don't understand them – though maybe they'd look at me on my crutches, the way Arthur did, shake their heads and go: 'You're an idiot.'

* * *

The traffic on the morning of Tuesday, 29 November was hellish. Danny was driving me to Ross Hall Hospital, a couple of miles from Ibrox, for an 11 a.m. appointment with knee specialist Colin Walker, but we were already 20 minutes late, a quarter of a mile away and going nowhere.

I hate being late. So out I got, grabbed my bag and jogged the rest of the way. It would be the last time I'd run until well into the next year.

As far as I knew, it was to be a simple tidy-up of some crap floating around a left knee that for the past couple of months had gone from feeling fine one day to giving me what felt like electric shocks the next. Warming up before training and games with Raith, I'd literally be hobbling around the pitch, but after 20 minutes or so it'd loosen up enough to be manageable.

On 5 November, we drew 1–1 at home to Partick Thistle. It was my 455th start as a professional – or at least, my 455th *competitive* start, because God knows how many more games I've played: reserve games, pre-season friendlies, testimonials, full-scale practice matches, bounce games specially arranged to get you or a teammate back to fitness. I wish I'd kept a diary of the past 23 years so I knew for sure. It must be another 200, anyway.

And don't think those 200 were just kickabouts, because we take non-competitive games just as seriously as the real thing. Or at least some of us do. You still want anyone who's watching to say you did well, that you gave your lot. The hardest ones are First Team v. Youths. The kids are always desperate to put you in your place, to remind you that they're on their way up, and that's the fire you hope they never lose.

That day at Stark's Park, I still had the fire, but that bloody knee wouldn't give me the spark to get it blazing. That night I went to a fireworks party at Dad's house – Barry had brought more rockets than the last night of the Edinburgh Festival – and when I bent down to help him light one, I got this agonising pain and that was that. Something had to be done. Quick scope, suck the debris out, home a couple of hours later, playing again in three weeks.

It turned out to be a few weeks before I could have the operation, so I played one more game, a 2–0 home defeat to Peterhead. Seventy-two hours later, they were telling me I was finished.

It's weird, but that morning was the first time in my long and complicated surgical history that I'd arrived at hospital totally relaxed. Didn't think for a minute there would be a problem. I'd been in for an X-ray the day before, and Mr Walker had shown me the bits of floating bone he reckoned had been bothering me. But the good news, he said, was that it wasn't too terrible for someone with my years in the game.

I even asked if I could walk down to theatre – because you know one of the main reasons people freak out before ops? They get wheeled through on a trolley and all they can see is the ceiling and those white fluorescent lights. If they let them make their own way there then hop up on the table, it'd be a whole lot less scary.

The last thing I always do before surgery is check my resting heart rate – usually 58bpm – then watch it shoot up when the anaesthetic goes in, then look at the clock. It was just before 1 p.m.; I'd be under for 15 or 20 minutes, so chances were I'd be ready to head up the road not long after two.

But when I came round, it was nearly 2.20, and that's when I knew something was wrong. When a physio came in with crutches and asked me to try them out, alarm bells were ringing big time.

Then Mr Walker appeared and told me there had been 'a wee bit more damage' than he'd expected. A wee bit? Turns out there had been so much cartilage and bone broken off it looked like the rest of the dressing-room had been emptying theirs into my leg when I wasn't looking.

To put it into perspective, the bone-on-bone wear and tear was eight times worse than the damage that stopped Daniel Prodan making a single appearance for Rangers.

All I heard myself saying was: 'Will I play again?'

The hesitation before he answered *was* the answer.

'Erm . . . yes . . . of course you'll play again . . . sure . . . why not?'

Then he told me I'd be on the crutches and totally non-weight-bearing for six weeks. The mental calculator went into overdrive. Six weeks? That would take me into mid-January. Then it'll be another six weeks of light work, then maybe some jogging, then . . . bloody hell, then the season would be as good as over.

And then he was gone, leaving me fighting back the tears. Soon after, Carol arrived with her dad, both of them all happy that they were picking me up to go home and get on with my career. Their faces fell when they saw mine.

I needed a second opinion and the man to give me it was Paul Jackson, youth-team doctor at Rangers and always good for the right advice. Except on this occasion.

'Derek,' he says, 'I don't think you should play in those shitty leagues any more.'

He said it for my own good. Or at least, he thought he did. He reckoned that as I'd been at the top and now I was near the bottom, I couldn't be enjoying it and that enforced retirement would be a blessing. He couldn't have been further off the mark – I wanted the chance to retire on my own terms, not to *be* retired. It had to be my shout.

All I've ever wanted to do is play. That's why when Paul told me to quit, all I wanted to know from him was what the risks were if I didn't. I wanted him to say: *'Derek, on a scale of one to ten, the gamble you'll be taking if you play even one more game is a six.'*

'I'll take it!'

One season in the Third Division. One more in the juniors. That's all I wanted before I finished. Then, when it turned out the knee was as bad as it was, I revised the game plan and told myself that even if I only got back for one *game* it'd be enough. Just one more Saturday buzz, one more 50–50, one more pass nobody else could see, never mind make.

The one fear is not being able to play with the kids as they grow up – and how many footballers must have been tortured by the same dilemma? Is pushing it for one more season worth it if you're limping home from the school run a couple of years later? Then, if you get through that season and feel not too bad, is another season worth the gamble? And on it goes.

As it turned out, Doc. Jackson didn't give me a scale of one to ten. He just told me to give up. He said if I was careful I might be able to run two or three times a month.

I told him I was looking to be training two or three times a week.

He gave me that Arthur Numan look.

For weeks afterwards, I couldn't get myself going at all. Didn't shave, lay on the couch all day, got the grumpy head on. I'm someone who needs to release the chemicals that training produces. If I don't get a sweat on, I get restless and moody – even spotty. By the middle of December, I had a face like a teenager.

I had one night out over the whole of Christmas and New Year and spent most of the festive period feeling about as ho-ho-ho as Santa with piles. The most exercise I got every day was hobbling the 800 yards or so from the house to the paper shop and back. And I also came far too close for comfort to getting myself hooked on the bottle. It was a wee glass of wine here, then maybe two there, then most of a bottle watching the telly. Once I could walk a bit further, I'd go round to my local – The Bully – perch myself on a stool and have a few pints of Guinness.

It doesn't sound much, but when you're doing it every day for nearly a month it starts to become a habit, and that was something I didn't want to happen. Thank goodness for that day when I got to chuck those damn sticks away and could get myself back into the gym.

To have one doctor tell me it was over was bad. For two to have the same view was pretty conclusive. But as I came out of the fug of self-pity and headed for the New Year, something inside me said not to make the call to Raith to say my season was over, not yet. Not until I was absolutely damn sure of it.

Big Kenny Brannigan once said to me that the time to call it a day wasn't halfway through a season or even in the summer. In his book, you owed it to yourself to come back for pre-season and give it your best shot – even if you only lasted the first half-hour of the first session.

You had to satisfy your own curiosity, to know within yourself that it either could or couldn't be done, that you were finished or you weren't.

Now, *that's* my kind of advice.

The decision was made in my head. I'd heard too many bad diagnoses and seen too many false dawns down the years to take anyone's word as gospel, no matter how qualified. This time, I'd rely on my own instincts.

Most people who get rushed to hospital for surgery feel like the bottom's fallen out of their world. For me, it was the opposite.

I went under the knife after the world fell out of my bottom.

Now, the tale I'm going to tell here – one of an endless list of injury stories – might put you off your tea and Hobnobs. Unless you're a fellow professional footballer, in which case you'll read and it go: 'I've had worse.'

Me? I never have. And hope I never will.

Injuries are part of football. Your body's the engine that

powers your game, so it stands to reason that you'll need to take it in for repairs now and again.

It's just that sometimes it seems mine's like Trigger's brush on *Only Fools and Horses* – it's been with him for 17 years and only needed 23 new heads and 14 new handles.

At the last count, I've been under the knife 21 times. That's enough anaesthetic to stop a herd of charging elephants. I've had dozens of wounds closed up with hundreds of stitches, had countless needles stuck into every part of my anatomy.

Aged eight, I broke my arm at judo in Easterhouse. Tony Jaconelli, who lived downstairs from my granny, was a black belt, and I went into it because of him. But within a couple of weeks I had a bad fall and felt my arm go.

They set it at the Royal Infirmary, but for nearly a week I was in agony, so Mum and Dad took me back. Turned out it hadn't set properly, that the bones weren't joining up, so I needed an operation. They said I might have a weakness for life, and Mum was livid.

They kept me in for a week, but every day I'd be running up and down the ward with my arm in plaster and one of those big metal brackets holding it up, kicking my ball about.

Another day I was playing football in the house with my dad; he body-checked me and I went right into the corner of the sideboard and ended up with a scar on my head. I've got another big scar down the outside of my left leg from playing tig in the house, trying to run away and ending up going through a glass door.

At 12, I had my first knee problem, a thing called Osgood Slatter syndrome, which affects a lot of growing children. The docs said it affected your tendons and the best cure was rest, but try getting a 12-year-old boy to sit around and do nothing. No chance.

They put it in plaster for six weeks, but I took a hammer to it after three and a half. Then I went to see the Accies physio

Bobby Reid, and he had me running up and down the terraces in my first-ever dose of rehab.

Playing for Rangers youths in Germany I damaged my knee ligaments, and since then I've had either seven or eight ops on either knee, I've lost count. The only bits of me that've never been chopped up are my ankles, but even then I've been told they're in the same state as those of a 70 year old.

As for my toenails, I'm always mortified when nurses have to see them. Most footballers would be the same. We always end up with worse feet than women who cram themselves into pointy-toed stilettos. At least they don't have to boot a leather ball around in them.

I had a thing called plantar fasciitis, or heel spurs to you and me. They give you cortisone injections in the sole of your foot for that one, and they had to hold me down to do it. It was torture on a marginally more sadistic level than getting a needle in the groin.

I've had my cheek caved in when Graham Roberts mistook me for a mitre. Playing for Rangers against Hearts, I went up to nod a high ball back to the keeper just as the big fella decided to do the same and everything went black. When I came round in the dressing-room, the doc said he was nipping out of the room for a second and warned me not to get off the table. But while he was away, I couldn't resist checking out the damage – and next thing there was a gargoyle staring back at me from the mirror. The left side of my face was hanging out from beneath my eye. I shat myself.

It had been hard enough getting a decent bird before, but now . . . ?

The following day I underwent microsurgery at Bon Secours Hospital in Glasgow. A really nice nurse held my hand all the way through, and in cold weather you can just about make out where they stitched me.

I used to be not bad in the air and a decent tackler. But both my shoulders have popped out of their sockets so often I can nearly fold my arms behind me.

My knees are like road maps of Lanarkshire, I've had both groins opened up, been for tons of scopes and scrapes and clean-outs and patch-ups, all of which means I've done more rehab than Keith Richards.

Never had a day's training in physiotherapy or sports science, mind, but I'll bet I could take any injured player and put him through a programme that would get him back playing right on schedule. In fact, where's that entry form for *Mastermind?*

'Your name?'

'Derek Ferguson.'

'Your occupation?'

'Occasional footballer.'

'And your specialist subject?'

'Techniques and timetables in post-operative recovery from football-related disorders, 1979 to the present day.'

'Derek Ferguson, your two minutes start . . . now.'

Two minutes later . . .

'Derek Ferguson, you have scored a zillion points and no passes. However, you have also slipped getting out of the big black chair and dislocated your elbow.'

And some guy in the audience who used to play for Yeovil Reserves will go: 'Yeah, I've done that. Six weeks, minimum.'

Players sit around and talk about injuries the way old folk discuss the weather. Why? They're as big a part of our daily life.

'What's the bandage on your ear?'

'Ruptured a tendon tripping over a mongoose that ran onto the pitch chasing a squirrel.'

'Did the same at Stranraer three years ago.'

However, I really and truly hope no one else in the game – or out of it – has been through what happened to me before a game for Hamilton against Partick Thistle back in August 2004.

I'm warming up, doing a wee stretch, and I look up to wave to Darren and Ross in the stand – and suddenly I feel wet underneath. I thought I'd peed myself, so I stuck my hand down my pants to check. And it came out covered in blood.

Scared? I can't remember anything like it on the pitch. I shouted over to our young physio Michael Valentine, and when he saw me, he nearly fainted. He called for the doc, who got me into the dressing-room and up on the table. Stuck the old finger up – nice way to get to know people, that job – and said I'd haemorrhaged and there was no way I could play without collapsing through excessive blood loss.

Funny what goes through your head at times like those. All I could think was: 'Did anyone see what happened out there? Did it look from the stand like I'd shat myself?'

Basically, part of my arse had fallen out. That's not the technical version, but it'll do. The doc blamed the synthetic surface at New Douglas Park and said that a lot of athletes get a similar problem when they change their underfoot training conditions. So the good news was at least he thought I was an athlete.

He booked me in for an operation at the Nuffield in Glasgow, and I can say without a shadow of a doubt that it was the sorest in history. It felt like they'd done it with a blowtorch, and my backside was screaming for days.

When it was done and they said I could go home, I phoned Carol and said she could get me at Reception, but she got caught in traffic and I ended up hanging around for an hour and a half. I was in agony, feeling sick, a right mess. For days afterwards I didn't know what to hold – my head, my guts or my rear end.

Now, you'd probably think a guy with that track record would toil to get a hire-purchase contract, never mind one with a football club. But here's a little secret.

Medicals? Most clubs don't even bother with them.

You hear about mega-money signings going through the full works for days at a time, but the only time I came close to that thorough an examination was at Sunderland. They did X-rays, the lot. At Hearts, though, I'd had a wee shoogle of the important bits from the doc, and that was that. Dunfermline never bothered with a check-up at all.

As for insurance, I give up trying to work out why more clubs don't take it out for their players. Yes, it costs a bit, maybe £20,000 a year for the squad. But when you balance it up against the wages they end up paying guys who can't kick a ball, surely it's good economics?

Thing is, though, no matter how badly you get hurt or how poorly you're looked after, when the op's over you just get back to normal again. None of it puts you off, not the jabs or the dislocations or the guff floating about inside you or the stuff that falls out. You shrug and you look at the fixture list and you set yourself a target for getting back in the team.

You try and be sensible each time, of course, to give yourself the right amount of rehab time. My theory is that you should always get to where you feel ready then give it another week.

My theory for other players, that is.

When it's yourself, you want to be back the day before yesterday. And even if you don't feel quite right when the call comes to play, you play. Wimping out's not an option. I've been down Strathclyde Park, hobbling around before daylight to get myself back to fitness. Why so early? Because once upon a time I reckoned that whatever time you went out running, as long as you wore a hat no one would recognise you. But people are smarter than you think, especially if they have eyes.

God knows how many thousands of miles I've run on my own, how many solo quick feet sessions I've done to get myself sharp again, how many balls I've kicked against a wall again and again to get my timing back. Or how often I've been so desperate to play again that I've pushed too hard and only succeeded in making things worse. Believe me, going to your gaffer and coughing that you've strained a hammy pushing yourself back from ankle ligament damage does not qualify you for Employee of the Month.

Which is where the little magic tablets come in handy.

I've asked plenty doctors about the long-term effects of taking as many anti-inflammatories and painkillers as footballers do, but they say that as long as you're on them for less than five years solid you'll be OK.

But the thing you've got to wonder is, if the stuff in them's strong enough to take away blinding pain and it then settles in your stomach, what does it do to the lining?

You take the prescribed amount, then one for luck. Then maybe a wee one before games just to ward off the jolt from the first kick. And a couple at half-time. Then maybe two at time-up. Then . . . well, then you're out and having a few beers on top of all the drugs.

Still, I suppose no one knows until later in life what the price is, do they? I mean, look at cortisone injections. They were meant to have no long-term side effects, but look at the state of some of the guys who took them week in, week out in the '60s and '70s.

Like poor Allan McGraw, the former Morton manager, hobbling around on sticks, his knees crumbling to bits. They can just lock at any time and, bang, he's down like a sack of spuds. We were invited to a wedding he was at, me and my lifelong pal Mark Paterson, and the knee went while he was sitting at the table. So he says to Mark: 'Here, son, snap it back into position, eh?'

Mark's face goes chalk white.

But Allan's saying it's fine, shows him where to dunt it, tells him not to worry. Mark looks at me, but I'm looking the other way. In the end he takes a big deep breath, does what he's told and – *crack* – in it goes.

Allan's face is a picture of sheer relief. Mark looks like he's about to throw up. It's scary to think how often the same thing must have happened over the years.

Allan's story started coming out when I was at Rangers and if there's one positive it's that it did every player in the business a real turn. From then on, we were all really wary of taking too much cortisone. I wouldn't take more than two jags into one area – Allan had been getting dozens.

The tablets are still obligatory, though. Brufen, Voltarol, you name it, anything with enough power to get you training without too much pain. And the good news was, there wasn't much of it when I took my first steps back from the brink.

Just getting my gear back on after my latest operation felt great, going on the bike in the Accies gym for 15 minutes a huge relief. After a few days, I was trying to lift some very light weights with my left leg. Carol even came with me and put in a few sessions walking on the treadmill.

And guess what? Once I'd stopped mumping about my bad luck, I thought: 'No, don't give in so easily.'

It's ironic that only now, when I finally understand physiology, fitness, coaching and formations, that I'm faced with giving up. As a kid, I knew nothing, played free, never worried. You weren't concerned with protecting a back four or supporting your strikers. You were just . . . well, *playing*. It was years before I understood that my body was what would earn me a living and that I wasn't looking after the tools properly.

Now, I can tell what's right and what's wrong, which is why it only took a week or so for me from getting on the bike to starting thinking that maybe the doctors had got it wrong. That maybe they'd been far too cautious when they said I shouldn't kick a ball again.

That maybe . . . steady on, son, one step at a time.

Plyometrics. That's what'll tell me if I'm up to a comeback. Plyo-what-rics? Exactly the questions I'd have asked in my young days. But it's simple stuff, really – skipping, bending, lunges. Impact exercises. If you can take the force on your joints, you can play football.

So, yes, if you want to know about injuries and how to get over them, apply within. And here's a wee bonus piece of inside info – never, *ever* get drunk when you're on crutches.

That one night out I had over the festive season following my op was the last Rangers TV Christmas bash and Carol never tires of reminding me what a clown I made of myself.

It was fine while we were in the bar, I could sit on a stool and have a beer and feel no pain. But the minute we got back outside and the air hit me, I turned into Lee Evans in *There's Something About Mary*.

What didn't help was the fact that the bar was in a basement and I had a flight of stairs to negotiate before getting to ground level. That was fun – I had Arthur Numan on one side and Carol on the other, along with the station's presenter Ali Douglas. The car was parked a few streets away, so Carol said she'd go with Ali to get it and bring it down to outside the bar. But that was too sensible for me, wasn't it? I had to try and walk the full way.

To be honest, it would all be a bit of a blur if Carol hadn't recounted every step several times now. Apparently she was terrified that I was about to take a header onto the pavement but didn't know whether I'd collapse to the left, to the right, forwards or backwards. By the time we reached the car, she was a nervous wreck – but also couldn't stop laughing at how stupid I looked. Apparently every time I heard high heels walking behind us, I screamed and tried to run away.

The final straw came while she was opening the passenger door and I keeled over and landed right across the bonnet. She reckons if I'd been sober I'd have done myself some damage.

But they don't call drunks rubber men for nothing, do they?

FOUR

BEANZ MEANZ BAZ

Our Barry was always full of beans as a kid. Maybe that's because he was named after a tin of them.

If you're as long in the tooth as I am, you'll maybe remember the telly ad. My favourite, it was.

The wee boy goes up to his big brother and says: 'Wot ya doin', Bawwy?'

'Writin' a letter.'

'Who to, Bawwy?'

'Mum.'

'What's it say, Bawwy?'

'It says: "Gimme HP Beans or I'll run away from home . . .".'

Bawwy. I loved that. I know now it was a south of England accent he said it in, but as a ten year old, with a baby brother on the way, it reminded me of holidays in Blackpool, the only place outside Scotland I'd ever been.

So one lunchtime I'm playing football at school, right across the road from Granny Fergie's, and my cousin Caroline comes to the veranda and shouts: 'Derek, you've got a wee brother.'

I went to see him and Mum that night with Dad. They wouldn't let me in: no kids at visiting time. In a maternity ward! Nice . . .

Anyway, I don't know if it was because of that or because they just didn't want me to feel left out full stop, but Mum and Dad said I could name him.

Well, they asked for it.

'I want to call him Barry.'

And that was that. They must have been daft – and I should have thought harder and called him Archie, after Dad. But that was my folks: always thinking about my feelings, always letting me away with just too much.

Having a wee brother was as exciting as it got. It was like having the best toy in the world. And you know how kids treat their toys.

I think he was about ten months old, not quite walking yet, when I was in the bedroom playing darts. Except that the board hadn't been put up yet. It was on the floor, propped up against the door.

Barry's always had good timing as a footballer, just not so much as a toddler, as he proved by crawling past just as the dart flew out of my hand.

Doink. Right in the head.

He looked up at me, puzzled. Didn't cry, which was a good sign. I crept over, got hold of the dart gently. Pulled it out. Then the screaming started, blue murder.

I picked him up, ran to the bathroom, opened the window and held him out. I thought if the noise went out that way no one would know. Once he'd calmed down, I tried to squash the hole back down. Luckily, it never bled, but I was still panicking.

My aunt Angela was living with us at the time, and she knew what I'd done, but she protected me. She's the sister I never had. Thanks to her and a bit of luck, it was ages before Mum and Dad found out, but they were OK about it, and they laugh about it now.

Naturally, Barry was kicking a ball before he could walk. Dad bought him his first one as soon as he was born, same as he had for me. We'd pick Barry up by his two arms and swing him at it, then give him a big cheer when he made contact. It was football, football, football for him from the off.

From the moment he was up and running about, he was round my ankles all day. A typical wee brother, always in the way, always hearing me tell him to shift in case he got hit with the ball when we were playing in the street. Sometimes I'd lock him in the garden, and he'd peep over the gate at us.

Other times, we'd go out the back, I'd go in goal, and he'd take shots at me. Even that young, he looked a player. Any empty room became a football pitch for us. Can you chip the ball onto the couch? Dribble round the house without touching a doorway?

We lived in Little Earnock and then moved to a new house when Barry was born. Then we moved to Bellshill and had a bigger garden, a new big patch of grass with a patio. We had a heady-tennis court, we'd stand on the patio and bend free kicks around the trees on the grass, play keepy-uppy for hours. We wrecked the fence and the plants, but Mum let us get away with it.

When Barry started coming to watch my youth games – he'd have been about 18 months – he'd kick a ball around with the boys at the side of the pitch. It was second nature to him by then.

Hairdressing? Not quite so much . . .

When he was four, we were going to Angela's wedding to Brian, and the wee man decided to cut his own hair. Then give the dog a trim as well. We had a corgi called Bosley, the only dog I've ever had who did what you told him. A smashing wee pet who was lucky to keep both his ears that day.

I came back from the Scotland Under-15 trials for the wedding, and on the way, Mum warned me what Barry had done. There was a huge chunk missing out of his fringe and even after being taken for emergency repairs at the barber's he didn't look right. As for poor Bosley, he was left with big baldy patches and a bemused expression for weeks.

If I'd been there, I'd have covered for Barry the way Angela had for me after the dart-in-the-head disaster. That's the way family should be and the way it's always been with me. Though that old theory about blood being thicker than water's been tested a few times.

One day when he was about nine, Barry kicked his ball into someone's garden, and the guy whose house it was grabbed him and shouted at him. I came home to find Mum in a state and Dad already away round there, so round I went as well to find Dad squaring up to a bloke about 6 ft 3 in. square.

He says to me, 'We're in bother, son, I've hit him twice and he hasn't even flinched . . .'

So the guy growls: 'Oh look, here comes Billy Big-Time.'

And that was the red rag for me. So I jumped up and broke his nose with the old Glasgow kiss.

He reeled for a second, then he grabbed me and ripped my shirt off. Dad was hanging off him but couldn't get him away. Then we heard the sirens, and I got off my mark, round to Ian Ferguson's house in Bothwell.

I heard later that the guy was going to press charges but that he drank in a pub full of Rangers fans and some of them, well, asked him nicely not to.

But never mind being in court, if I'd ended up in the papers, Graeme Souness would have gone off his trolley. So there I was, hiding like a daft wee boy at my mate's place. What a halfwit.

It was that protective instinct, though – and where Barry's concerned, it's never left me. As I proved one day at a windy junior ground in West Lothian once he'd grown into a Rangers starlet.

Their reserves were playing Motherwell at Bathgate, at a time when I'd been on Barry's case for not being tough enough in the tackle. I'd warned him that if he went in for the ball with his leg loose he'd come off worst – and, sure enough, that was the day I was proved right.

From the outside, it's easy to point the finger at players who seem to go in over the ball, but as Claudio Gentile once said to Kevin Keegan: 'Thees is not dancing school, Senor.'

In the professional game, your first instinct is to protect yourself. Which means that if an opponent comes in at you with the boot high, you have to go in with yours higher or you'll be the one who gets hurt. It's not nice, but it's true. Hang back, and you'll never make it.

So that day, on a bobbly pitch a million miles from the big-time atmospheres he's so used to now, Barry's faced with a 50–50 against 'Well defender Greig Denham and he gets done, big time. A snap, a scream and my wee brother crumpled in a heap.

Maybe it was shock at seeing him lying there. Maybe it was anger at him having ignored everything I'd told him. But next thing, while they were waiting for the stretcher to take him off, I was ranting and raving at big Greig. I can't remember why, but he'd got taken off as well, and I followed him into the dressing-room, yelling that he'd wrecked my brother's career. I was miles, miles out of order.

As it happened, Barry was lucky. The snap had only been his shinguard, and the worst he came out of it with was a mass of bruising and a nice imprint of a set of six. No. Greig was the one in real danger – because I wouldn't let it go. I was challenging him to a square go, goading him to have a pop at me instead of a wee boy. I was still going when Archie Knox and John McGregor came through and ushered me away.

What a tube I feel about that now.

Yes, Barry could have lost his career if it had been his leg in bits out there. Yes, it would have been his own stupid fault for not protecting himself. But what did it have to do with me? Why was I having a pop at another pro whose only crime was that he *had* looked after Number One?

I suppose it was just a family thing again, wanting to look after your own. If a loved one's in trouble, you're there.

Who knows, though, maybe the whole incident helped Barry in the long run, because now he definitely does leave in the foot – and the elbow if need be – if he's under threat.

And to be fair to him, even if I've gone over the score in protecting him at times, one mad incident in August 2000 proved that he's not one for running away and leaving me in it either.

The Battle of Bothwell.

It was the night when Barry's Rangers career could really have gone off the rails, and I'm just thankful that it never worked out that way. He could have taken a really serious kicking. He could have ended up in the nick. He could have been booted out of Ibrox.

And all because a bunch of neds decided to have a go at him in the wake of one of the most amazing Old Firm games in recent history.

Celtic had beaten Rangers 6–2 in the first derby after Martin O'Neill took over at Parkhead, and with nine minutes to go, our Barry's day went from bad to worse when he was sent off.

I was in the Rangers end that Sunday, and it wasn't good fun. When I phoned my brother after the game, he was absolutely miserable, and we agreed to meet up at the Bothwell Bridge Hotel for a beer and a chat before going up the road. Had we stuck to that plan, Barry would never have been splattered all over the front pages the next morning. But instead, we decided to walk down to the Cricklewood for a quick one before heading home, and that was when the trouble started.

It's not like we were charging down the street singing 'Come And Have A Go If You Think You're Hard Enough'. There were half a dozen of us, and we were chatting in pairs, maybe ten yards apart.

I never really thought anything of it when we spotted a couple of guys coming out of the Douglas Arms then shooting straight back in when they clocked Barry. But next thing, we turned round and about 20 young boys were steaming at us, one of them shouting: 'Ferguson, you're getting it.'

I told one of the boys to get Barry away from it and said the rest of us should just keep walking. Barry, though, wasn't for running away. He stood his ground.

So it was him, me, Mark, Jim (known as Quiet Man), Ian and John the Gardener, being followed by this big squad, some of whom had started taking their belts off and swinging them around their heads.

'Boys,' I said, 'we're going to get a tanking . . .'

Pretty soon they were all round us and we were backed up against a jeweller's shop. It was like the OK Corral. We managed to get a few smacks in at them, but only one for maybe every six they landed on us. The only positive thing I can say is that it was an old-fashioned punch-up – thank God none of them pulled out knives or any other weapons.

Even then, I looked down at one point and saw John the Gardener lying sparko on the pavement and I really did think for a moment that he was dead. Barry had taken a smack that would leave him with a black eye, and the rest of us had cuts and bruises and grazes as the fists and boots flew.

There was a Chinese restaurant across the road and through a gap in the crowd I saw this giant of a man run out and lumber across the road. I had a fleeting moment of hope that he was maybe there to give us handers, but no such luck. He waded in with the rest of them.

It was one hell of a relief when we finally heard the police coming, and as the gang got on their toes, we also bolted, because no way were we hanging around to give descriptions or explanations. It was not a good situation.

I couldn't work out why it had all happened, because having been around Bothwell for years I'd never seen a gang fight anything like that. It just goes to show you what Old Firm games do to people.

Next day, the papers made out that Barry was right in there wanting a fight with Celtic fans, yet the contradictions in the copy showed how little of the facts the reporters really knew. In one paragraph, it told how he was wearing his club tracksuit; in another, it claimed he'd taken off his belt and waved it around.

Now, I know that footballers are all guilty of a few fashion disasters at times. But a belt with a tracky? Never mind Barry Ferguson, not even Barry Venison would go out in that get-up . . .

Luckily, what happened that night didn't harm his Rangers career. The last thing he needed was to go the same way I had – and from my point of view, I'd invested too much time and effort in trying to mould him into the ideal professional to see it all go down the drain thanks to a few angry halfwits.

It scares me to think what would have happened had the thumbs-up not come from Rangers all those years ago. Look at him: the whole lifestyle suits him. He needs good players around him; he loves the big games, the big challenges. The material rewards really matter to him.

Plus, he already knew Ibrox nearly as well as he knew his own living room. Being shown the door for good would have crucified him.

As soon as he was big enough, I started taking him into the

stadium as often as I could. Even that early, I had this idea that it would help him settle in better if he eventually signed.

Guys like Ally McCoist knew him from when he was five or six. These days, it feels like he's been around the place for ever. Once he goes over that white line, he owns the place. *'I'm the Man. Give me the ball, and I'll do the business.'*

In the last few years, I've also taken my own boys in behind the scenes at my clubs – though not at quite such glamorous surroundings. They've hung around at Recreation Park in Alloa, New Douglas Park in Hamilton and Stark's Park in Kirkcaldy. It's football in the raw, and I hope their visits do them good.

Back in Barry's schooldays, though, it was top flight or nothing. So he was immersed in the ways of Ibrox from before he went to secondary.

When the place was quiet, usually on a Sunday, I'd get him into the big communal bath. It was fantastic, even if I can't imagine Darren's generation being impressed.

Dear God, never mind them, what would health and safety people make of it now? Fifteen big hairy blokes all using the same water, sharing all their germs and blood and snotters and who knows what else? I mean, when it was busy you had to push a layer of scum away from you before you got in.

One of the first days I was with the first team, I was lying back and got this smack on the top of the head. When I looked round, I realised it had been Alex Miller's big bollocks. They were like rocks.

First thing some boys did when they got in the bath? Grab a bar of carbolic, shove it straight down into the wedding tackle. And meanwhile, at the other end, somebody else comes up from beneath the surface *gargling* and spitting the water into the air like a fountain.

Today, the stadium would be shut down in two minutes, but

that was how we lived. It didn't strike us that someone going in there with a skinned knee full of dirty red ash off the training park might be spreading infection around the place. We just jumped in, mucked in, had a laugh.

Washing together was part of the whole team thing. Now, clubs fine you for not wearing flip-flops in the showers. Everybody's more hygiene conscious.

The dressing-rooms at Ibrox were as big then as they are now but far more rough and ready. It wasn't until Graeme Souness arrived that the place was kitted out to suit the superstars he wanted to attract to the club – he'd have flipped if he'd been there in the early '80s to find that our training kit was handed out to us clean on a Monday and you wore it all week.

At the end of every session, you took it off and put it on your own hanger in a heated airing cupboard. By Thursday, you'd open the door and the stench caught the back of your throat. Everything was solid with sweat and ash and dried blood and whatever else. You were banging your socks on the floor to soften them up and stuff was flying out of them.

We'd have slips – cotton underpants – with our kit at the start of the week, but as the days went on they'd get mixed up and we'd all be wearing someone else's and . . . well, you know where I'm coming from.

If I coach kids now, I'll hand out bibs and if they've not been laundered from the day before they're like: 'Eeewww – Ah'm no' wearin' that!'

How come we didn't react like that 20-odd years ago? Because guys didn't really bother about stuff like smelling back then. If you moaned, you'd have got slaughtered; if you had deodorant, you were a poof.

Look at that picture on the cover. My face is beaming with pride at having my wee brother in there with me. His seems to be saying: 'One day, all this will be mine.'

When it was taken, Barry had just started playing for Mill United. These days, they're playing organised games at five and six, but he was nearly ten before he got going. I went to as many games as I could, but by then I was with Rangers. Dad went to them all, though, wouldn't miss one. He'd moved on from me to his next son. You could see Barry was better than the other kids, different. He was always in the middle, running the show, and my only worry was that he was wee for his age and that might count against him. Those fears seem justified when he missed out in the trials for Scotland Under-15s. I know I'm biased, but I thought he'd played well enough. He just lacked the strength of some of the other boys.

Making that squad had always been the yardstick for young talent in this country, but I told him that of the eighteen I'd been part of, only four or five had even come close to making it to the top. He was lucky that he had me and Dad in there backing him, encouraging him, getting him through the first big disappointment of his footballing life.

It made me wonder, though – how many youngsters who *don't* have that support just give up and fall out of love with the game?

The streets are full of late developers, yet our game's so quick to discard anyone who's not ready for the rough stuff by the time they're in third year. That's why I don't like the new youth system, where boys are reviewed every six weeks. That's far too often; it was far better when clubs took them on at 12 and let them develop through till their 16th birthday before making a definite decision.

Apart from anything else, kids are naturally nervous with adults looking over their shoulder and will only improve if they're not constantly on trial. One thing's for sure: Barry would never have made it the way things are done today. He'd have been regarded as too slight, and that tells you all you need to know.

Everyone has a different idea of what makes a player – is he strong enough? Does he beat men? Does he score enough goals? – but in Scotland it seems as if what everyone looks for is commitment, for the game to seem a real effort. Barry's always made football look like the easiest thing in the world. I'm certain that's why a lot of people have never taken to him – and why I'd loved to have seen him go abroad and take himself to another level.

Look at Paul Lambert. He plodded away with St Mirren and Motherwell without anyone ever settling on what his position was. Then he got the big break of a move to Borussia Dortmund, who made him into a Champions League-winning holding midfielder, and it was only then that Celtic and Scotland realised what they'd been missing all those years.

Had Barry been born overseas, they'd have treated him like a boy genius, but here it was all about whether or not he could tackle. Me? I loved ploughing through the bigger guys to prove myself, but Barry didn't want to be involved. He made an art form out of avoiding the hurly-burly from a very early age.

The Dutch would have loved him, as was proved when Dick Advocaat took over at Ibrox and rescued his career.

After the 15s turned him down, he trained with Everton – while Mo Johnston was there – but always wanted to join Rangers. Question was: would they take him on? We were wound up like watches waiting to find out. I wanted so much for him to get the same chance as me. Then to grab it with both hands and never let it go.

I had decided, though, not to fight his corner with the club. I'd coached him and pushed him since he was a toddler, but he had to make it as a pro on his own. The day he was called in for the big decision was the biggest of his life. Dad went with him, and I can only imagine how they felt when they were told he was being given a YTS deal. For me, the feeling was more one of pure relief than joy.

We weren't the kind of family to pop open the champagne at good news. We knew it was just the beginning, but the good news was that he wouldn't be scraping about for a proper job. My wee brother had been given the chance we'd dreamed of. It was up to him now. But I knew he'd be looked after.

Ian Durrant was virtually his uncle and took him under his wing, christening him Billy One-Tie. He was accepted straight away. But after a year or so, things changed – once they realised that Derek's wee brother was now a threat to their places in the team.

That was when the wind-ups really started, and he had to stand on his own two feet. One minute he'd been the wee fella, the next it was 'Me against You'.

He was up to the scrap, used to come home and tell me he'd gone through Durranty or Coisty or whoever in training, just to make his point. I liked that. The experienced guys were looking over their shoulders, and that's how it has to be in a dressing-room.

As soon as he started at Ibrox, I tried to mentor him. Asked for his training routine every day, always encouraged him to be at his best. He was an extension of me. That's a Ferguson thing.

Of course, the next stage in his life outside Rangers was the advent of girlfriends and all the other teenage distractions, and that's when I really stepped up being on his case. A big part of it was not wanting him to make the mistakes I had. As I'll probably repeat throughout this book, I didn't know any better, but there was no excuse for Barry to be saying that in his mid-20s. And I didn't want anyone at Rangers having excuses not to give him another contract.

There would be no Sunday afternoons on the beer, no falling in with the wrong crowd. Lee McCulloch, who's now at Wigan, was his big mate, and they were the same kind of character. Liked a laugh but were determined to make it.

Mum and Dad had been too soft with me, I knew that. Dad should have rattled me when I came home late, made me feel guilty, but Mum would have given him a row if he had.

I knew what young footballers got up to, knew how girls threw themselves at them, knew every idiotic trick in the book. I'd have hated to hear anyone calling my brother a Big-Time Charlie.

The easiest thing in the world's to see the wide boys in the dressing-room and want to be like them, to overdo all the off-field stuff. I tried to tell Barry to be his own man, not just follow the crowd and go daft.

If I had a quid for every time I've wished a Ray Wilkins or a Joe Jordan had been on my case when I was 16, the mortgage would have been squared off years ago – and for a long time as a young guy, Barry accepted me being on his.

I pushed him quite hard, constantly wanted him to improve, didn't let him get away with dropping those standards. Even when he broke through at Ibrox he needed kept right, and I never hesitated to say what needed to be said. I saw nothing wrong with that and still don't, but pretty soon he'd feel differently.

He got his first-team chance just before Christmas 1997, a couple of years older than me but in a team peppered with far more superstars. It was the final half-season of Walter Smith's reign and an uncertain time for everyone.

But especially a young local boy whose face didn't seem to fit.

He came on as a sub with 13 minutes to go of a 1–0 home win over Hibs and started eight times after that through to February, often at the expense of Gazza. I missed most of his early games, but he wouldn't have expected anything else with me playing for Falkirk. Dad was always there, so I'd hear about it from the pair of them then catch the telly highlights.

Even on the small screen, he looked the part. To break through into that team with all those midfielders was some job, and he was handling it so well. Didn't stop me chinning him, though. We'd speak after training, and I'd want to know how hard he'd worked, if he'd bossed the place. I'd ring after seeing him on TV and point out little things that he needed to work on.

He was so happy when he played under Walter, but from early on he got really down when he was left out. He needs to play, and I really started to fear he'd end up falling out with the club and lose his big chance. Luckily, that was when wee Dick Advocaat came on the scene.

What did I say earlier on? That the Dutch would have loved him when he was young? Well, the new gaffer's attitude seemed to prove it. Almost from the off, my wee brother became a fixture. His whole game seemed to take off. Arthur Numan arrived and moved in round the corner from him. They started rooming together. And pretty soon he wasn't welcoming my input as much.

In fact, let's be honest here. He blanked me.

For a long while, he wouldn't take my calls – though I kept making them and I also knew where to find him, because he was never away from Mum and Dad's.

Barry's definitely someone who needs approval, who likes to be surrounded by people telling him he's done well, and I've not always been that person for him. I'm more likely to pick him up on things he hasn't done as well as he could, but only to help him maintain the high standards he's set himself.

Barry would be like: 'Did I do all right? Did I do all right?'

And I'd say: 'No.'

He'd be hurt. But I'd rather he was hurt and went and did something about it than believed he was doing well when he wasn't. Yet these days when Barry asks him for an opinion on his performance, Dad nearly always says that it was fine, even when I know that's not what he really thinks.

As a kid, I knew I played well if Dad said nothing on the way home. That was his seal of approval. It was only when I'd made mistakes that he'd be talkative, though even then he was only ever constructive, never had a dig. When Barry was young, mind, I was forever telling him how well he played, and I do the same with my boys now. Maybe it's because I'd wanted to hear the same things more often.

But Dad's a product of a different era, a time when men didn't show their feelings. He used to go to Ibrox with his dad, and afterwards he'd get left outside the pub with some crisps and lemonade until it was time to go home. That's just the way it was then. Now you'd get shopped and the Social Work would be at your door with a court order.

I didn't want to run Barry's life, just keep him right where I could. If I told him twenty things and one stuck, that was a result. Unfortunately, it was the other nineteen that pissed him off.

Even Dad was asking me to back off after a while, but I'd say: 'No, he needs to be told.'

Then, out of the royal blue, something huge happened and changed my attitude for good. With results going wrong and the fans getting stroppy, Advocaat took the captain's armband off Lorenzo Amoruso . . . and gave it to our Barry.

It was just three months after the Battle of Bothwell. He was three months short of his 23rd birthday. And suddenly, he wasn't my wee brother any more.

So one day when we were down at Strathclyde Park watching Darren play, I turned to Dad and said: 'OK, *now* I'll back off.'

He looks at me and asks why. And I say: 'Because he's the captain of Rangers. Not an awful lot I can tell him now, is there?'

And there wasn't. I'd wanted him to follow me into football, and he did. I'd wanted him to make it with Rangers, and he did.

Advocaat pulled a smart move when he made Barry room with Arthur. It was great management, and I used to think: 'Why didn't Souness put me in with Richard Gough? Why let me do what I wanted with Durranty?'

No offence, mate.

We all called Goughie boring and, well, he was. But what a pro and what an example. He'd have given me all the good habits Arthur must have been passing on to Barry.

So even though I'd tried to keep him right all the way along the road, it would have been a bit rich for me to try reading the riot act to someone who'd reached the position he had as young as he had.

I mean, by the age of 22 years and 9 months I'd already appeared in court twice, been on the front pages for being a naughty boy on a night out and talked my way out of the only club I'd ever wanted to play for. Barry had taken a stretch in height and in status. He was on his way to achieving everything any of us had wished for him.

Yet no matter what his manager thought, a hell of a lot of fans just couldn't take to Barry. I used to hear them murmuring about him playing too many safe balls. They never sang his name. He just couldn't win their approval, and it was only when he started getting forward and scoring a few goals that they finally warmed to him.

I wanted to get a grip of every one of them and tell them what it was like to be up close and personal with him on the pitch, a privilege I would finally get to enjoy on a memorable Sunday evening at Dunfermline in 1999.

I'd seen him play in the front room and the garden and on public parks all his life, but this was the first time we'd ever played on opposite sides, and it gave me a whole new appreciation of how good he is.

His passing was brilliant, he covered every inch of the park, and he smashed a tremendous goal. What more could you ask from your playmaker and captain? We had a bite to eat that night at the Esporta club in Hamilton, and I tried to kid him on that his goal was a deflection, but he knew I was only at it.

By then he was on a five-year contract and had just won his first Scotland cap in a 0–0 draw away to Lithuania. He was halfway to matching his big brother's international record already. There was no hiding his quality if you knew anything about the game. Which kind of suggests that a lot of the people who watched him week in, week out from the stands *didn't* know the game.

When the 2001–02 season was drawing to a close, word went round that he might be leaving. There wasn't exactly outrage around Ibrox – in fact, plenty of fans even reckoned the club should take the first reasonable offer. But one game changed all that.

No, make that one kick.

Celtic had won the title by an embarrassing *18* points and, with 21 minutes of the Scottish Cup final to go, were 2–1 up and heading for the Double. A League Cup final triumph over Ayr in the February, when Barry had scored a penalty in a 4–0 canter, wasn't going to be enough for the Rangers fans. They needed a hero – and they got one. My wee brother.

He placed the ball for a free-kick 23 yards out at the Rangers end, took aim and curled it over the wall and beyond Rab Douglas and was off and running, lost in that childlike excitement again.

And suddenly, the chant went up: 'Oh, Barry Barry . . .'

Hearing that brought a lump to my throat, and next thing, the chant of 'Barry Must Stay' went up round half the stadium. Then, in the dying seconds, Peter Lovenkrands headed a dramatic winner, and Rangers had begun a run of last-gasp trophy wins at the expense of the other half.

As the kid I'd schooled from before he could walk climbed the steps to the VIP box and lifted the cup, I had tears in my eyes. A few rows in front of me, Stuart McCall was leading more choruses of 'Barry Must Stay'. It was a magnificent moment that will never leave me.

Now that he'd finally won over the troops, Barry could pretty much write his own cheques. He really was The Man.

A year later, he'd lead his team to the Treble, scoring 19 goals including a hat-trick against Dundee United at Ibrox. He was about to fulfil his ambition of leading Rangers into the Champions League. But it never happened.

I've heard so much crap over the last few years about how I was the one who told Barry to leave Rangers to play for Blackburn Rovers. A lot of fans seem to think that, because of what happened to me at the club, I had a chip on my shoulder and wanted him to quit as some sort of revenge.

But hand on heart, it's simply not the case. Yes, I'd stated publicly plenty of times that I'd like to see my brother playing down south or in Europe – but the decision was ALWAYS his to make.

And isn't it obvious by now that even if I'd been shouting through his letterbox night and day to get himself a move, when Barry doesn't want to listen to me, he doesn't listen to me?

Plus, after what *did* happen to me in my final couple of years with Rangers – a devastating time for me that I will go into later – can anyone seriously believe I'd have sold him on a move to play under Souness, the then Blackburn manager? To say he and I hadn't seen eye-to-eye at Ibrox is . . . well, read on a few pages and you'll see for yourself.

So no, Barry's exit from Ibrox was nothing to do with me. In fact, four or five weeks before he left, he told me he was ready to sign a new deal and I was delighted. That would have taken him through to his 30th and settled him down for life – just the way I'd wanted it for myself.

But if you want the truth, I think his agent showed him the pound signs and that swayed him. You can't blame a guy for taking the money if that's what drives him. You can also understand the agent realising there was more to be made by moving his star client rather than keeping him where he was.

Plus, if it didn't work out, he could always negotiate a deal to go home.

When Barry then said he was going to Blackburn, I asked if there was interest from elsewhere and he mentioned Arsenal, Liverpool and Villa. For me, any one of those three would have been a better prospect. He needed a club with the same history and status as Rangers – and Blackburn simply didn't have that.

Barry at Arsenal would have been fantastic. With all that pace and touch around him, everything could have gone through him and he'd have made goals for fun. But the rotation policy at a Highbury or an Anfield would have worried him, because he needs to know he's playing.

The only way I thought Blackburn could work was if he was going there with a view to making his name in England and *then* stepping up to one of the big boys.

Was he capable of hacking it in the top six? Of course he was. So why didn't he end up at Liverpool or Arsenal or Man U? Only he – and his agent – can tell you that for certain. All I know is that it was all too short-lived and too troubled a stay down there for anyone to know for certain what he was capable of.

He was only just making his mark when he dislocated his knee at Newcastle, and once he was fit, Souness was off, Mark Hughes was in and the look and feel of the team changed from pass-and-move to press-and-tackle. I felt so sorry for him that his dreams of becoming a major star in England were dashed the way they were, but coming back soon gave a lot of people shooty-in practice at him.

He'd failed. He'd bottled it. He'd run back to his pals. All nonsense, as anyone who knows him will tell you.

Blackburn was simply the wrong move at the wrong time and it was probably better in the end that he cut his losses and went back to Rangers – better, that is, for both parties.

They'd missed him terribly in the year and a bit when he was gone, lost the title and didn't look much like recapturing it. Yet after he returned, right in the final hours of the final night of the January 2005 transfer window, they staged that unbelievable comeback to snatch the flag in the final seconds of the final afternoon of the league season.

That tells you his value to Rangers.

People assume Barry and I live in each other's pockets – and that my hand's usually in his. But nothing could be further from the truth.

Barry's money is his own business. Why should he give me handouts? And why should I want them anyway? I don't have a single twinge of envy about a single penny *he* earns, because he deserves it.

See, it's one thing knowing how to do what Barry does, to sit there and sniff that all he does is play simple passes. But it's another thing altogether going out there and doing it when the bullets are flying.

Try keeping your head up and picking those passes – seemingly simple or not – with ten charged-up athletes right in your face. Disciplined guys, whose sole aim is to stop you running the show.

Look at that Inter Milan game. Now, if Rangers were playing a regular SPL team, the playmaker's first thought might be to get the ball forward as early as possible and find their right-back out of position – but the Italians just don't lose their shape that easily.

They think so much harder about the game than we do. They stick to their jobs for 90 minutes, don't just decide to have a wander. Which means a guy like Barry has to think even harder and the guys around him have to work overtime to make their runs count so it all comes together. It becomes a game of chess and that's what Scottish fans don't seem to get.

Yes, our job is to send them home happy, but they have to help us do that. Players feed off the fans, their emotions get through to us – but sometimes I wish they could try a little harder to get their heads around the pressures we face.

It's really hard to sit in the stand watching Barry play and hearing people giving him stick. Dad's ended up walking away from Rangers games when punters have been slagging his boys, but I have to bite back – even though I used to tell Barry if he was watching me and the same thing happened he should bite his lip.

I remember one day he came to see me playing for Clydebank at Albion Rovers and ended up having words with a guy who was slaughtering me. Then he got embarrassed because people started looking round, but like I've said, it's natural to defend your family.

And there's no doubt that sometimes supporters *can* go over the score with their criticism and get very personal.

There are few places in the world where that's more true than Italy, yet for very different reasons than here.

There, you'll hear the crowd boo a long hopeful ball that runs out for a goal-kick. Here, that punt will get a sympathetic round of applause if a forward chases it in vain and slides into the advertising hoardings.

For me, they've got it right and we've got it wrong.

I love a full-blooded game as much as the next man, love

seeing guys going right through each other in 50–50s. I also want to see the ball in the box as often as possible, just the same as the punters do.

Watch Barcelona, though. They tackle and press and chase and attack like demons, all when the time is right. Yet there will be times in every game when they keep the ball, roll it around, bide their time. They're not being boring or negative, simply playing the waiting game.

When you're up against an organised defence, it plays into their hands to hoof the ball and hope for the best. Far better to keep it, move it around, use the width of the pitch and eventually draw the opposition out of position. That's when the great teams spring into top gear.

The speed Barca counter-attack at is frightening. When our teams are defending corners, we'll nod the ball out of the box, someone will chase it and hump it and hope that the one or two guys left on the halfway line can hold it in and bring us up the park.

Within ten seconds, Barca can switch from having almost everyone behind the ball to having five or six men charging into the opposition's penalty box. That's the difference.

Keeping possession at the highest level in football these days is almost like scoring a goal. Give it away cheaply and quality opposition will punish you, simple as that.

Count how many times in a game Barry gives it away and then tell me he doesn't impress you.

These days, we have an odd relationship. We don't talk much straight after games and we don't have that many nights out together. There have been times when he's looked uncomfortable in my company. We've both been down in Hamilton watching our kids train and I've had to shout him over to come and talk to me.

I hear from him most often when he's injured, when he needs an arm around his shoulder. When things are going well, he rarely calls. Carol gets upset at that, but I don't. It's the way of the world.

At his last birthday, he wouldn't let me sing down the phone to him and that got my back up. I always sing down the phone at family birthdays.

Anyway, Carol went down to see him to give him his present and he'd bought our three PSP consoles and gave her £100 to get them games. That was quality.

And I knew I'd get to play with them when the boys were out.

What would I change about Barry? I'd get him to lighten up, for a start, because he takes criticism too much to heart. He got this letter from a fan once slagging him off and kept it for ages on the fridge door at Mum and Dad's. Me? I'd have binned it straight away – pay too much attention to that stuff and it'll drive you daft.

Look at the Hotline in the *Daily Record* every day or tune in to the phone-ins on Clyde and Real Radio and the BBC. He's constantly being talked about, more often by punters wanting to slaughter him than praise him – because, at the end of the day, these shows are all about controversy, not patting people on the back.

Dad's aware of it all and it really gets to him, but you're better to ignore it. Fans know what they want and understand the game to a point, but 99 per cent don't have the first clue about the pressures a player's under out on the pitch, the injuries they carry, the off-field problems they have to try and forget when the whistle blows.

That's why, even though there are times when I'll be annoyed at him for something, I'll hear someone having a go at him and I'll leap to his defence in an instant. Because he's my brother and I love him.

I want him to do well. I want him to keep getting better. I look forward to the day when he's finished playing and we'll get to sit down and have a beer and get closer again.

The problem isn't with him, it's with so many big-time footballers today. They live in a bubble and sometimes not even family can break through.

You wish they'd take a step back and look at the world as less well-off people see it, appreciate stupid little things like nightclubs letting them in for nothing, restaurants giving them good tables, fans waiting in the cold and the rain to ask for an autograph. But it's hard to make them see it that way.

We've only ever had a couple of proper fights. Once, he brought home some stuff that had fallen off the back of a lorry and I went through him. Dad stood up for him and I fell out with the pair of them over it.

The other time, a few of us were in his house playing pool and I thought he'd taken two touches at one of his shots. We ended up rolling about on the carpet, but next day we were right as rain.

He's a good boy, Barry. A terrific footballer, a good dad and a loving son. He has a lovely home and looks after his money, and if fate deals him the right cards, he should be set up for life.

Who knows, maybe there are people out there who'd think me a hypocrite for telling Barry to behave himself in the first place, because maybe it didn't help my case when he grew up seeing guys like Coisty, Durranty, his brother and more up on chairs and tables in my mum and dad's house singing and dancing after a session on the bevvy.

Maybe I should have butted out altogether and let him be what he was going to be on his own terms.

Maybe. But I don't think so. The fact that I wasn't a bad influence on my wee brother has been proved in the fact that he doesn't run about like a madman. The fact that he has such good habits on the pitch hopefully reflect well on all the time we spent together kicking a ball.

Overall, I hope he'd say he has more to thank me than begrudge me for. I hope he understands that what he saw as nagging was actually important advice.

Put it this way. If I've gone even 10 per cent towards making him the star he is today, then I'm a happy big brother.

FIVE

TUNNEL VISION

This is the bit I want my kids to read – then tear out and pin it somewhere that ensures they never forget the message.

It's the easy guide to setting yourself up for a middle age when you haven't a clue what to do with your life.

In that way, football's no different a drug to alcohol or heroin. Get yourself hooked on it early enough and you think there's no tomorrow.

Now, let's get one thing straight. I don't regret a single second of the way my career's gone. I just wouldn't want the boys to go the same way.

I wasn't a dumbo at school, far from it. But my real brains were in my feet, and like so many others with the same talent, once the clubs came calling all thoughts of exam certificates went right out the window.

Especially when THE club came calling. My club. Rangers.

I'd trained with Celtic and Man United and Dundee United, but Ibrox was the only place I wanted to be. When I was 12, they got my signature for the first time. And school was out.

All I could see from that day was the vision of myself running out onto the Ibrox turf for my first-team debut.

When you have that kind of tunnel vision, nothing knocks you off track. Teachers sneer that you won't make it and you vow to prove them wrong. Then you're in there and you were right and they were wrong.

You're part of the furniture at the club you love.

But what happens to furniture? Eventually it gets chipped or scratched or simply goes out of fashion and its owners put a small ad in the papers to get shot of it.

That's football.

And that's why although I'd be the happiest dad in the world if Darren, Ross or Lewis followed me and their uncle into the professional game, it most definitely won't be at the expense of something to fall back on.

At 12, I had no idea what I'd do if my chosen career didn't work out and nearly 30 years later I'm still none the wiser. That's not clever. The boys need to be smarter than that.

No regrets? Not quite. Yes, I've lived life for the moment and always firmly believed that what's for you won't go by you.

But one thing sticks in my throat and gnaws at my guts and unfortunately it's a big thing. Messing up at Earnock High School in Hamilton.

It gets to me so much because here I am trying to tell the boys to work hard at school, but until now they haven't known that I don't have a single qualification. That's why I'm writing this, so they go the opposite way from me.

Like I say, it's not that I was a thicko. I was actually pretty bright in primary school. But by secondary time, my mind was made up that I was going to be a star, so there didn't seem much point in normal lessons.

In my second week, I got into a fight with someone who was

trying to bully my aunt Angela. He was third year, I was first and he was giving her stick. We were coming downstairs at the science corridor, he stepped out of line, I dropped the schoolbag and went for him. That kind of thing gets you a name and not one for academic achievement.

Plus, the crowd I got in with wanted to play football up the tennis courts all the time and that suited me fine. The teachers knew I was bright, but the more they told me to stick in, the more headstrong it made me.

Now, at this point it would be easy for me to tell my boys that I was right and the teachers were wrong. After all, here we are, nearly 30 years on, and football's been my living every day since leaving school.

That wouldn't be right, though. Because the teachers *were* right. I *should* have made sure I got some qualifications behind me and *then* went on to play football. It wouldn't have been hard to do both.

Wonder how many guys who made it in football but not in real life would tell the same story?

Because, let's be honest, the irony is that the attitude I had back then was really no different to the one that would cost me dear years later when I'd gone on to break through at Rangers.

All it would have taken was a little give and take, for me to bite my lip and not be right all the time and do what the gaffers said, just knuckle down.

Easier said than done, though.

By the time fourth year came, I was down to sit either three or four O Levels, I can't remember which. English, Arithmetic, Geography, maybe something else. That's how interested I was.

Anyway, however many it was, the Embassy world snooker was on the telly and the game was just taking off big time and we

71

all decided we'd rather be watching some blokes pot balls than writing essays or doing sums.

So we struck a pact.

The exams rules were that you had to sit in the hall for twenty minutes, so that was what we did. Twenty minutes and not a second more, then we all got up and walked out.

It was my way of getting back at the teachers, but a blind man can see I was only getting at myself.

Today, I couldn't be more embarrassed about it all, because I meet people from school and they've all got qualifications and good jobs, and although they look at me like the one who made it, I'm ashamed of how my school days ended.

My days revolved around PE and the football team and the rest of the time I'd dodge about, missing classes and playing games instead.

George Cummings, who went on to be head of the SFA refereeing set-up, was my Geography teacher and the man you got sent to if you misbehaved. Mr Sims, the PE teacher, used to belt me a lot as well – so even in the subjects I took seriously, my attitude was all wrong.

My mindset was simple – I was going to be a footballer and I didn't need anyone's help. A lifetime down the line, I know better. But it's too late.

The only consolation is that other guys pulled the same strokes and swung the lead as much as I did in a bid to be footballers but didn't make it, so I suppose I was lucky.

Thing is, everything happened so young for me at Rangers. I was still in school when I became the club's youngest-ever first-team player. I'd played in Europe by the time I was 16 and a bit, faced Celtic at 17, won my first championship at 19.

When life's as good as that, you're convinced it'll never end. Being 25's a lifetime away, never mind 40.

And so it should be. There's no better way to live than being young and fit and playing football for money. They should just make it compulsory that before they hand you a shirt, you show them your qualifications for the real world.

There weren't many around the place back then who had ambitions to do anything outside the game. Well, except maybe Gordon Ramsay – though he was a million miles from the Gordon Ramsay you see larging it on the box these days.

He was a posh boy from the Borders who ended up as one of the many who the scouts net but the bosses throw back in. I think he played at East Kilbride in a testimonial and had half a game on a Highland tour and that was that.

The irony is, he was quiet as a mouse back then – yet if he'd been half as loud and cocky as a footballer as he is as a chef, he might have stood a better chance.

Where did it all go wrong, big man?

My road to Ibrox and beyond began in the schemes of Glasgow, where I spent ten happy years before we moved out to Hamilton round about the time Barry came on the scene.

There was a big overspill from the city to Lanarkshire in the mid-'70s, but I think Mum and Dad were fed up with tenement life by then anyway. When we lived in Garthamlock, in a top flat in Coxton Place, we got broken into and my mum was heartbroken. They came in through the communal loft you got into from the stair landing and it was never the same there again.

From there we flitted to Barlanark, near my Granny Fergie and my primary school and I loved it there, but there was a lot of stuff going on that made my folks want to get away. The biggest thing was the gang fights. They got really naughty – I'm talking swords, the lot. We played football down near the Edinburgh Road, right on the boundary with Easterhouse, and that's where they got stuck into each other.

The gangs were the Bar-L from our bit and the Toi from

across the road – one minute we'd be kicking the ball about and the next we'd be doing a runner, up the close and out onto one of the verandas to see what was going on. Then the police would scream up and scatter them and we could get on with the game.

We'd play until ten, half-ten at night, until my granny shouted me up. We played on the street, at the school, in the mouth of the Close, heady football out the back of the tenement. When we weren't playing football, we were playing tig, jumping on and off the bins.

People talk about kids today having no co-ordination and there's no doubt one of the reasons is that they don't play the games we did. We were always on the move, jumping and twisting, and that really helped my balance improve. I wasn't aware of it at the time, I was just enjoying myself. But I still get the benefits today.

The bit we played heady football in wasn't the same width all the way along, so you'd switch ends at half-time to make it fair. You always had a favourite end, though, because you knew where to put the ball so the other side had no chance of getting it back to you.

That never changes. When I was at Rangers we played in the tunnel after training and there was a drainpipe at one end. When you played Davie Cooper, every serve went right into the pipe. He simply never missed, the guy was uncanny. He is one of my all-time heroes.

You don't see enough of that at football grounds now. Too many players don't play daft games after training, probably because they didn't play them as kids. We've got out of the habit of always having a ball at our feet and it's hurt the game.

I was the only Rangers supporter in our street in Barlanark, but all the Celtic fans looked after me because I was the smallest in the crowd. Different story outside your own territory, though.

One day when I was six or seven I got this Rangers rosette off somebody and put it on my jumper when I went out. I didn't have a clue why it had a drawing of a guy sitting on a white horse, just that it looked quite smart.

My cousins Paul, Caroline and Eileen and my Auntie Margaret and Uncle John all stayed near us in Barlanark and they were all Celtic fans, so it hadn't struck me that anybody would want to batter you for not following the same team as they did. You live and learn.

Round I go to the shops, not a care in the world, when I bump into some boys from another street and they give me a right doing. Talk about getting what the bigotry business is all about knocked into you. A fat lip and a pile of bruises soon told me what it meant to wear the wrong colours in the wrong place.

The rosette never went on me again.

Still, I came back with what I'd gone for – my weekly pair of gutties. They were those black canvas slip-ons with the elastic at the sides and the brown rubber soles, the ones you still see Primary One kids wearing today. They cost £1 and every week Granny Fergie would send me down with the money to replace the ones I'd kicked the toes out of the week before. They were my first football boots.

Granny Fergie used to swear like a trooper. The only time I remember her biting her tongue was years later when Carol started coming round, because she thought Carol was posh. When Granny died, we went back to the house after the funeral and there was this old woman, who was one of her pals, sitting there with the good coat and hat on, not saying a word. I can't remember what sparked her off, but she suddenly went into a rant and every second word was f*** or c***. Carol sat there absolutely shocked.

My first-ever game was for Barlanark Primary, when I was nine, and I couldn't sleep the night before because they wanted me to play right midfield and I wasn't sure how to keep myself in the position. But of course, as soon as the game started I was off, chasing the ball wherever it went – the way I played until Rangers took me in hand.

All I remember is that my boots had huge rubber studs the size of Rolos. That and the fact that they were solid black – I've always liked no-nonsense kit. I also never liked boots to look new, so even when I got my first Nikes with a yellow swoosh I took them straight out of the box and blackened it with boot polish.

Why? Probably because if you see a guy running onto the pitch in flash boots you know he fancies himself and you clatter into him twice as hard.

It's usually the wingers or strikers who have the daft boots and that's bad enough, but at Raith Rovers our captain, Todd Lumsden, had silver Predators and that's just not on for a centre-half.

I was sitting watching Rangers playing at Motherwell last season, just me and my dad, when Barry ran out of the tunnel with his short-sleeved blue shirt on and a long-sleeved white top underneath. Dad turned to me and fumed: 'What the f*** is that all about?'

He was not a happy man, because in his eyes the way his son had gone out on the field was not the Rangers way. I have to say I was with him on that one.

You get two tops left out for every game, a short sleeved and a long sleeved. If you're cold, you either wear the long sleeves or both of them. But if you want to wear something different under the short sleeved, you should make it the same colour as your strip.

I think Barry was just being trendy, but it didn't really work. Early in the game, Dad shook his head and said: 'He'll not have that on in the second half.'

And he was right.

As well as the school, I played for Blue Star Under-10s in Easterhouse and kept that up for a year after we moved to Hamilton, until it got too much for Dad to ferry me about all the time.

I was about 11 when I started going to the games myself. It was a half-hour walk from Little Earnock to the town and my parents never had to worry about me. It's hard to imagine you letting your kids wander about as freely now without checking up on them.

I loved the old Accies ground, Douglas Park. I used to go there a lot as a kid and still went to a lot of games whenever I wasn't playing.

As wee boys, we'd try and get a lift over the gate but once we got a bit more cunning we dug a tunnel under the wall at the tyre and exhaust place next to the ground to get ourselves a freebie. Sometimes when the ball was kicked out of the park, wee boys would dive under the wall again and run away with it.

We were so keen to get in without paying that even when they put up barbed wire around the top of the wall there were days when we took our lives in our hands and punted over it.

One of the great things about Douglas Park was listening to old Fergie, the legendary die-hard with the foghorn voice and the world-beating vocabulary of sweary words. One day when Rangers were playing Accies he just tore Souness apart all day and we were knotting ourselves.

I know he was an embarrassment to the Accies and he was banned from watching them countless times, but I also know how much their reaction to him used to break his heart. He was one of those guys who had nothing else but his football team and it wasn't his fault that the way things came out of his mouth offended people in the directors' box.

On the way home we'd stop at Equi's for chips and two

pickled onions and wander back up the road again. You can't beat childhood days like that.

Years later, one of the first dates I took Carol on was to see the Accies in a midweek game. We went in my Ford Fiesta XR2 and when we came back out it had been nicked from the car park at the County buildings.

I still say to this day it was her fault.

We were walking to the game when she remembered she had left her handbag in the car – though why she needed a handbag to go to the football is beyond me. She went back and got it and we thought nothing else of it, but after the game we wandered back across and it was gone.

The cops found it later in the Whitehills scheme, where by coincidence my previous XR2 had also ended up. That one had been found with the wheels and the stereo gone, which I was just about able to accept. This time, they'd also ripped the seats and kicked lumps out of the body work and that wasn't on.

I know why people nick cars, strip them and dump them – but mindless damage does my head in.

Hamilton had two big juvenile teams, Burnbank and Mill United. Years later, Barry started out with United, but back then I knew someone at school who was with Burnbank, so I went there too and won the Under-13 Scottish Cup.

The final was at Kilmarnock's Rugby Park, my first-ever big match on a senior ground. Just walking through the front door with my bag over my shoulder was great. It gave you the buzz. I knew by then this was what I wanted to do every week of my life, nothing else came into the equation.

It must have been a big game, because even my mum, Maureen, went – but, typically, never watched it. She was downstairs under the stand, pacing up and down. She gets too het up and she'd knock your head off if you sat behind her criticising one of her boys.

Even now, if I'm at her house and Barry's on the telly, she won't even glance at the screen. She'll wait until the end, then come in the room and ask two questions:

1. Did they win?
2. Did he do well?

Even if he hasn't done well, we say he did, just to keep her happy.

What struck me that day at Kilmarnock was how big the pitch was. I was in the middle of the park and I'd never been happier not to be shunted out wide. We won 2–1 and I remember getting stuck right in – I had Wee Guy's Syndrome, was never happier than charging in at someone twice my size. Still love seeing that in players today.

Afterwards, we got Pomagne in paper cups and felt like heroes.

Manchester United invited me down two years in a row, when I was 12 and 13. Their scout, Jimmy Dickie, would meet up with a bunch of us at Central Station and we would stay in bed and breakfast places. The real player among us was Sammy Johnston, who went on to play for Partick Thistle, St Johnstone and plenty more before ending up as a manager in the juniors. He was top man at our age group.

Being down there was top drawer. Every morning a bus would come to the digs and take us to The Cliff, and when you're that age, just turning up for training at the same place where Best and Law and all these legends had done their stuff really made you want to crack it as a footballer.

We trained inside a big shed with an ash surface or out on the main pitch, which had a wee stand for when they played reserve games. It was magic. And one afternoon I was in the gym and ended up playing badminton with Gordon McQueen. One minute you were watching him play on telly, the next he's your partner.

But as a kid, the best thing of all was drinking cold milk out of those wee white machines you used to get. That was a revelation – some folk back home didn't even have a fridge in the house – and I'd down pints of the stuff at lunchtime then barely be able to run about for it all sloshing around in my guts.

I always wanted to play in the centre of the park, but with my height – or lack of it – whenever I went for trials anywhere they stuck me out on the wing. When I got a trial for the Scotland Under-15s, the trainer David Livingstone put me at SWEEPER.

He was the guy who discovered Paul McStay and took loads of players from our area to Dundee United, so he knew a lot about football. But I couldn't help thinking I was wasted where he was using me, because in those days I had bundles and bundles of energy. I could have run all day. People wouldn't believe it seeing me now, but as a kid I'd run and dribble for fun.

Anyway, I got into the squad by the skin of my teeth and ended up getting a game on the right wing. I just used to get the head down, beat three or four and have a crack at goal.

By this time a guy called David Skinner had started up Gartcosh United and I went there; by the time I was coming up to Under-16 level Rangers had scouts watching me all the time. And that was when they gave me the shock of my life.

Out of the blue, I got the word that Greigy wanted me out of Gartcosh and in the reserves at Ibrox – they reckoned the way I played was giving me too many bad habits. I could see what they were doing and there was no way I was ever saying no, but I've never been sure it was totally for the good. You have to entertain the punters. They pay a fortune and deserve more than safety first.

I remember getting pelters from experienced guys like Derek Johnstone because when they were screaming for passes I'd be off on a mazy run, playing for myself. DJ used to moan at me all the time, really give me some stick, but I could see why. He'd made the run and he expected the ball. He wasn't going to check back out and go again because some wee boy was doing his own thing all the time.

The drill at Rangers was constant – touch and hit, touch and hit. It wasn't my game, though they must have brainwashed me well, because as the years went on two-touch was pretty much all I played.

Rangers changed me, no doubt about that. Through time, that took something out of my game. But whether you're a kid or an established star, you do whatever the manager wants. Your life revolves around keeping him happy – and whatever people think of me, I can cross my heart and swear that once I cross that white line I've always done what the manager tells me.

If they wanted me to tackle, to touch and hit, there were no mumps and moans. I just got on with it.

I was in awe of Greigy and still am. I was at a Rangers Hallowe'en do in 2005 and he was at the next table. It really riled me that some of the players were talking to him like he was just anybody, because he's not. He's a hero and that never changes, no matter what you think you are yourself.

If I see Bobby Russell or Alex MacDonald or any of the Rangers players I watched as a kid on the terraces, they still give me butterflies. They might not believe that, but it's the God's honest truth.

Once you've idolised guys in your schooldays, you should never look at them any differently. What they were to you then is what they are for ever. I hope I never lose that.

Something's changed, though. The Bobby Russells and John Greigs were mad about football, it was all they knew and all they wanted to know and that's how it was for me. But I see guys playing these days who plainly aren't in love with the game. For Greigy, for Bobby, for me, it was a job – a fantastic, exciting job, but still a job. Now it's a way to make money. And that's a huge difference.

You can get rich in football now without caring about it. Then, everybody wanted to be a football player and only a few of us got the privilege. Far better players than me fell by the wayside, but it was all about how much you wanted it.

I never went to school discos. I never really had girlfriends. You were more likely to find me running up the hills around Hamilton. But if missing out on a few nights out with my mates was the price to pay for giving myself a better chance of achieving my dream, it was a small one.

Dad was a huge influence as well, always there, making sure I did the right things – but never getting on my back. He'd just say stuff like: 'You trained today? Done a wee bit?'

That was enough for me. I knew he'd be proud of me if I'd done it without being forced to. I just wanted to please him.

The same went for Greigy. I'll always hold him in the highest respect simply for what and who he is. The Greatest-Ever Ranger, that's what the fans voted him as ahead of Coisty, Coop, Laudrup and all the other heroes from down the decades.

So you can imagine what an honour it was for me when he made me the club's *youngest*-ever player on 27 March 1983.

What a day. What a feeling to walk into Ibrox Stadium not as a fan, not as a kid turning up for training with the other kids.

But as a member of the first team.

I was 15 years and 239 days old. I was still a schoolboy.

You get mascots aged 15, never mind players.

Yet here I was, already fulfilling my greatest dream. God bless John Greig.

It was big Tam Forsyth's testimonial and the big man played the first 15 minutes then went back on for the last 15. I got the last half hour in the middle of the park and loved every single touch of the ball.

We were presented with engraved decanters at time-up and my mum still has mine. It was a big thing for me.

Yet what sticks with me most of all about my debut in light blue?

The memory of Tam coming off after his first stint, slumping down in the dugout . . . and lighting up a FAG.

I was shocked. I don't think I'd ever seen a footballer smoke before. And definitely not during a game.

These days, a lot of the foreign boys smoke, which amazed me considering the way they tut-tut at the way us Scots live our lives. But the only other homegrown guy I've know to be into the ciggies was Kevin Drinkell.

I think he kept a packet of Woodbines rolled up in his shirt sleeves.

I wore the No. 17 shirt in big Tam's game, the first of *twelve* I'd have on in my time with the club. I wore every outfield number bar 3.

My first competitive appearance was as a sub in a 4–0 League Cup win at home to Queen of the South the next August, but my first start wasn't until the last week in October in the same competition.

By which time, the Greatest-Ever was gone.

My dad had told me all about Greigy from when I was wee and back then, as now, I held him in huge esteem. A true legend – though plainly not in the eyes of some of his other players.

As I found myself around the first team more and more, I'd hear some of the boys talking behind the boss's back. It wasn't a nice feeling – though, as the years have gone on, I've come to see that it's just how dressing-rooms can be sometimes.

Back then, though, it was a eye-opener for a young boy who thought everyone felt the same way about the manager as I did. Greigy? Slaughtered when he wasn't around? Surely not.

To be honest, I think some of the boys were happy to see the back of him. As a player he'd been hard as nails, but it just wasn't the same when he was in charge and some players took advantage of him.

Greigy was too nice as a manager, too busy trying to please everybody. He didn't have the arrogance to go with his knowledge of the game and his love for the club.

Finishing fourth, as well as losing both cup finals in that 1982–83 season, pretty much ended his reign and come the first week in October, out he went and back into the hotseat marched big Jock Wallace.

At this point, by the way, I should point out a pattern that will develop as the book goes along. Just about every time a manager signs me, he gets the bullet.

It started with John Greig, the man who gave me my break in the professional game and who kept an eye on me for a lot of years after that, and continued through Alex MacDonald, John Lambie, Terry Butcher, Tam Coyne and more.

Think it was something I said?

I can still see Jock before his first game, saluting the fans with a clenched fist and bringing the whole place to its feet, roaring and believing. He just had that aura about him, you knew he was a fighter. And when he talked, you listened for all you were worth.

He ran Ibrox like an army camp and for me was a brilliant manager. He believed in a clip round the ear, sometimes while you were sitting in the dressing-room waiting to go out for a game, just to keep you on your toes. When you were walking along a corridor and you spotted him coming the other way, you'd find a cupboard to duck into in case he was in the mood to test your strength with a punch in the guts.

He demanded the highest standards from his players, in the

way they dressed, played and behaved. Socks up and tied, shirts tucked in, no facial hair. Shirt and ties every day of the week. It had been that way from when I was 12 and it made you feel special, part of something that mattered.

And when you let those standards slip, you soon found out about it.

The call would come to go up to the office and suddenly the marble stairs weren't nearly high enough. All too soon you were chapping his door and hearing his voice boom 'Come in', and you were being reminded about what was expected of you. Whether you were 16 or 36, it was an experience you don't want to go through more than once.

Jock had only been in charge for a couple weeks when he gave me the shout for my debut against Hearts at Ibrox, though the team sheet went up so close to kick-off, the only way I could let my dad know was to put a wee note on the back of my comps envelope saying: 'I'm playing.'

Sitting in the dressing-room, I just couldn't wait to get out and get started, for Dad to see me. I also knew I'd have pals from school up in the stands with *their* dads and I wanted to put on a show for them.

Then there were the other players – Robert Prytz, Craig Paterson, Bobby Russell, guys I'd watched from the old Centenary Stand. Any Saturday when I didn't have a game, a guy called Willie Houston, who was two or three years older than me, used to take me in on the train to Glasgow Central and we'd scoot across to Ibrox from there.

And now, all of a sudden, there I was waiting to go out and entertain boys like me and Willie and all the other guys we knew who were Rangers daft. It wasn't frightening, not a bit. It was just a massive thrill.

I sat there thinking back to my debut in the reserves, when big Derek Johnstone gave me pelters for dribbling past full-backs instead of delivering the ball to him exactly when he wanted it.

It was years later before I realised why he'd been like that, but even then I didn't think it was the right way for him to react. I'd rather have a quiet word in passing with a young lad and try to encourage him to do it differently next time, not dent his confidence with a bollocking.

Mind you, Big Derek was going through a rough time in his career and he was a grumpy boy at the best of times, so when some daft wee boy tried to beat every defender twice instead of crossing for him it must have driven him nuts.

Craig Paterson was superb. He was a bright lad, and he'd come across in the dressing-room and have a quiet little word in your ear. I always appreciated moments like that and tried to follow his example down the years.

Then you had Kenny Black, Andy Kennedy, Eric Ferguson, all of them only a couple of years older than me but with masses more experience. It wasn't the greatest Rangers team of all time, but every one of the boys would have run through a brick wall for the club.

I was out on the right wing that night, up against George Cowie. I was told to get at him and I did it from the off; ran at him, committed him, tried to make the yard for the whipped ball into the box. There was so much excitement inside me. Give me the ball and I'll go for it.

We won 2–0 and I remember cutting the ball back for Prytzy to hit the clincher. There can't have been more than 10,000 there that night and with the place also being in the middle of being reconstructed it was an eerie atmosphere. But it felt like Hampden when it was full to the rafters.

Come the Saturday, though, I was back down to earth with a bang – and I *mean* a bang. We were at Love Street and I was up against a real hard nut in Billy Abercromby. The kind of guy who looked across the line at a wee boy like me and made his mind up to dish out the facts of life.

I was all football, wanting to be on the ball, looking up, making my passes. He wanted to win. So near the end of the first half, he came right over the ball, topped me a cracker. One broken leg.

That was a sharp – and extremely painful – reminder of what it takes to play at the top. You have to be intimidating or be intimidated. I was naïve, doing all the things I would later tell Barry not to do, going in loose, not winning my battles.

So there I was, two minutes in the first team and suddenly heading for nearly a year out of it. By the time I was fit again, it was a case of grafting and grinding my way back into the plans.

I changed in the reserve team dressing-room and played for the reserves, but trained with the big boys. That suited me fine, because I was happier around the boys I'd grown up with.

But very little else about the situation suited me. I'd been on the verge of doing something and then it all fell apart again. Abercromby really set my career back – yet the strange thing is that in the long term he maybe did me a favour.

After that tackle, I realised that there are guys out there who go to do you because they think you're going to do them first. It's the hard side of football, the ugly side, but you have to learn to deal with it.

I lost my first big on-field battle because I had no intention of doing my opposite number. That taught me . . .

I came back into the plans from the bench in a 1–1 draw with Hearts at Ibrox in early December and two weeks later made my Old Firm debut – a game when I received the strangest advice of my career.

The day got off to a bad start when I turned up with blond tips in my hair and the gaffer went berserk. I actually thought for a second that he was going to punch me, but then he took a deep breath and leaned into me and said menacingly: 'That'll be gone by Monday.'

And it was.

It was a big game for Jock, his return to the battlefield he loved after six years away, and he got us pumped up in that away dressing-room until we were growling for raw meat. It was an astonishing buzz. My mates were in the Rangers end, ten guys in hooped shirts were coming after me with 50,000 bonkers punters as handers – and I couldn't wait to get in about it.

There's a part of you that hates the other side in these games, not for all the stupid sectarian reasons, but just because they're what stands between you and ruling the city. Everything depends on the result, all the usual need to make the fans happy is magnified by a million.

I used to love the bus pulling into Parkhead and hearing all the abuse and seeing all the faces. It didn't disgust me or frighten me. It was just part of the build-up.

Then you'd come out that tunnel and it would just be a blur of noise and colour. Sometimes, especially when it's sunny, it's hard to even see the ball. All your senses are being assaulted at once.

Your head spins like crazy; you're constantly fighting with yourself to stay in control. In the Souness days we used to freak the foreigners out in the dressing-room with how hyper we were, because you're definitely more aggressive than in a normal game. It's still only three points, that's what they tell you. I'll let you argue that one with the punters. All I know is that some Friday nights before a Celtic game I could barely sleep for running it all through in my mind.

So when you're ten minutes into your first experience of the madness on enemy turf and you hear a calming voice in your ear telling you to stay cool, keep it simple, you're doing great, it's probably a good thing.

It's just when you realise it's the most Celtic-y player in Celtic history who's dishing out the advice that you stop dead in your tracks.

The voice belonged to Tommy Burns.

'Play two, three touch. Don't get wrapped up in it all . . .'

I'm looking at him, baffled. Some guys try and talk you off your game, but he was talking me *onto* mine. And he kept it up the whole way through.

'*Good ball, son, you're doing well. Keep the head up, get the big picture . . .*'

It was the most surreal experience I ever had on the pitch and afterwards I couldn't wait to tell Dad.

'Hey, see that Tommy Burns . . .'

'*Aye? What about him?*'

Up go his hackles. He's waiting for me to tell him the so-and-so had a fly kick at me behind the ref's back.

'He really helped me through the game, Dad.'

His jaw was nearly on the carpet. And any Rangers fans would have been the same.

I mean, my first Old Firm experience was in a reserve game when I was 15. I was up against Jim McInally and he called me a wee Orange bastard then spat on my shirt. That always stuck with me. I've met him since then and shaken his hand after games and it's never been mentioned, but I'm sure he's probably embarrassed, because that can't have been his true character.

Young guys – and, let's be honest, older guys as well – just get sucked into the nastiness that goes with games between Rangers and Celtic. It's hardly surprising with everything that's going on around them.

It makes me laugh when players are accused of causing trouble in the crowd. You've got 60,000 there screaming religious hate at each other, re-enacting the wars from Ireland. And some left-back scythes down a winger and *he's* the one lighting the touchpaper.

Nonsense. We all have a responsibility, but the punters can't have it all ways. They can't want to tear the heads off each other then get all moral when there's handbags in the centre circle.

Anyway, how could I have run about calling Celtic players Fenian bastards then or shout it from the stands now? Half my family – Granny Buchanan, cousins Carolyn and Paul, Uncle John – are all Catholic. There's absolutely not a shred of bigotry in my family. Carol's from a staunch Catholic family. Her dad's Celtic daft. Her brothers Danny and Jim were in Seville.

Yet I've been on the team bus with Big Jock when The Sash got played or in the dressing-room when the party songs started and I'm giving it laldy with the rest of them, drumming on the treatment table, the lot. Before one Old Firm game we were marching up and down the floor with Jimmy Nicholl.

But it was all just how we got wound up. It was just words.

And yes, I've been to a lot of Rangers functions and yes, I've sung the songs there as well. I'm not ashamed of that and I can put my hand on my heart and still say that I don't have a bigoted bone in my body.

I should just be grateful that back in those days there weren't sneaky swines hanging around with camera phones primed to land you on page one.

Donald Findlay lost his position as vice-chairman of Rangers after being caught on video singing 'The Billy Boys' at a club party. And more recently, there was outrage when Celtic stars John Hartson and Stephen Pearson were captured on somebody's moby singing 'The Fields of Athenry' while IRA chanting went on in the background.

I have sympathy for all three of them and for anyone else who's been turned over after thinking they were among friends. Unfortunately, these days it seems someone always wants to get you – even if you're all meant to be on the same side.

I used to go with Durranty to pubs around Ibrox and places like The Grapes and The District are filled with incredible characters. People would ask for your autograph but would want a little message with it, something like FTP – big Bob Malcolm actually did it one night and got caught, the silly boy. It cost him a doing in the papers and a £5,000 club fine.

I know that admitting these things go on and that you were part of them won't impress some people, but going through it all was part of my growing up and I don't regret any of it.

The whole sectarian thing is so big and complicated you could write whole books on it and only scratch the surface, so I'm not even going to start taking it all apart and analysing it. All I know is probably the same as Hartson and Pearson know – that when you go to a supporters' function with either of the Old Firm you're expected to be one of the boys and not make yourself bigger than the fans.

I felt completely relaxed at Rangers nights, and when the singing started after a couple of beers you joined in. When you went on stage to collect an award, they wouldn't let you down until you gave them a song – and they weren't looking for 'Moon River'.

But outside those walls? I would never ever be dragged into anything that would be seen as bigoted or sectarian.

These nights are astonishing at times. Carol used to come to some of the Hearts ones and she was amazed by how blatant the women were. They'd come over to some of the players – even if they were sitting with their wives or girlfriends – and basically put themselves on a plate.

At some Rangers supporters' clubs, guys would actually come over and offer you their wives. No kidding, they'd go: 'See her at the bar? That's my missus, feel free . . . '

And you'd think, thanks for offering, but I'm OK.

Jock tried like a bear to turn things round and managed to win the League Cup in his first two seasons, but fourth in the league both times was a hell of a hard one for the fans to take.

They were fair with young guys like me, because they knew we were trying our hearts out and that most of us had been fans before we signed.

Others, though . . . well, let's just say that the abuse Alex

McLeish's men took during their lean spells seems like a carpet of rose petals compared to what was dished out in the winter of 1983 and the early months of 1984.

Ringing up phone-ins or writing to the papers calling for the manager and his under-achieving stars to get the axe? A few dozen of them hanging around outside the front door for half an hour after a 0–0 draw with Aberdeen?

The dressing-room windows open right onto the street at Ibrox and I've sat in there after games with crowds outside literally baying for blood. Seen guys walk out the front door and have fans right up in their faces, spitting venom.

To be honest, when you're 16 and 17 booing's not an issue, you barely even notice it. You're too young and full of optimism to let things like that eat away at you – but in any case, if I gave the ball away the fans would actually get behind me and will me to win it back. It was the older guys who got no leeway. They had no hiding place and it wasn't pleasant.

Look at the way they treated Coisty when he came at first. His movement was great, his enthusiasm was infectious, but the goals just wouldn't go in. He missed chance after chance and it seemed as time went on that each one was easier than the last. During one Scottish Cup replay against Dundee, the whole of the Copland Road and the Govan just seemed to have had enough all at once. Thousands of punters just stood up and started booing him, a solid wall of hate aimed at this guy who was sweating blood to try and please them.

What those punters didn't realise was how good a player you had to be to get into the position to miss those chances. What they didn't appreciate was that, no matter how often he missed, Coisty kept coming back and back and back for more. They should have been giving him a standing ovation for that level of guts, not trying to drive him out.

He has tremendous belief in himself, that guy. Always told

himself he was the best and slaved tirelessly to prove it. But that day, he sat in his sweat-soaked strip at time-up after we'd lost 1–0 while the rest of us got showered and changed and he cried his eyes out.

In the depths of his misery, you could hear them outside yelling his name. I looked at him and listened to the abuse and thought: 'Jesus Christ, is this what it comes to?'

Yet look how quickly things can turn. Within a matter of weeks, he was scoring a hat-trick against Celtic to win us the League Cup and suddenly he could do no wrong. What an example to any young player – if you have the strength of character, you can come through anything.

I admired Coisty so much during that spell and again a couple of years later when he kept his discipline in the face of some awful treatment at the hands of Souness.

And yet when I first met him, I didn't like him. Why? Because he'd knocked Rangers back twice before finally signing and I didn't understand why anyone would ever need a second invitation, never mind a third.

Later, I realised how smart he'd been in planning his career. And he really is smart – as well as incredibly difficult to stay annoyed at.

Carol never used to like Coisty either, she thought he was too much of a ladies man. In fact, she told me about this lunchtime when she was in Di Maggio's in Glasgow with some pals and they were slaughtering him for all the jumping around he was meant to be doing.

Then who walks in but Coisty himself? And don't the whole lot of them just fall at his feet?

It went like: 'Carol Ferguson? How ye doin', darlin'? Ye're lookin' gorgeous – and who's yer pals? Every one better lookin' than the last. Hey, you, shift up – waiter? Two bottles of white over here, please . . . '

That's as big a talent as the one he had for putting the ball in the back of the net. He could get a biscuit at anybody's door.

Mind you, by sitting down with the girls and doing his Mr Loverman act he probably kept someone else waiting impatiently somewhere else for an hour. He was always late, mainly because he'd never walk past anyone he knew or even strangers who just wanted to natter.

The following season, I was involved in 20 games in all competitions and really started to feel part of things. It was starting to happen for me – but not, sadly, for Jock. Hearts and Celtic were fighting for the title and by April he was gone.

No one likes to see a legend suffer and it was sad to see the pressure mount and mount on him. He went from this bellowing, sergeant-major of a leader to someone quiet, withdrawn. Beaten.

When times are hard and a new manager comes in, you rely on him to give you a lift and get things going again. Then, when he's the one feeling the heat, he needs you to return the favour for him.

Unfortunately, not many get the response they want from the whole dressing-room. Some feel responsible for their boss's plight. Too many others are only too happy to sit tight and wait for change.

In the end, what it came down to for big Jock was that the game had changed since his first, triumphant spell at the helm.

A clenched fist just wasn't enough any more.

Rangers had the swish new stands, but too many of the seats were empty as fans voted with their feet. They needed to produce something special – some*one* special – to get the place rocking again.

Enter Graeme Souness.

SIX

SOUNESS

Ten minutes into the second half, another lung-bursting run. Really pushing myself now. Pounding the legs and arms until they hurt.

Sweat's pouring, head's starting to swirl with the effort. And also with the pain of doing it all so far away from where the game's on.

Rangers are playing at home, but they don't need me. The manager needs me less and less these days.

Which is why I'm here, in my second home.

God's Country. Strathclyde Park.

When you're left out of a football team, you're meant to stay and support the ones who *are* needed. But that's not my style. It's not that I'd ever want them to lose, it's just that me sitting in the stand watching isn't going to do anything for either of us.

The guys who get picked don't want or need anyone else around them. The guys who don't get picked would be better off getting the hell out the way and doing something useful.

So there I'd be, while my mates were grafting for points and bonuses, hammering myself in the wide open spaces of the place I also go back to when I'm coming back from injury or simply feeling down.

During my time under Graeme Souness, I spent far too long doing both.

Niggle after niggle in my body, niggle after niggle in my ear from the gaffer. Over four troubled years, it all gradually wore me down until all my dreams of forging a long and happy career at the club I loved lay in tatters.

It wasn't all his fault. I should have bitten my tongue when he got at me, played the game the way he wanted it played, stayed in sometimes instead of running around with my mates.

But all it would have taken from his side was an arm on my shoulder now and again rather than a ton of bricks on my head, a few words of experience from his own youth rather than growls of disapproval. A bit of come and go.

Instead, the day he came they started the countdown to the day I'd go.

It didn't need a genius to work out that when he arrived in the summer of 1986, I'd be playing second fiddle to him. We played in the same position, but he was a world-class operator, fit as a fiddle. And he picked the team.

Being left out, though, never got any easier. In fact, it began to feel like a personal slight. So it got to the stage that when he broke the bad news before home games, I'd go and find my dad and he'd drive me to Strathy so I could have a run and get the frustration out of my system.

I'd do lap after lap of the park, thinking with every step about why the bastard hadn't picked me. I'd push myself, trying to hurt myself physically. It felt sometimes like I was going to explode. I'd be fuming with jealousy about the guys who were playing. That bit never changes – you wish them well, but inside you hate them. Not for long, mind. It subsides, because they're your

THE FIRST TEAM – with Carol, Ross, Darren and Lewis,
the most important people in my life.

WHO ATE ALL THE RUSKS? – chubby
Barry, not long after the time I
pinged a dart in his wee head.

MR MUSCLE – comparing biceps in
the bath at Mum and Dad's with Barry.

HAIR-RAISER – holding off Roy Aitken on my Old Firm debut, aided by the flowing blond tips that drove Jock Wallace tonto, December 1984.

HAT'S AWFUL – Durranty and I celebrating an early Scotland call-up. The bunnets are magnificently stylish.

COUNTRY BOY – in the Scotland strip I didn't get to wear nearly as often as I had dreamed of.

FLAG DAY – bursting clear on the Saturday we celebrated
winning the 1987 league title by beating St Mirren 1–0, May 1987.

FIT FOR LIFE – I never worked harder in my career
than I did to reach peak condition with Hearts.

TOGETHER FOR EVER – in Barbados on the holiday when I proposed to my first and last girlfriend, June 1991.

BLUE DO – with 14-year-old Barry and best man Jim 'Quiet Man' Gillespie minutes before Carol and I were married, June 1992.

ISN'T SHE LOVELY – Carol takes centre stage after the wedding. With (from the left) Aunt Angela, her son Kevin, me, Mum and Dad, Granny Fergie, Barry, Granda Buchanan, Auntie Agnes and Angela's husband Brian.

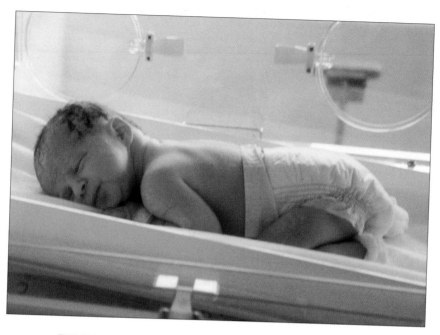

THE BRIGHTEST STAR – the picture of Lauren we had turned into a painting that hangs in our lounge. She never looked more beautiful.

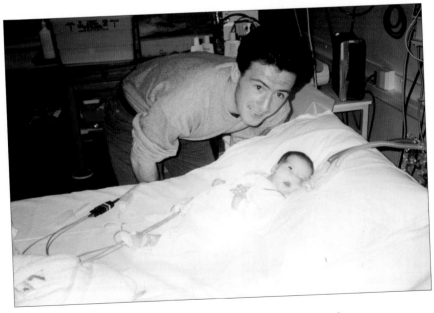

CLINGING TO LIFE – seeing Lauren with all those tubes and drips and clips broke our hearts every single day.

HOME FROM HOME – a few weeks after joining Sunderland, we played Rangers in a pre-season friendly. Here I am taking on Stuart McCall.

MEET THE PARENTS — my mum Maureen and dad Archie (on the right) with Carol's folks Danny and Millie.

SCARF ACE — I owe John Lambie a lot for taking me to Falkirk and Thistle as well as getting me off the dole.

ALL GROWN UP – my wee brother's wedding day. Carol, Barry, his new wife Margaret and big brother.

EBONY AND IVORY – in St Lucia for Barry's wedding – note big brother's far superior muscle tone and tan, June 2001.

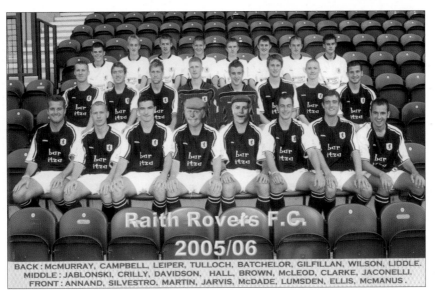

FAIR GAME – Scott Crabbe and I came in to training at Raith one night to find the boys' team pic doctored in tribute to the TV grumps Jack and Victor.

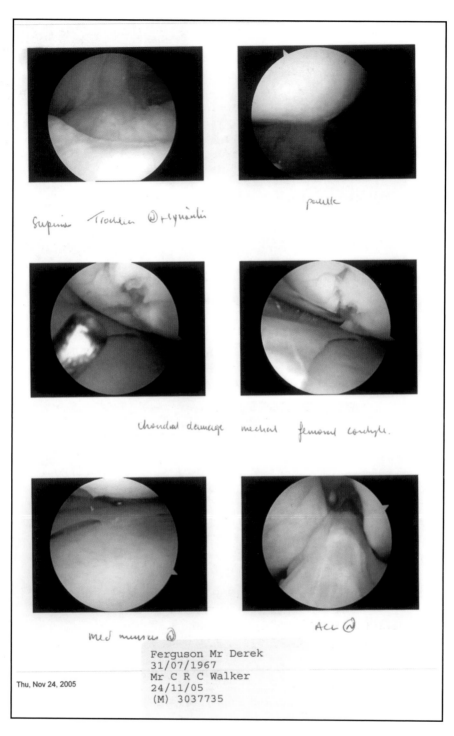

Supra Trochlea ④ +synovitis

patella

chondral damage medial femoral condyle.

med menisci ④

ACL ④

Thu, Nov 24, 2005

Ferguson Mr Derek
31/07/1967
Mr C R C Walker
24/11/05
(M) 3037735

PICTURE OF MISERY – the X-rays taken the night
before my fateful final knee op, November 2005.

mates and you want them to win. It hurts, though, or at least it should if you're a real pro.

Some guys numb the hurt with a beer and say 'F**k them.' Sweating my guts out was always better than alcohol. Either that or I'd take a ball down the park, find a wall and boot, boot, boot against it for ages. It becomes hypnotic. You imagine you're on the pitch, in a real game, picking your passes through a crowded midfield. You're a wee boy again, dreaming of stardom.

You play it, take the rebound in, turn, move. Switch direction again, pass, take the rebound . . . repetition's the only way to make the real thing second nature. You use a rough bit of the wall to make the ball come back at you at unpredictable angles, a smooth bit for volleys, use air vents for target practice. Once Barry was big enough, I took him down to the park to practise all the same skills and today I do it with my own boys. We all owe that place a lot.

Those game-less Saturdays, I'd finish my laps, then batter out ten 100-metre sprints, have a warm-down and then go up the road with Dad, listening to the results coming in. I needed my dad so much then and he was always there for me. He knew how hard the whole Souness thing was for me, because he knew how much it meant for me to be part of things at Rangers.

The club and everyone in it were like family to me. So imagine thinking everything was great in the house, only to find out your dad wanted you out. That's what it was like between me and Souness.

So what went wrong between us? Where do I start?

For one, there was the difference between the way I played and the way he *wanted* me to play. I think he saw bits of himself in me and expected me to take my lead from him, but I was never going to be a replica.

When he picked himself it was all touch-and-give, touch-and-give, the way he'd done it all his life. But I wanted to do more than touch and hit, had done ever since Rangers picked me up at 12 years old. I wanted the flick, the nutmeg, the little ball over someone's head. And it started to bug him after a while.

He'd constantly pull me up in training about how many touches I was taking and the subs would tell me how he'd been doing the same during games.

And the more he nit-picked at me for it, the more I started to believe he simply didn't like me. He'd come off the park and tell me that the way he'd just done it was the way it should be done. But all he'd do was make me more determined than ever to show him that it wasn't.

Yes, I could have knuckled down and played the simple ball more. Yes, doing it my way caused conflict. But it was instinctive, off the cuff. That was how I played. That's how I *was*.

I was fiery then, full of beans, fearless and up for anything. Big players didn't intimidate me – I was excited about facing them, getting stuck into them. That was my strength. Unfortunately, in his eyes, it was also my weakness.

Now, I hope I'd be smarter about it all. Then, I just wouldn't back down.

Pretty soon, he brought in guys like Ray Wilkins, guys who *would* touch and play. After that came Terry Hurlock, who'd put the foot in. And I was caught in the middle, not the hardman but not the guy for the simple stuff either.

So our attitudes to the game were never going to dovetail. Our attitudes to life? Just as far apart.

I was bubbly, always up for a laugh. I don't think my mood ever changed back then. Souness? You never knew how you'd get him. Some mornings he'd be brand new, others his face would be tripping him. You were constantly walking on eggshells around him.

You knew what was what with Walter Smith. He was on the

same level all the time – until you riled him, at which point it was time to run for cover. Only once did he ever even appear to turn against me. When I left to go to Hearts, I did an interview in the *Rangers News* saying that I hoped the fans didn't give me a hard time when I came back to play against them. It was how I genuinely felt.

But a while back I met Terry McGeady, the guy who'd done the piece, and he told me that after it went in Walter pulled him up and said that he hoped the punters gave me stick. That took me aback – mostly because it just didn't sound like Walter. When I got left out of the 1989 Scottish Cup final, he was the one who'd put the arm round my shoulder. He was Good Cop. But Souness? He was moody as hell.

Plus, he seemed to need to prove himself to us all the time. He'd go through young guys at training, as if to leave his autograph on them. But we all knew who he was, what he was, where he'd been and what he'd done. We were in awe of the guy when he arrived. He was this almost mythical figure, a true footballing giant – and working with him should have made me. I was a young guy desperate to run the show in midfield, he was the gaffer who'd been there, done it and worn the Armani T-shirt. Yet in the end, he broke me, forced me out of the team and out of the club I loved. To him, it probably meant nothing. To me, it meant everything.

I didn't hate Souness then and I don't hate him now. But I didn't like him because his methods were wrong and his attitude stank at times and he could be a bully.

It was so hard to work out why all of that should be when we'd have jumped through burning hoops to make him happy. It takes a lot to start out with people hanging on your every word and make them turn against you, but somehow Souness managed it with me and many more besides – ask Coisty about that one.

Why did the gaffer turn against him? Simple. Because everybody loved Coisty and the gaffer wanted to be the centre of attention. For me, it was jealousy, simple as that. But what does that say about Souness, an international star, the bee's knees, rich and famous and successful and respected? Pissed off because one of his players was a nationwide personality.

Grannies, models, kids, dads – they all thought Coisty was fantastic. But not Souness. You could feel it about the place, sense it in training and in games. Coisty was a complete one-off. He didn't have the best touch, wasn't the quickest, but his movement was second to none and upstairs he was sharp as a tack. He'd have been an asset to any side, yet the manager's attitude to him held his career back.

Despite everything, though, he never showed his feelings in the face of it all and I wish so much I could have been more like that when it was my turn for the treatment. Coisty was cleverer than me in that if he got angry, he did it in private. I bit every time and paid a heavy price.

Then there were the injuries. I picked up too many silly little ones under Souness and I know how much that frustrated him. At one point he told the press that the club had invested a lot of money in me for no return.

But how frustrated did he think *I* felt at missing my chance during the most exciting period in the history of Rangers? That I wasn't in there showing what I could do alongside the conveyor belt of superstars arriving at the club? Did he think I was swinging the lead? Or getting hurt to spite him?

Because that's how it felt at times.

And then, of course, there was the other wedge between us.

Me.

Or rather, the Me he thought was out there making a tube of myself.

I was a daft boy, no bones about it. There were times when I did myself no favours. But I wasn't the only one – just the one he seemed to come down on hardest of all.

The incident that really got to him was when I put my shoulder out trying to throw a big bottle of a water dispenser at Durranty when we were messing about in the gym after training one day.

Souness was in his office – right through the wall from us – and heard the boys yelling for Doc Cruickshanks to come and see to me. He was absolutely raging when he saw the damage, and no wonder. But there were other times when he'd hear us generally laughing and messing about and it still pissed him off. I reckon he was jealous of our youth and freedom.

Some mornings, he'd pop his head round the dressing-room door and look right into Daft Corner, where it was me and Durranty and Scott Nisbet and Coisty, all loud and giving each other pelters – and I'm damn sure he made his mind up that we'd been on the batter the night before.

I don't think The Game Of Death did us much good with him.

If you've never played The Game Of Death, you've never lived – and never nearly died either. You take four or five guys, you sneak into the physio's room and grab scalpels, scissors, anything sharp that's lying around. Then you lock the door and turn out the light – the physio's room has no window, by the way – and then you start throwing lethal weapons at each other in the pitch dark.

We always made sure we took a senior pro in with us, big Tel, somebody like that. They always bricked themselves at The Game Of Death. The rest of us were too stupid to be scared. It never crossed our minds that a scalpel could get stuck in a scalp or take out an eye.

Team bonding? Team bandaging, more like.

One of our other favourites was switching on this electronic box they had for speeding up tissue repairs. You were meant to strap sponges on either side of your knee or ankle or whatever and turn up the current. We'd stick them on our temples and crank it up to full blast.

You don't think Durranty's frizzy hair was natural, do you?

But that's what players are. That's what they do. They have so much energy and if clubs aren't smart enough to channel it in the right directions, it comes out in all the wrong ones.

And you know what? I can't believe Souness never got up to stupid stuff like that when he was a kid. I've read about his problems as a teenager at Spurs, how he ran away because he couldn't settle there.

Surely back then he'd have loved the manager or some older pro to come and sit him down and make him feel better about himself, tell him what was expected of him? The last thing he'd have needed was someone calling him all the stupid bastards of the day. Yet that's how he was with me, instead of taking me aside and sorting me out with a few quiet words.

He'd also been on the wrong end of enough rumours and inaccurate newspaper headlines down the years to know that you can't trust a fraction of the off-field stories you hear about footballers.

Yet this was where our relationship eroded worse than my dodgy knees. He just never seemed to give me the benefit of the doubt when the gossips got going. It became accepted fact that I was going off the rails.

So, let's get this bit out of the way once and for all . . .

Derek Ferguson and Ian Durrant. The Kray Twins of Ibrox.

Yeah? More like the Chuckle Brothers.

Even now, I keep hearing all the stuff about the pair of us having gone off the rails at Rangers – and it's all rubbish.

We didn't run about wild. We never once went looking for trouble. We certainly never had a season ticket for the nick. We were just two ordinary guys living a dream.

Should somebody have reeled us in? Of course they should. But when you're that age, with a few bob in your pocket and there's nobody setting you straight, what do you do?

You go for it.

We were young, we were fit, life was brilliant. We felt invincible.

And I tell you what, I'd have needed to be had I got up to even a tenth of the nonsense that was churned out by the rumour mill. It got so out of control it was almost laughable.

Except that mud sticks – so much so that, despite playing nearly 500 games for a dozen clubs across 23 years, the thing I'm most remembered for is a mythical late-night brawl.

The Kebab Shop Incident.

Durranty and I have been slaughtered about it for years on *Only An Excuse?* and *Off the Ball,* after-dinner speakers still make gags about it and if you mention our names in the same sentence to most football fans, they'll automatically say the word kebab.

Yet here's how much of a myth the whole thing is.

We weren't even eating kebabs. It was pizza.

It was a midweek night before a day off, so we were OK to go out. We'd gone to The District Bar and then, as you do, we'd fancied something to eat. So we wandered a couple of hundred yards up Paisley Road West to a takeaway place opposite the Grand Ole Oprey Country and Western Club and ordered up.

I was inside with Ian, while our mates Donnie and Gordon waited in the street. They were carrying on, somebody got bumped and next thing there was an argument. Donnie and Gordon thought nothing of it and turned away, but this bunch of young guys and girls didn't let up.

Then one of them spotted Ian, whose stookie and crutches from his latest knee op made him stand out a tad, and asked what he was saying about it. We just laughed and went back to waiting for our pizzas.

When it started getting iffy was when they started heading for their motor and one of them shouted at Ian: 'I hope you break yer other f*****g knee!'

That wasn't on. So Donnie grabbed a bin and emptied it on the motor. They got out and there was some shoving. The guy in the shop rang the cops and said Ian Durrant and Derek Ferguson were in a fight.

And next thing, the cavalry arrived. Sirens, lights, action. Panda cars and Sherpa vans screamed up, officers made a bee-line for Ian. The other boys were telling them neither of us had anything to do with it, but suddenly Ian was being nicked.

Not gently, either, but shoved roughly into the back of a van. I wasn't having that. I asked them – politely, by the way – if they'd mind putting him in a car to help his leg. They gave me a rubber-ear.

So I started wrestling with them to help my mate. And I was off down the Govan Hilton with him.

By the time we got there we were giggling about it all. Until, that is, the reality set in.

Souness. He'd kill us.

How fast did he find out? Probably before it even happened. And he was as angry as you'd expect, even though the truth was we'd done nothing wrong.

Thankfully, when it came to court the truth came out. As each police officer took the stand their story was different from the last one. I sat and watched the sheriff shaking his head and knew the case would rightly be thrown out.

Yet still it stays with us. Life is strange.

That night was my second in a cell. The first was as a teenager in Hamilton, when my pal Ray Jack and I kidded on we were breaking into a bank after a night out. No masks or guns or anything, you understand, just two drunk boys battering on the door shouting: 'Gie us money!'

Waiting for my mum to come and get me in the early hours was a nightmare. She was mortified and so she should have been. I got a £50 fine for breach of the peace and a thorough feeling of shame.

It still embarrasses me that the conviction's on the disclosure form I filled in to work with kids. Yet here's an odd one for you. If you ask most fans to pigeon-hole me they'd say Bad Boy and if they did the same with Paul McStay he'd come under the heading Role Model.

Know what, though? We have the same criminal record. When he was a young player, his mates pushed him in a shopping trolley after a night on the beer and he also got a fine for breach. So if I'm a baddie, so's the clean-living Mr Nice Guy of Parkhead.

I always seem to have been painted as a baddie, a lunatic who went around looking for trouble. But at very, *very* worst I was mischievous. All you can do is try and laugh the reputation off and hope that those who matter know the truth.

I always hoped Souness would be one of those people. But sadly, he was in the other camp.

He was hearing stuff that I was meant to be doing the night before games and that really got to me, because anyone who knew me knew that I never stepped out of line on a Friday. The game meant everything.

And to be honest, if I'd got up to even a tenth of the capers that were reported back to him, I'd have been dead on a slab years ago.

Didn't stop him suspecting, though. In the mornings, I'd look a state and Coisty would be running in late and Ian would be messing about and Souness would stick his head round the door and clock us and you could see his mind working.

'Yeah, they've been up to no good again . . . '

But he was wrong. That's just how we were back then.

Yes, if I'd known then what I know now about how long it

takes the body to recover from a drinking session, about what alcohol does to your muscles, then my weekends might have been very different. But nobody told us anything much about diet and drinking – or anything, really.

Even when we got perks like our first club cars we didn't take it seriously. We were taken out to the track and there were Montegos lined up all round it and they just told you to go and pick the one you wanted – so we all went sprinting for the colour we fancied and you would have this daft game of musical chairs where someone was at a blue one then changed their minds and wanted a red one.

It goes without saying that Ian and I didn't treat our company wheels well. We'd be sitting behind each other at traffic lights dunting each other's back bumpers, stupid stuff like that. It was like having your own dodgem car and we got into bother for not looking after them. Young guys back then didn't realise what they had, so I can only imagine how some of them get their heads messed up by the money and the extras that come their way today.

As long as we turned up for training in a collar and tie and we were clean-shaven, as long as we worked hard every day, as long as we were on time for games and gave our lot, that was all that mattered.

What a job football is, though. How many other people do you know who get a day off during the week to get together with all their workmates and go out drinking or golfing or to the races? Money can't buy perks like that.

We used to go to the Cricklewood in Bothwell a lot on Wednesdays and again on Sunday afternoons. Maybe that was a mistake as young lads, carrying on our Saturday nights into the next day. But what did we know then?

Sometimes later on a Sunday we'd end up in the Burnbank

Masonic club in Hamilton, not because we were masons, but because it was a safe haven. That might sound daft, but anybody who's played for Rangers or Celtic knows that sometimes you need to be somewhere that you won't be bothered by anyone trying to give you a hard time.

But believe it or not, one of our favourite spots for a beer was the bar at Glasgow Airport.

After home games, I'd go to my mum's and have a salad, then pick up Ian and head down there. I loved it. There was something really special about seeing so many people going off on holiday and looking so happy, so free. It doesn't matter what people are, or what they do, or what they earn – if I see them happy, I'm happy.

So we'd sit there and have a few Buds, watching the world go by and chilling out and it became a real favourite haunt for us. It wasn't flash, but it was where we were happy.

At weekends, we'd spend a lot of time at the Rococo in Hamilton, then everyone used to pile back to my flat, and even after I'd hit the sack they'd drink till six or seven in the morning – but they always respected the place.

Everyone in the gang seemed to have a party trick. Ernie – his real name was Sandy Steel, but he was a milkman – did somersaults. Then one night he did one on a table in my living room and smashed it. Mo Johnston was there and got really upset for me, but I knew Sandy would replace it.

When I look back and see us sitting there, I see lucky boys, playing football for money for the club they loved and living for today.

Then there were the summers, when it seemed like tomorrow would never come.

We'd go away on an end-of-season trip with the club and after that we still had anything from six to eight weeks off. So Durranty and I would have a fortnight in Tenerife with our mates, then come home, get the laundry done – and hop on a plane to somewhere else warm.

And I'm talking the *same day*.

While our mums were washing our gear, we'd nip into Glasgow for a few beers then pop in to a travel agency and simply book the first trip to the sun that took our fancy.

We'd scoot back home, pack the bags again and be at 30,000 feet by ten that night. We did that for two or three years and it was magic. It was never anywhere fancy – just your usual package destinations – but that suited us just fine. All we wanted was a laugh and a beer, and maybe a few girls, and we were sorted.

One year in Magaluf, Majorca, we stayed in a flat above a pub that belonged to the Scottish darts player Harry Heenan and the best thing about the place was that every night about seven o'clock his missus would make us a plate of mince and tatties. It tasted better than the lobster in the poshest restaurant in town and always set us up perfectly for a night on the batter.

These days when I'm on holiday I do some kind of training just about every day, even if it's just a light jog. But back then, if we played the odd game of fives we were pushing it. You can get away with that when you're young, as long as you remember to start doing a bit a couple of weeks before pre-season gets going.

Most teams are back these days before the start of July, but at Rangers we didn't see each other until halfway through the month, so you really did have a tremendous break from the game.

The Tenerife trips were one long party, really magic times. We went there five years on the trot from when I was about 17 and the second you got back you started looking forward to the following year.

We used to drink in the Caledonian Bar on the island, which got loads of Rangers fans in, and one year Ian and I worked behind the bar for a week. It was just a laugh, and although I wasn't bad at pouring a pint, I just didn't quite get the hang of asking for the money, so they must've wondered what happened to the takings some nights!

It was a fantastic laugh, plus – although it didn't cross our minds at the time – those Rangers punters must have got a real kick out of being served by two guys they paid to watch on a Saturday. And in our game, you should never forget what it means to the fans to get some time with their heroes. Not that I'm calling myself a hero, but you know what I mean.

It takes nothing for a footballer to stop and talk for two minutes and maybe sign an autograph. You may not have a clue who the boy is you're chatting with, but he knows you and the impression you make on him will last for ever. Act the Big-Time Charlie and that's what you'll be in his eyes and in the minds of all the mates he recounts the story to.

You have to strike a balance, though, because if you stopped and chatted to everyone who gave you a tug on a night out it'd be last orders before you'd even got a pint up. That's why I always used to prefer getting settled down in a corner where we could stick together and fade into the background. It was safety in numbers in more ways than one, because it meant there was less chance of anyone taking a pop at you.

That didn't happen very often, thankfully, but you are always aware that it might. Now and again you'd walk into a bar and realise within seconds that this was not the place for you. It was always best to cut your losses and hit the road before it got the chance to hit you.

One night, down at Bobby Jones in Ayr with my Rangers mate Davie McFarlane, I was on the dancefloor with a girl when next thing a tumbler bounced off my head. I was hell of a lucky that it didn't smash.

Davie and the other boys came rushing over to make sure I

was OK, but I kept dancing. It's a bit like when you take a free kick in the balls during a game – you're in agony, but you won't give the opposition the satisfaction of showing it.

The thing was, I hadn't even been trying to pull someone else's girlfriend – she was Davie's cousin and we were just having a laugh.

You took the scrapes in your stride, though. Like I said, we were invincible.

Of course, today's players take far better care of themselves in general – especially, as I've found out, at part-time level.

But one thing never changes.

They all still love the end-of-season blow-out.

I've seen absolute fitness freaks down shandies for breakfast, men who wouldn't dream of missing a single day on the training pitch bevvying 24/7 for an entire week. And, of course, laughed my bollocks off at the ones who've been all talk about what they're going to get up to out on the lash and who then land upside down in a plant pot after two local measures of vodka in the Spanish heat.

Me? I fall somewhere in between – and yes, sometimes fall is the operative word. I tended to go at it like a bullet from a gun for the first three days, then spend 24 hours in bed, then get back in the saddle but more at a trot than a gallop.

Magaluf's the place at the end of every season, the permanent venue for an unofficial World Club Championship of drinking squads. You walk into one bar and there's Cardiff City, in another there's Burnley, you're sharing a hotel with Dunfermline or Airdrie or Southend United or any other name you care to pluck out of the Rothmans Yearbook.

There's rarely any hassle between rival teams, even if you've had issues on the pitch during the season. Come Magaluf time, the ball is most definitely locked away in the boot room.

But there's still competition. Too right there is.

To be honest, the way guys try to outdo each other over how long they can make a session last, over who can sing the loudest or pull the most birds borders on the stupid. If we all just gave it a miss and lay by the pool with an ice-cream and a Pina Colada, we'd only have to work half as hard come pre-season.

That wouldn't be half as much fun, though.

Thing is, when you spend as much time with the same guys in the confined spaces of a dressing-room or a bus as we do, when you're under as much pressure as we are to deliver results week after week, you need to let off steam or it could all simply get too much.

The release valve on pre-season trips came after a fortnight of battering it on the training pitch when we got a full day off on the batter.

With a few drinks in us, tongues got loosened, things that needed to be said got said and any little niggles got ironed out – and with the work we'd done, two beers and you were hammered.

For two or three years on the trot at Il Ciocco, the Italian training camp that Souness loved to take us to, we'd go into town on the bus for a bevvy, then have a rumble on the way back. Everyone up the back and just pile in. It was mostly in fun, but if there was someone you had the spur with over something that had happened in training . . . well, this was payback time. It was the chance for a wee guy like me to get in a free whack at a big fella when he couldn't see whose fist was coming through the crowd.

Ian and I always picked on Terry Butcher and Chris Woods – a real Glasgow thing, that, punch as far above your weight as possible. Of course, quite often they then put you back in your place, but that was all part of it.

When I was a kid, it was always Peter McCloy I noised up and I usually got a tanking for my cheek. Same went with big Tel. If he got a slap in during those back-seat play-brawls, you stayed slapped.

At Raith, young Brian Fairbairn was always wanting to have a dig at me because he was the young wide man and I was the old geezer. Showing you his willy, that's his big thing. Although I say *big . . .*

These days, Barry moans that the foreign players have a different attitude to nights out, that they come along and have their meal and a glass of wine, then they bow out and leave the homegrown boys to go mental. But you can't slag them for that, just as it's not right for them to question why our lads need a good blow-out now and again.

In all my time at Ibrox, only Goughie ever took a step back when the nonsense started. Play-fights were our thing, throwing each other across tables. I've seen million-pound superstars lying in piles of broken glass. We must have been off our heads, but we were only letting off steam.

And throughout those magic days, my fellow Superman was always Durranty. It seemed from the moment he walked into the dressing-room that we were together 24/7. We played together, roomed together and went out together for so long we were almost inseparable.

Like me, he didn't know enough as a teenager about taking care of himself and it was only when he was into serious rehab after his knee operations that he began to develop his body.

By the time he came back he had this broad chest and big arms – to go with his big ears – and he needed that upper body strength when he became less of a runner and more of a playmaker.

He also became a moaning git, thanks to the frustration of being out of football for so long, but that was all part of his charm.

He'd have been a scaffolder had he not been spotted playing on a public park, and when he signed aged 16 I was the one who showed him the ropes. He was a mad Rangers fan and just loved being part of it all.

We started playing together in the youths, then the reserves, and by the time we got our big break we had a genuine, lasting understanding and we should have played at the heart of the midfield together for years.

And off the field, we partied together and had a ball. We simply got on brilliantly.

We only drifted apart twice, in the months when he was recovering from the cruciate injury that made massive headlines and wasn't around as often, and then in my final four or five months at the club, when it was me who was missing.

When he was out injured, he spent more time with his old mates. When I wasn't in the plans, he drifted more towards Coisty. That didn't piss me off; it's just the way football is. Out of sight, out of mind. Harsh but real.

I wasn't there at Pittodrie on 8 October 1988 when, at 3.08 p.m., his world turned upside down. I was playing for the reserves and had arranged to meet him in The Nile, so when he didn't trap I was raging. No mobiles in those days of course, so I phoned his mum's and his brother Alan said he'd been injured but would be OK.

So I went out with a couple of the boys, ended up back at the dancing in Hamilton and it was only when we came out and bought an early edition Sunday paper that we saw what had actually happened.

There was me giving him a hard time, telling the boys that I'd managed to meet up with him on Saturday nights after having stitches or my teeth broken and that he caved in after one wee kick.

Our motto had always been: It's Saturday night, so strap it up and get out.

But not this time, not for Ian. That infamous Neil Simpson studs-up tackle had left his knee in bits and him in a hospital bed after an agonising trip back from Aberdeen lying across the back seat of the bus.

It's not just the players themselves who have learned a lot over these past couple of decades, football as a whole has wised up. Today, Ian would have been immobilised and taken to the nearest hospital for the promptest attention. But all those years ago, he was screaming to get off the park and our physio Phil Boersma panicked and carried him off on his back.

You can't think that was helpful and neither was being battered up and down every time the bus went over a pothole during those three long hours back to Glasgow.

When I walked into the hospital, Ian was fairly bright, considering. I said I'd pick him up after his op and he was happy with that – but here comes another one to add to that long list of daft things you do when you are young.

Because where did we head straight from the hospital?

Where we should have been the night he got hurt.

The Nile.

When he said he fancied a pint, I wasn't sure it was the smartest idea, but we went anyway. We got him settled down with his leg up on a table, but after a pint he felt crap, so I got him up again and back into the car and it was no surprise that when we got round the road his mum was not happy.

We were the dressing-room clowns back then, the same kind of daft boys I've seen since as I've got older and a wee bit wiser. I just hope I've shown them half the same example as the great Ray Wilkins showed me and Ian.

What a lovely guy, a real class act. The way he dresses, the way he speaks, the way he looks after himself, the way he always has time for you; it all screamed quality.

No, not screamed. Whispered.

Always one for understatement, Razor.

I think he enjoyed all our nonsense, but he also worked away subtly to try and educate us away from the daft life. He even introduced me to a wee glass of wine, for which I'm eternally grateful.

When I switched over from the beer, a lot of guys wouldn't ask for it. 'Wine? Are ye a poof?'

But Ray knew better and he taught us what was what.

In Dubai for the British Cup game with Everton, they gave us a night off and the two dafties headed for the bar to neck beers and look for mischief. Ray and Trevor Francis, meanwhile, ordered up a nice bottle of Frascati and settled down on a pair of comfy sofas for some civilised chat.

After a while, Ray shouted the two of us over. We brought our beers, but he suggested we try a drop of vino. We told him we didn't like wine. He promised we'd *get* to like it.

So he shouts up another bottle and two more glasses and pours us a glass each and we take a wee sniff and then – *bam* – down them.

'No, no, no,' he says. Trevor just sits there looking horrified. 'You don't gulp it, you sip it. Here, try another one . . . '

So we tried to take our time, then we ordered another bottle, then some beers, then another bottle as a chaser for the beers . . .

Ray just used to laugh at us. But Trevor? Sometimes we just drove him up the wall.

Like later that same night, when we met up with the Everton boys and got battered into a few more drinks, we noticed him sitting quietly on a couch reading a big pink Italian football paper. And we decided to torch it.

Ian went across, perched on the edge of the couch and distracted him. Then I flicked a lighter on the edge of the paper and disappeared pronto.

Next thing, it was blazing – and so was Trevor. He was swearing in Italian, always a sign that he'd lost the plot.

He used to do it in training if he didn't like the drills. One day we were doing some strides and he was shouting about how it was too windy and they wouldn't make players do this in Italy. We thought it was hilarious.

But for all that we wound him up, we respected him. We hung on his every word when it came to preparation and how to play the game, and needless to say the same went for Razor.

The wee man was just the best. At the end of that drunken night in Dubai, I found myself standing in a corridor above the comatose Durranty. I was dragging him by the leg when Ray appeared, took an end and helped me carry him back to the room.

I was for slinging him on the bed and leaving him to sleep it off the way he was, but Ray insisted on getting his gear off and tucking him in. He was even a gentleman to unconscious pissheads.

And when you think about it, that whole episode summed up everything about how life was for me and Ian back then.

Two rough-edged boys from Govan, sitting in a five-star Middle East hotel learning about fine wines from the former captain of Manchester United and the first £1 million footballer.

We were in heaven.

One of the nicest things Ray ever said was an article during the 1990 World Cup about how he rated Durranty higher than Gazza – and I completely agreed with him.

Gazza would give you a special moment in every game. But Durranty gave you moments, plural. He was a Heineken of a player, he got into areas others couldn't reach.

You were never short of a passing option when he was on the same pitch. One second you'd be closed down, the next you'd see him out of the corner of your eye, in the perfect position to receive the ball.

He was so easy to play beside, a master of his craft from the same mould as Coop and Bobby Russell. His was a priceless knack.

He could also have been a successful runner, 800 or 1500 metres. He was a whippet, not electric off the mark, but soon got up to a hell of a pace.

In another era, with better education and a hugely better slice of luck, he and I might have been the best midfield partnership in the business. But in the end it was a toss-up what held us back more, the injuries or the reputation.

Personally, I don't think we deserved either.

Anyway, back to the action. And what action it was, an incredible explosion of spending and promises and controversy that shook Scottish football until its head was spinning.

It all started at Easter Road at the end of July. I was on the bench for Souness's debut in that infamous 2–1 defeat at Easter Road – and what an eye-opener that was.

You'd always been under pressure playing for Rangers, always had the microscope trained on you. But now the glare was so intense it blinded you.

To be honest, when it all kicked off in the centre circle, I was laughing – mainly because of the sight of Coisty running and dinking someone from the back then disappearing into the crowd scene.

But the smile disappeared from my face when poor George McCluskey was carted past our bench and down the tunnel. The gaping gash in his knee told the whole story. Mr Souness had certainly made his mark on him.

A year earlier, in a World Cup qualifier in Ireland, he'd made a fearsome challenge on young Siggi Jonsson, who had to be carted off in a stretcher. And I'll never forget seeing him going over the top on a Steaua Bucharest player at Ibrox while he himself had the ball. We'd just lost a goal and he couldn't handle it. Now, I want to win and it's a tough playground out there – but behaviour like that was beyond anything I'd experienced.

Mind you, so was the thrill of the late October afternoon when I won my first senior medal.

The 1986 League Cup final was always going to be fiery enough. What Rangers–Celtic game isn't? But this one had everything – us going behind then fighting back to win, Mo Johnston sent off for Celtic then teammate Tony Shepherd almost following him for hitting ref David Syme until it was pointed out a coin thrown from the crowd had done the damage.

Incredible stuff for the fans. So just think how it felt being a young guy right down there in the middle of it all.

Brian McClair put them ahead, but then Durranty made one of those trademark runs onto a through ball to slide home the shot – and kept running behind the goal towards the massed ranks of the Rangers End.

When Coop then won it from the penalty spot, it was just an unforgettable feeling. But then, so was the whole day and the night that followed.

In the build-up, you fret and sweat about whether or not you'll be picked, then when the list goes up and you're in, it's an almighty buzz.

On the morning of the game, Durranty and I got up, got the papers and went down for breakfast. Alex Ferguson had done one of those man-by-man ratings jobs in one paper and had given me a really low mark, saying that I was inexperienced and maybe a weak link.

He was absolutely right. I was just a pup and Celtic would probably go out to exploit that – but still, his comments got my back up and made me more determined than ever to have a blinder.

On the bus to a final, you just want to be there and getting changed. Once you get out on the pitch, you see the bands marching up and down and know this is no ordinary fixture.

The noise is even greater than usual, the venue's spectacular. And you're playing for so much – even more than the season's first piece of silverware that's waiting up in the Royal Box. When you go a goal down, the pressure really bears down on your shoulders. Everything hangs on your ability to come back. There's a do planned for back at the stadium, there's the feeling all your fans will get the following morning when they wake up and remember their team lost, there's the fallout at training all the next week.

Seeing the sea of faces all around us when the final whistle went brought it all into sharp focus. We'd made half that stadium – half a *city* – absolutely ecstatic. And the great thing for me on our return to Ibrox was that it wasn't all about the players and the manager. Everyone was there, cleaners, cooks, doormen, the lot. We'd all done it together. We stayed at the stadium for hours before heading off to a supporters' party. As we were leaving, Durranty saw one of the groundsmen, a boy called Dougal, admiring the cup and told him it'd be fine if he took it home for the night. The poor boy was halfway up Edmiston Drive with it under his arm before they caught him . . .

Great lad, Dougal. In the summer you'd wonder why he was out mowing the pitch in a mohair jumper. Then you'd realise he was just incredibly hairy.

Anyway, off we went to be with the fans – we tended to drift away from the other players as the night went on because most of them had their wives with them – and finished off the celebrations in style.

There can be few feelings in life better than the sheer happiness I enjoyed that night.

Had we not turned a 1–0 deficit into a 2–1 win, though, it would all have been so different. Drowning our sorrows, not swimming in champagne.

It's always the same when you win something, no matter how small-time the trophy may seem. Souness was just in the door when we played Celtic in the Glasgow Cup final, now downgraded to a youth tournament, but in May 1986 a full-blown, full-house, full-on showdown.

It was on a Friday night in May, right after the end of the season, and big Ted McMinn had arranged a weekend away to Blackpool after it. What a game it was, a thriller from start to finish won 3–2 for us by a Coisty hat-trick, and we couldn't get in and get changed quick enough before getting off for the trip south.

On the way, we popped in for a quick one at The Granary over in Shawlands. Though, as quickies go, Sting's tantric sex sessions have been shorter. It was gone four in the morning by the time we rolled back onto the bus, which by then had been pelted with stones by Celtic fans who'd got wind of whose it was.

When we arrived at the seaside sometime after 7 a.m., we headed straight down the beach for a big kickabout. The tide was out, though we barely noticed. We were down there for the day, then went back up to Dumfries, which was Ted's country. We went to a Rangers club and they were still giving it yahoo from the Friday night.

Had we lost, it would all probably have fizzled out for us before we left the South Side a couple of hours after time-up. Blackpool probably wouldn't have happened. That's what winning means. Being involved in big games is everything.

Which is why, even though I started 26 games and came off the bench in another 4 in that first season under Souness, and felt like I'd contributed a lot to our title push, it still flattened that when the flag was finally clinched, I was 150 miles away playing in front of two men and a dog.

Players had been in and out all the time as Souness picked teams to suit games, and while he was playing – and being sent off – on a nerve-racking afternoon at Pittodrie, I was in the reserves. Word got through to us that big Tel had scored and the point from a 1–1 draw had been enough to clinch things, and after that we couldn't wait for the bus to get down the road and the party to start.

At the same time, though, it wasn't the same. Half of you'd be delighted to know you'd been part of it, but the other half was utterly gutted at not having been in there for the kill. A weird feeling.

In 1987–88, Souness went crazy in the transfer market, bringing in Trevor Francis, Ray Wilkins, Mark Falco, Goughie, Bomber Brown and Mark Walters, but I was involved even more, starting thirty-one league games and another half dozen in the cups and five in Europe.

On 24 November, I even scored my first Rangers goal in a 3–0 win at Morton and felt things were going pretty well – but it seemed Souness had other ideas. For all the reasons I've already catalogued and some others I'll never understand, we were already drifting apart.

When things boiled up between me and him, I always wanted to get him on my own and thrash them out, but he preferred to have a go in front of people.

This was his style. One-to-one, he was great. We actually got on well at times, on our own. But with an audience? Sarcastic and dismissive. He'd sit back in his chair and put his feet up on the table and play to the gallery for all he was worth. He was everything that I hope never to be.

When he pulled that stuff with me, I knew exactly how Coisty felt. I just wish I'd known how he handled it so well.

The euphoria of his first season in charge soon faded as Celtic charged back under Billy McNeill to win the Double in his second, and as he dipped deeper and deeper into the transfer budget, I got further and further out of his plans.

Between losing the league to Celtic – we were 12 points behind in third – and all the other stuff going on between us, he seemed to make up his mind about me and come the new campaign the appearances dried up.

I only started a dozen league games and four more in the Scottish Cup, and although injuries played a part in my absence, the fact is that I simply wasn't in his plans any more.

After training I'd duck and dive to stay out of his way, because when he had me in his sights, he made life as uncomfortable as possible.

It was a case of me constantly getting on his nerves, him constantly trying to punish me for it, me constantly trying to prove he wouldn't piss me off: a spiral of stupidity that would never stop until one of us took a step back and admitted we were in the wrong.

But neither of us ever did. We were both too headstrong by half.

So there we are, in Il Ciocco the pre-season when Mo signed, and I'm a couple of minutes late for the bus to training. It was Durranty's fault. He was still getting fit and wasn't involved with the rest day-to-day, and he was mucking about in the bathroom so long I was chasing my tail.

When I came hammering down to the front door of the hotel, the bus was still sitting there. But that was when Souness saw his chance and told the driver to go without me.

He could have waited another 30 seconds and given me a bollocking. But no, that wouldn't have been enough. Better to make me look daft, to leave me standing there like a diddy.

The boys were all up the back seat, giving me pelters. And I did *feel* like a diddy. But no way was I going to stand there like one.

So I ran after them.

It was uphill all the way from the hotel to the training pitches, a good mile and a half in the Tuscan heat of early July. The sweat was pouring off me, but a good run never hurt anyone.

Once or twice I actually thought I might catch up with the bus – which would have made my morning. Every time I got close, though, it pulled away again. Wouldn't surprise me if he was getting the driver to slow down and speed up again to make me look even dafter.

When I got to the top of the hill, the boys were off and warming up. My heart was going like a big drum. But I plunged straight into the running with the rest of them as if nothing had happened.

Yet another example of stubborn manager and even more stubborn player thinking they'd scored points off each other.

Round about the time of Durranty's injury, there was talk of Chelsea and Nottingham Forest bidding £1 million for me and maybe the move would have done me good. I met Ken Bates on a Scotland trip and he as good as confirmed they wanted me. I just nodded along with him; I hadn't a clue.

I'd have loved to have gone abroad, though. Facing foreign teams was magic, they were always so sharp and alert and you had to raise your game to match them, the way Scottish teams did against us.

If I'd gone then, though, as a single boy, I'd have needed Mum and Dad to go with me. With Carol, I'd have flown anywhere, done anything.

In the dressing-room, on the park, things would have been no sweat. It's away from football, being in a new country with a new language and new customs that would have been the problem.

Back then, Spain or Portugal or Italy seemed a long way away. Now, though, it's a small world. You've got satellite telly, texts, emails. You're never far from anyone or anything. It's a wonderful time for a young guy to go away and improve himself.

And if you're a young guy who takes his football seriously, all you need is your Sky and your moby, because the rest of your life should be training, eating, sleeping, training, eating, sleeping.

But nothing ever came of all the rumours.

Then, early in 1989, my shoulder became almost as big a pain as the manager. Eight times it came out and eventually it didn't even wrench, just fell from the socket like a well-cooked chicken wing. All it took was for me to swing my arm for balance as I made a pass and, pop, I'd be hanging in bits. I used to play with a big Vulkan support that went right across my chest, but it was so uncomfortable that I'd come over to the touchline while the game was going on and rip it off.

I originally did the shoulder playing against Bayern Munich in the Olympic Stadium. Went into a tackle, their guy went flying and landed right on top of me. It only came halfway out and Doc Cruickshanks and the physio had to work together to put it right.

Soon after, though, I went into a challenge in training and out it came, this time for real. I used to dive in too much and I paid for it this time. So I'm lying there screaming – and who decides he's going to play at *Holby City*?

Dr Souness.

He's obviously seen the doc doing it before, thinks he knows the ropes and next thing he's got his foot under the shoulder, he's turning and as he turns he yanks the arm. No weakling, Graeme. But no medical expert, either.

At the hospital, the doctor gave me a wee jag and slipped it back into the socket like he was mending the wean's Action Man. It was a job for a professional from the off.

After that, I decided that I'd go for an op and that was me out of the plans again. It drove Souness daft, it drove me daft. Another wedge between me and the boss. Another step nearer the Ibrox exit door.

The shoulder also forced me out of at least a couple of Scotland games, but the fact is that Souness wangled me out of many, many more.

I got two caps, in Malta and at Hampden against Columbia, and it hurts that the total's not a lot higher.

But whenever the squad would be announced, he'd be going: 'Well done, son, you've been called up.'

'Cheers, gaffer.'

'But . . . er . . . there's a big game for us next week, so are you sure that wee strain's going to be OK?'

'Yeah, I'll be fine.'

'Sure you won't do yourself more harm?'

'Absolutely . . . '

'I mean, it's a *really* big game next week and you don't want to miss out, do you . . . ?'

And in the end, out you'd come. Of course, it wasn't him who got the stick from the fans, it was me or whatever other player was missing his chance. We were the ones who in the eyes of the fans didn't fancy playing for our country – but what a load of crap *that* was, because being a regular for Rangers and Scotland would have been my ultimate dream.

No matter what I thought of Souness, though, he was the manager and if he said jump in the Clyde, I'd hold my nose and jump. It's only now, with experience, that you realise how stupid you were. You wish you'd had the savvy to talk him round, to make him see what it meant to you.

That's why the five-day rule is so good. It means it's the national team doctor who gets to make the call, not the club. I'd have had a stack more caps if that had been in operation back then.

Souness had a chip on his shoulder about Scotland, no doubt about that. Being left out by Fergie for the Uruguay game in Mexico back in 1986. Kenny Dalglish being left out of the squad altogether. The fans giving him stick at Hampden in a few games. I think that all stuck with him.

When we played Scotland v. England at training, he always went on the English side. What's that all about? I used to look at him and think: 'How can you play for them? What's wrong with your own country?'

For me, he should have remembered how being snubbed made him feel and wanted his own players to get a better deal.

That was him, though, a poor man-manager in my eyes.

Those training games are the pressure valve when you've got a problem in the dressing-room and, sure enough, one day the moment came when things boiled over between me and Souness.

We were all going at it full pelt when – wallop – he flattens Durranty. It was a belter and for a second or two Ian sat there, working out what the hell had just happened.

Then he picked the ball up and threw it at the gaffer.

That started the verbals.

Then people were squaring up.

There was a scuffle, Ian told him he was out of order, Souness said something along the lines of 'Dry your eyes', then it all simmered down.

Me? I was raging. You train as you play, but the line gets drawn at injuring your own guys. If it had been Walter or someone else on the staff I might just about have let it go, but not Souness.

So the game got going again – and first chance we got, we battered the ball right at him. We almost raced to get there first, actually turning away from goal to have a pop. And it all kicked off again.

Things like he'd done really upset us and we couldn't help but get back at him. He had two fiery buggers in me and Durranty, who weren't going to take his bullying style lying down.

It went on for the rest of the game that day, us biding our time to get a whack in as revenge. He caused that and, for me, it was poor management.

Mind you, he was bloody hard to get near enough to for a good kick. That was his talent, knowing that when the ball came he had to pop it off quick or he'd get cemented.

Others, like me and like Ian, wanted to get it down and play football. That day, he made Ian pay.

I can't imagine myself as a top manager crumpling one of my top players. It just doesn't compute. It was another strike against Souness as far as I was concerned.

I'd go home at night and tell the folks my tales of woe and they'd be 100 per cent on my side, the way families should be. But then I wonder: should they have been harder, told me to dry my eyes and get over it?

Then again, would I have listened?

I mean, Greigy always told me it like it was, but no matter how much respect I had for the guy there was still a part of me that believed I knew best. He was the club PR man by then and one day, at the height of my problems with the manager, he shouted me into his car when we were coming back from training and gave me a real talking to.

He tried to tell me what it would be like the day I left Rangers, that it was all downhill from there and I took it in because it was Greigy, but I had a real thing about Souness by then.

Years later, I read in Greigy's autobiography that he felt I'd had my chance and had blown it by going off the rails. But it wasn't as black and white as that.

Then it was David Murray's turn. When it was all getting really tit-for-tat with Souness, I got a shout after training one day that I was to go to the chairman's office in Edinburgh the next afternoon.

It wasn't made to sound like a bollocking. I was to meet him for lunch. But believe me, as my mate Robert drove me through, eating was the last thing on my mind.

I'd met Mr Murray before, when he'd come into the dressing-room after taking over, but never one-to-one. The fact that it was happening now told me how frustrated Souness was getting with me.

It was like the teacher sending a naughty pupil to the headmaster.

But to be fair to the big head honcho, he didn't hammer me. He only seemed to want to play peacemaker, to get me to screw the nut and knuckle down – just the same as Greigy had said.

Walking into that massive office was really strange. His secretary brought the food in and, as much as he tried to make me feel at ease, all I could think of as I sat opposite this big, powerful multimillionaire was: 'Am I slurping the soup? Have I spilled anything down my front?'

We chatted for about an hour about what Rangers meant to him and what it meant to me and how I had to cut out the silly things if I wanted things to settle down and improve.

See, Souness had a certain way of dealing with players. It was the old my-way-or-the-highway routine. So maybe he really did think I could be something, because instead of showing me the door, he was getting *his* boss to try and get through to me.

But you know what? It was the manager I wanted to sit down with face-to-face. A lunch or a dinner with Souness and maybe we could have sorted a lot of stuff out. The chance never came, though. He never seemed to want it to be just me and him – and if I ever manoeuvred the situation, Walter or Boersma or someone would always walk in on us.

Back in the car, I don't think I spoke for the first ten minutes. Still couldn't believe I'd just been for showdown talks over lunch with the Big Fella.

Then I told myself, yes, it *was* time to really knuckle down. I convinced myself things could work out. But the reality was that things had already gone too far. Souness had had enough of me long before he finally got me out the door.

Still, life's all about opportunities and on this occasion I was really glad to have been given one to spend time with David Murray. First impressions matter and he made a big one on me.

He was great that day and every time I've met him since he's been just as good to me.

Not long ago I was doing a bit of hospitality work at Rangers and the club secretary, Campbell Ogilvie, gave me a tug. He was about to leave the club and whilst clearing out his stuff he'd found the records of my first wage at the club.

When I walked into his office, Murray was in the room. He was lovely, asked all about my mum and dad and the family. Then he said he'd seen me on Rangers TV and told me to smarten myself up a bit.

That was him all over. A gentleman, but always the boss.

The killer for me was the 1989 Scottish Cup final. I'd hurt my shoulder – again – six or seven weeks earlier, but with ten days or so to go I was ready. I really thought I'd be on the bench, at worst.

Then, sitting up the back of the bus to Hampden, one of the directors went round all the boys, going 'All the best, give it everything' and then he comes to me and says: 'Never mind, Derek, your time'll come.'

It didn't register at first. Then one or two of the boys were looking round at me, puzzled. And it sunk in. I wasn't getting stripped. He'd left me out.

It was an absolutely sickening moment. Yet that wasn't the worst of it.

Because it was only once we got into the dressing-room and the team was read out that it came to the subs and the name Souness was among them.

Not only had he axed me, he'd taken my place.

That shattered me. I had to get out before the tears came. Just to be involved, even sitting in my tracksuit for 90 minutes, would have been something special. We were going for the Treble. It was Celtic. It was a packed house at Hampden.

It was horrible.

I remember standing behind the dugout, watching him warm up and feeling like he'd stolen something precious from me. I'll never forget that.

The following season, I started just four domestic games and the European Cup tie against Bayern when my shoulder first went and the writing was all over the wall in huge, luminous letters.

By Christmas I wasn't even in the home dressing-room any more, and things were so bad I started pressing the self-destruct button.

Ian McCall had become a pal, and we decided we'd be smartarses and go on the reserve-team night out *and* the first team's 24 hours later. As clever moves go, plankton would have shaken their heads at us.

Out we go and have a kick at the ball the first night, come in next morning for what we knew was going to be a light session, then we go out with the big boys. But what happens the next morning?

We both sleep in.

I was the lucky one, I woke up just in time, leapt in the motor at about twenty past nine, hammered it in and was half an hour late. The squad were already away to training, and I knew I was in bother, but at least I'd made it. McCall didn't bother. That was him, Mr Laid-Back. He was late, so he might as well go the whole hog.

We were over at Jordanhill in those days, so I raced there and joined in as quietly as possible. But at the end I was told to wait and see Souness when we got changed.

He and Walter had me in and told me I'd be fined two weeks' wages. I could live with that, it was only money.

But then they dropped the bombshell.

I was to stay away from the ground for two weeks.

Oh, and I was on the transfer list.

My guts started going round like a tumble drier. Banned from

Ibrox? I couldn't think of anything worse. There was nothing like being in there every morning, laughing with the boys, running and kicking a ball and filling your lungs.

Doing laps of Strathclyde Park on my Jack Jones for the next fortnight just wasn't the same. They really knew how to punish me.

Keeping me out of that dressing-room was like me bursting Darren's favourite ball for him not passing it straight. It seemed really harsh, and it didn't make sense that they wanted me to be a better player and a better pro but wouldn't take me in and show me what they meant by that.

Even now, I love going back into the home dressing-room at the stadium. It feels good, feels like . . . well, it's still my second home. The people change around the place, sure. The likes of old Stan Holloway, the English boy on the door with the medals and the sparkling toecaps on his boots, have long gone.

But walking through the front doors and retracing the steps I took when I was a player, the corridors where we played bowls and heady football, the doorways we had chipping competitions through? It feels sort of right.

Souness slammed those doors shut in my face with that suspension.

It was a long, long two weeks – and even once it was over, I wasn't allowed back where I wanted to be.

Walter's pal Gordon Wallace was in charge at Dundee, and it only took a phone call for me to be sent on loan up there. It was another kind of punishment, but this time I could handle it, because at least I'd be playing first-team football.

The guys at Dens were brilliant, the Jim Duffys and Ray Farninghams and Alan Dinnies. They had a decent team and made me feel really welcome. It was strange, though. I'd never played for anyone but Rangers and never wanted to. But if I wanted to get my career back on track, I'd no option.

So who's my first game against?

Celtic.

And what happens the second I run out the tunnel?

One of their fans spits right in my face.

I can still feel it now. You come out the dressing-rooms, down a concrete slope, and the away support are in the corner, hanging over the wall. One of them screws up his face and – *ptoo!* – direct hit. Disgusting.

For a split-second, I almost stopped and reacted. But suicide's not a great career move, so I kept running, pulling my shirt out to wipe the grog off. All it made me think was: 'I'm going to rattle into these people even harder now.'

It made me realise, though, that in the eyes of the Celtic punters I was a Rangers man no matter whose colours I had on. Truth is, they were right.

No matter how good it was to be playing – and I did OK in a 0–0 draw that day – and how pleasant the guys at Dens made life for me, I didn't belong there.

Apart from anything else, I was very aware of taking someone's place, and that had to hurt him and his mates in the dressing-room. It's not the best situation if you start analysing it too much, and maybe it worked out for the best that I picked up an ankle injury and was shipped back to *Ice Station Zebra.*

It had been great being wanted, great to play even a few games. But now I was back to the reality of a manager who definitely *didn't* want me around.

I knew then for sure that I either had to mend this with Rangers or get out permanently.

Being left out of that cup final had taken Souness to a new low in my estimation. But after we'd lost to wee Joe Miller's goal, I truly despaired for what was going on in his head.

As we trooped back into the dressing-room, he made a big

performance of bursting through the door and chucking his medal away. Just threw it on the floor with the dirty socks and went: 'I don't want prizes for losers.'

I was furious inside. That medal would have meant something to me, second prize or not. I'd have given it to my folks so they could say their boy played in a game that big.

Little things like that really bugged me about him.

That night I went back to Ibrox and went out into the stand with a bottle of champagne, me and Durranty and Ian McCall, drinking and feeling sorry for ourselves.

Walter came and looked for me and apologised for the way I'd found out. That was the difference between him and Souness. He had time for people.

Anyway, when his fit of disdain for the medal was over that afternoon, Souness went and showered and while we were all getting dressing he suddenly said: 'Never mind, we'll have the last laugh.'

We soon found out what he meant.

Mo Johnston was signing for us instead of Celtic.

Tin hats on for the fallout from the transfer sensation to end them all.

It was announced officially when we got to Il Ciocco for pre-season, but Coisty had already told some of us before we went, because Coisty always knew what was going on, no matter how secret.

We'd thought he was at the wind-up, but, sure enough, out came the gaffer in Italy and it was for real. Coop jokingly said he wouldn't play with him. Or at least, I think he was kidding . . .

But the truth is that none of us in the squad ever had a problem with Mo. He was brilliant – a fitness fanatic, a sensational player who proved his fantastic mental toughness just by putting himself through the whole experience.

He was one of the first guys I ever knew who went away and did his own body circuits, who conditioned himself separately from training. Sure, he had his nights out. But he drank champagne not just for the image, but because it didn't have the calories of beer.

At Il Ciocco, in the restaurant, there was a table set for one at dinner. That was our kitman Jimmy Bell's one-man protest. He hated Mo and made no bones about it. Wouldn't give him so much as a Mars bar.

I heard tales that Coop was the same, that he left Rangers because of Mo, but no way. He'd played in Scotland squads with him and was fine with him. He was Rangers through and through, Coop, but he was no bigot.

Me and Durranty? We just wound Mo up, mercilessly. First few days in Italy, we did his room in – waited till he went for dinner, then rearranged the furniture. Bed upside down, wardrobes in the bathroom, the whole Mensa job.

The boys all talked about what Mo had done, but mostly from the point of view of how he'd handle it. We all agreed he had more bottle than all of us put together.

We knew what he'd go through once we got home, but as far as we were concerned, if he won us football games he was one of the lads. It'd have been different if he'd been all about himself, a fanny merchant. Not Mo. He was all for the team, totally unselfish, the ultimate pro.

His superstardom wasn't on paper. It was earned on grass.

I had pals back home who wanted me to do him in training, but I'd just laugh. They only knew him from the pictures in the Celtic strip. They didn't realise how much he wanted to be successful with Rangers.

Could I have gone from Rangers to Celtic? Not for all the dosh in the world. The grief would have been unbelievable.

Mo got it from Celtic fans like my Granda Buchanan, who called him 'that wee bastard' and loathed the fact that he'd jumped the dyke. And he got it from plenty of Rangers fans horrified at a Catholic playing for their club. It seemed like a total no-win situation.

So how did he do it? The million in the Swiss bank account helped, I suppose. But the fact is that he was a man with a plan, and Rangers were just part of it. Even then, he wanted to end up in America, playing and then coaching in the sunshine with a lifestyle that suited him.

The price he had to pay for that plan coming together was the loss of his privacy and any normal sort of life for a while. We went out together a few times, and he always had minders with him. We'd go to the Cotton Club on a Wednesday night, and every pair of eyes in the place was on him from first to last. The rest of us would get clocked when we walked into places, but then they'd all go back to their own night out. Mo? He *was* their night out.

I'd have stayed in the house rather than go through that. Needing two 6 ft 3 in. bouncers to keep me alive for the sake of a pint and a bird isn't my idea of fun.

It was the same on the pitch. Every terracing chant, every opposition wind-up, every camera, every reporter's pencil, they were all centred on him.

I don't know how he did it, but the fact that he came through as well as he did is a mark of what a man he is.

More of a man than the one who signed him, in my opinion.

SEVEN

FIT FOR LIFE

Tuesday, 17 January 2006

Wallace Mercer is dead. And it feels like I've lost a friend.

A giant of a man, cut down at the age of just 59 by liver cancer. It just doesn't seem fair – I mean, he was only my dad's age.

It took me a while to realise it, but I owe Wallace big time for helping change my career for the better. He was the one who convinced me that Hearts were the right club to join when Rangers no longer wanted me. And it was only once I went to Tynecastle in the summer of 1990 that my eyes were opened to the full potential of my fitness.

Had I stayed at Ibrox for as long as I had originally wanted, I might have picked up more medals and made more headlines – but I doubt if I'd have been as good an athlete or a person.

The first day I walked into that Hearts dressing-room, I got the fright of my life. Everyone in there seemed to be built like a boxer or a weightlifter. They were like nothing I'd seen before in football.

Here was a club where they clearly worked on conditioning

the body – and it soon became obvious that they also put more graft into looking after their legs than I'd ever known.

When I was a young player, we weren't athletes. We were fit, but nowhere near the fitness levels players have today.

When I look at pictures of myself in training with Rangers as a 20 year old, then check myself in the mirror now, there's no comparison. I'm a different shape, my muscle tone is completely different and there's no doubt I could outrun my young self no problem. The understanding footballers have of their bodies today as opposed to when I started out in the early '80s is like night and day.

Even the way we run is different – as a kid at Ibrox I used to go round and round the track to build up my stamina. I remember when they were building the new stands, looking up and seeing my dad hanging from one of the roofs he was sheeting. He told me later the guys were meant to wear safety harnesses, but clipping them on and off wasted too much time, so they just hooked one leg round a girder and hung on. That terrified me, yet he never turned a hair.

Anyway, I'd be doing my laps, thinking I was doing myself good. But it wasn't until after I'd left Rangers that I realised there were so many better ways to get myself fitter.

These days, I still love a good run – but the real benefits come from working on quick feet exercises. My garage is full of little cones and hurdles and markers that I take down to Strathclyde Park or the field across the road from our house or even just the back garden and set up for little sessions on my own or with the kids.

All that was sparked off by signing for Hearts.

Pretty much as soon as I signed, we were into pre-season. I'd done a lot of running to prepare, but didn't realise they were also used to three days a week in the gym.

They already had that fitness in them and I really struggled, didn't have the technique for the speedball, was behind them on jumps and squats and dips.

Yes, it was a hard shift for them, but it was an absolute killer for me. It probably took a year to get to their level.

After our initial work at home, we went off to Romania, where we'd do 15- to 20-minute fartleks – runs where you constantly lift and drop the pace – building up to nearly an hour. It was hellishly hard work, but really enjoyable and perfect for a midfielder.

That Heriot-Watt campus where they still train must come second to Strathclyde Park in my favourite places to train. I'd run for Hamilton Schools up there, then I trained there and now my boy Darren's there with Hearts.

I became utterly immersed in a training regime that I absolutely loved and which set me up for the rest of my career. Under Jock Wallace it had all been sand dunes and running in straight lines. Under Souness, little more than five-a-sides. Here, the quality of preparation was light years ahead.

Wee Alex MacDonald was responsible for that, and even though he was gone by the middle of September – two clubs down, two managers binned in no time – I'll always be grateful to him for setting me on the right road.

Luckily, the man who came in to replace him with the season barely under way was Joe Jordan. And he wasn't just out of the same mould when it came to setting up training. He actually led from the front. He was a magnificent example to all of us.

And then there was Mr Mercer, a man the like of whom you're unlikely to experience very often wherever you go in life.

When I think back now, it should have been obvious he didn't have long to go. Observing him as he sat in the main stand on New Year's Day watching the Jambos play out a classic title clash with Celtic, he simply wasn't the man so many of us had known and loved.

Wallace always looked prosperous, was always pear-shaped,

but carried his weight like an expensive accessory. His face was full, tanned. His clothes were always immaculate.

Now here he was, pale and drawn, his cheeks and chin sagging, has body wrapped in a raincoat whose putty colour matched his complexion.

When I close my eyes and re-live that scene now, it's like having death itself stare you back in the face.

Not that you think of these things at the time. Truth is, when the news of Wallace's death broke it was still a terrible shock to the system.

All you can ask of people is that they're good to you and good to those around you. That was always how Wallace Mercer was with me.

He worked wonders for that club, dragging them from the gates of financial despair to the brink of winning the championship and over more than a decade made them proud again, a truly big club once more.

Sure, he could come across as pompous, maybe aloof, but there was a wonderful genuine side to him that I truly admired. He used to love coming into the players' lounge for a natter, and I remember one day he flopped down and put his feet up on the table. When I looked at the soles of his shoes, he had a huge hole in one of them. I said, 'I'm not being cheeky, Mr Mercer, but do you not have a better pair than that?'

He just shrugged and grinned: 'I like these ones, they're comfy.'

That was him, the real Wallace Mercer, a million miles from the egomaniac so many painted him as.

Once, he took us to Nice in the South of France for a mid-season break and on a bus trip down to Monte Carlo he got up at the front of the bus and grabbed the driver's mike. So we're all thinking: 'Oh no, here goes Waldo again . . . '

Within minutes, though, we were all in stitches as he gave us a brilliant guided tour of an area he knew and loved so well. He sent himself up superbly and set the tone for a cracking trip.

And as I found out from the very first time we met, he was a generous man who did things in style. I went over to Edinburgh grudgingly. Somewhere deep inside I still had this idea that I could turn things round, so for about three weeks Souness and I shadow-boxed over the interest Hearts were showing in me.

Two or three days a week, I'd go into the gym at Ibrox and would end up talking to the gaffer. We didn't argue, but it was obvious our positions weren't getting any closer.

He'd say: 'Look, you might as well go, because you're not in the plans.'

I'd say: 'Fine.'

So he'd say: 'You'll be in the reserves.'

I'd say: 'No problem.'

So he'd threaten to put me on the *bench* for the reserves. Still I wouldn't back down. I simply refused to even talk about leaving. Then he turned up the heat and for about five days on the trot pushed me harder and harder. I just went into my mule act, but it couldn't last. My dad hit it on the head when he asked me: 'What do you want to do most of all?'

'Play football,' I said.

He just shrugged. And I knew what was what.

You train every day to play on a Saturday. If you train all week and you're not good enough for the team, fair do's. But to come in every Monday knowing there was no chance, no matter how hard you grafted, was a waste of everybody's time.

Even then, when I finally agreed to speak to them I think I was just trying to buy time. I didn't really have any intention of signing. When I met Wallace, though, he really impressed me and I started coming round to the idea of biting the bullet and signing. I even got myself an agent – though in the end, he got his money for doing the square root of not very much.

John Hollins, the former Chelsea player and manager, had been doing some work for Durranty and when it was suggested that he came with me to see Hearts I thought: 'Why not?'

There turned out to be quite a few reasons why not.

On our way into the meeting, he grabbed my arm and told me: 'Listen, when we sit down here we play hardball. We get the deal we've come to get and nothing less.'

That was good enough for me, so in we went for some tough negotiating. Except that as soon as we got going, John agreed to everything the other side suggested. He even told them I'd probably be happy to move to Edinburgh, which had no chance of happening.

In the end I called a halt and asked him if we could go outside for a minute. When we were alone I asked him: 'What did we just agree? What was all the hardball stuff about?'

After that I did most of the talking and eventually got what I wanted – which, ironically, was only the same wages as I'd been on at Rangers. It was hardly Rio Ferdinand and Man U stuff.

Oh, and John got about £3,000 for his day's work.

Before then, contract negotiations had been simple for me. I'd be told that the manager wanted me, I'd walk up the big marble stairs, chap the door, go in and sit down and ten seconds later I was signing on the dotted line. Money was never an issue for me at Rangers – they started me on one wage, the next manager moved me up to another level and the next moved me up again. Happy days.

Back then, I'd never even have dreamed of having an agent and my experience dealing with Hearts didn't change my opinion. But the next time I moved, to Sunderland, I got a crash course of what a good Mr Fixit can do for you.

This time, I took Bill McMurdo with me. He was The Man, he'd done the Mo deal with Rangers (and Celtic, but that's another story) and seemed to have a finger in every pie. Clubs would publicly slate him for holding them to ransom, while privately using him to buy and sell players.

I used to wonder how he managed to get his own way so often. In the space of a couple of hours in Terry Butcher's office, I was left in no doubt.

It was the complete opposite of the Hearts talks. This time, everything big Terry offered me was exactly what I wanted to hear. The money was the best I'd ever earned, the conditions were great and, apart from anything else, I really wanted to play for my old Ibrox skipper.

I was about to ask for a pen when wee Bill slapped me on the shoulder and said: 'Get your jacket, Derek, we're not sitting here listening to this shite!'

Terry looked stunned, but not half as stunned as I felt. One minute I'd been over the moon, the next I was half way up the A1 in Bill's roaring Porsche.

We sat in silence for a while, then I mumbled: 'Er . . . what just happened in there, Bill?'

He just smiled and said: 'Don't worry, we'll be back down in a day or two.'

And he was right, of course. Sunderland phoned, new talks were arranged – and I ended up with stuff on my contract I hadn't even asked for.

Still, it's all relative. When Mo joined Rangers, he got a Swiss bank account.

I went to Hearts for the equivalent of a Toblerone.

My signing-on fees for those two moves – both Hearts and Sunderland paid £750,000 for me – weren't huge, but every penny went straight into my pension anyway. So did almost all the extra cash I ever made on top of my basic wage until I was kicking 30.

The magic date was 31 July 2002. That was when I would turn

35 and my policies would mature, even if I hadn't. I worked out that I had around £400,000 coming to me. However, here's another date to remember: 11 September 2001. The day the Twin Towers crashed and took the financial markets with them.

The pensions people told us the Al-Qaeda attacks robbed families like us all over the world of billions we'd salted away for our old age. Never mind George Bush going after Osama Bin Laden, I was close to hunting the bastard down myself.

But when you think about it, the human cost of 9/11 was far, far greater than any effect it had on me and Carol. OK, so you worry that you won't be able to provide as well for the kids as you'd hoped – but then you think of all the little ones who were orphaned in those terrorist attacks, or look at the tots caught up in the Tsunami, and you realise that it's only figures on a bit of paper.

The night of 9/11, Clydebank were playing Dumbarton in the League Cup down at their place. When we met up in the afternoon, everyone was talking about it, sat glued to the screens watching the towers fall, over and over again, watching those bodies plunging from the windows.

It was beyond belief, too much for us to understand. For a while, we talked about whether or not the game should go ahead and I'm sure the same debate went on right around the world. In the end, we played. But for maybe the only time in my life, losing didn't really matter.

The pensions crisis, though, was more than a decade away when I signed for Hearts. The only worry I had then was over whether or not I would fit in and I have to admit that in the early days it felt weird.

Even though you knew the faces, even though they made you welcome, it just wasn't the same. It wasn't Ibrox. I'd been with Rangers since I was 12 and there were plenty of faces around from my first day to my last. Souness apart, I'd never felt I had to prove myself to anyone. Now I had to set about earning the respect of an entirely new dressing-room.

That's why it didn't just take me months to get as fit as Doddie demanded, it needed just as long for me to get Rangers out of my system. And there was no way my career could progress if that didn't happen. Not that those first few weeks weren't fun. We went to Romania for a four-team pre-season tournament and after the final we were all invited to this big outdoor banquet that turned into the Food Fight at the OK Corral.

The place was pretty rundown and the people were skint, so the massive spread they'd put on obviously meant a lot to them. But you can't take football players anywhere. Or their managers, for that matter.

When it all started to drag, Doddie picked up a trifle and shoved it in Craig Levein's face. Big Shoes picked up another one and splattered the gaffer back.

And we were off.

First, we were only pelting each other. Then, we took aim at the next table. Pretty soon, all four teams were at it. The dignitaries at the top table just sat there, jaws on the floor.

Later, back in someone's room, as one of the new boys I was told to sing a song. Well, having been to so many of those Rangers functions, one *did* spring to mind . . .

Long story short, by the end of the night, I had a telly above my head, kidding on I was about to hurl it through a window. The boys thought I was for real. I think the madman reputation had gone before me.

Me playing for Hearts was strange for Dad as well. I don't think he liked the Edinburgh punters all that much, judging from the fact that when they gave me stick, he turned round and called them 'teabag-squeezers'.

But if people around him hadn't earned his respect, his son

was working overtime to earn some from the guys in the dressing-room and you don't get that by mouthing. The worst thing you can do is walk into a new club and act like you own the place. I've seen new signings strut about boasting that they're here to do this and prove that. Never goes down well. The best thing you can do is be friendly, get your head down and graft your way into the scheme of things as quickly as possible.

And the best place to do that is on the training pitch and in games. As with Mo and the Rangers boys, you put your shift in, be a team player and after that it doesn't matter who you are or where you've come from. You're in.

There are complications, mind. As I'd found in my short loan spell at Dundee the previous season, for a new guy to get a shirt an established guy has to have his taken away. And he has pals who might not be happy at seeing him lose his place.

And then there's the other side of the coin – when you're the one who is facing a threat from that new signing. Whenever it's happened to me, I've shaken his hand, made him welcome, then upped the ante from the first minute of his first training session. If he wants to beat me, he's got to be up for it big time.

I have total belief in my ability as a footballer, if not in many other areas of my life. But then you get boys like Gary Mackay, who have all the talent and desire in the world and yet seem to live in constant fear of being dropped. He used to sit there every Friday going: 'I'll be out when the team goes up. You'll play, he'll play, he'll play. But not me.'

He was a worrier without a cause, because you couldn't have got him out of that Hearts side with a crowbar. Yet every time he saw his name on the sheet, it was like a huge weight had been lifted off his shoulders. He was on cloud nine.

Gary was Hearts daft, they meant to him what Rangers had meant to me and the same went for wee John Robertson. Losing really hurt those guys. They were living in the city, their mates were Hearts fans as well. I was going home every day and the punters didn't get to dig me up in the street.

It was the same thing down at Sunderland. They had a lot of local boys who took results to heart and I liked that. I like people who really care.

That's why, when Souness started to bring all those big English names to Ibrox, us locals set about teaching them what the club was all about. By that, I don't mean all the horrible stuff that goes with the Old Firm, we just needed them to know how much it meant in the Old Firm goldfish bowl to win, win, win – and, more importantly, what the price was for failure.

Mind you, they soon found out about it all on their own.

Guys like Butcher and Woods and Graham Roberts would go to the kind of supporters' club functions I've already mentioned and be made to feel like kings. These were the nights when it really was burned into them how much the club meant to its people. Of course, the trouble was that some of the imports thought they had to act up to the demands of the fans and it got them into trouble.

Terry and Chris landed in court with Frank McAvennie after their infamous Old Firm scrap in October 1987, which was also the day when Graham decided he would conduct the crowd in a chorus of The Sash. He thought it was just a laugh. But as those of us brought up in it know too well, it's no laughing matter for an awful lot of people.

Now, those people can tut-tut and criticise these guys all they like for going over the score in full view of the watching world. But if one single, solitary supporter can tell me that he or she ever went to a Rangers–Celtic game and didn't lose the plot for even a single second, then they must either be a saint or they somehow managed to fall asleep amidst the mayhem.

Tynecastle was never quite as mad as Ibrox or Parkhead when it all kicked off, but it was still one hell of a theatre to perform in. I loved running out into the frenzied atmosphere of a full house there, with the fans hanging right over you and baying for blood.

It helped that I also played maybe my best-ever football at times there – in fact, one of the few 'if onlys' in my life is the thought that if I'd started there and then moved to Rangers I'd have been a fitter, sharper and wiser player. But if only your auntie had an extra bit, she'd be your uncle.

The Rangers team of my last few years there was full of great players brought together by a manager who felt they didn't need to train hard. We had the ball most of the time and the other side did all the chasing.

Winning four and five nothing never did much for me. I prefer a challenge right to the final whistle. The environment under Souness made me lazy.

Now I had the hunger back. Which is why I got so bloody angry that people thought I'd already blown my career.

Guys I'd been at school with would come up and shake their heads and say I'd wasted my chance. They wanted a reaction. They went away disappointed.

I think the common opinion was that now that I was away from Ibrox I'd play for a year or two then go down the pan. Some people might still reckon I did. But I stayed full-time until I was 35 and even then never stopped.

It's easy to say that Rangers was the peak of my career because that's where I always wanted to play and because they were the biggest club in the business. But football-wise, the Jambo days were tremendous.

The only downer when I was on form at Hearts was that I never resurrected my Scotland career.

Tell a lie, I got one call from Andy Roxburgh asking about my availability. But the irony was that, after all the times I'd been pulled out of his squads by Rangers for little or no reason, I actually had a genuine injury this time. A dead leg. He said he understood, but the phone never rang again.

Anyway, back to that summer of 1990 and good old Waldo. He really couldn't have done more to sell his club to me. He even took me to see this lovely penthouse flat out in Barnton that he wanted to put me up in. He didn't have to do that, I hadn't asked for a place to stay, he was just trying to make me feel at home.

He wasn't daft. He'd heard all the stories about my supposed off-field behaviour and thought it would be better if I stayed in Edinburgh. I told him I didn't want to move, that I was happier being with my mum and dad and that if travelling wasn't an option then I wouldn't be signing.

Again, that was probably just me being pigheaded, still harbouring this daft notion that Rangers might change their mind. Back came Wallace, though, and said that as long as I screwed the nut then I could stay in Hamilton and travel through with Nicky Walker, Ian Ferguson and Davie Kirkwood.

(A wee aside, by the way. I'd known Nicky from when we were 16 but it was years before the penny dropped that he was heir to the shortbread fortune.

Once it did, I thought even more of him than I had before – not because he was going to be rich, but that he hadn't bragged about it.

He always had a second-hand motor, never dressed flash. The only unusual thing was that he always seemed to be handing out boxes of biscuits.

One day, Wayne Foster had a big tin of shortie and I asked him where I could buy one. He laughed and said: 'Ask Nicky.'

Still it didn't click. So he said: 'Read the tin . . . '

Ping!

What a top-class guy. You liked him because he was Nicky Walker, not because he was Nicky Walker the soon-to-be multimillionaire.

Though once I knew his background, it explained why he was different from most of the other boys. He didn't seem as desperate to make it big – in fact, I've seen him walk away altogether more than once.

We played together at Ross County, and one training session the boys were ripping the piss out of him, so he just walked off and we didn't see him for three weeks. That's how he was. He liked football, but he didn't need it.)

Yet here's where timing comes into it again.

It was only a few months later that I met Carol and if we we'd been together when Hearts came calling I'd have bitten Wallace's hand off for that flat. Carol would have loved it and the two of us would happily have set up home in a lovely part of the city and started a new life together.

Carol was my first steady girlfriend. Until I met her, I'd only ever had what I called 'pals', girls who I either saw or didn't see. I'd meet them when I was out, we'd have a laugh, we might go home together. But then we might not see each other for weeks on end.

Why? My old-fashioned values again, I suppose. I couldn't see the value in a footballer having a steady girlfriend when there were so many distractions every time you went out. I saw too many guys who were in relationships but who thought nothing of jumping about. That was never going to be my style, so I kept myself single.

There's no doubt you got more women hanging around when you're a footballer and especially when you're with a club like Rangers. Sometimes players start to believe they actually *are* good-looking, but the truth is they're simply famous and earn a lot more than the other blokes in the pub.

Not long before leaving Rangers, I'd bought a terraced house for £25,000, about 70 yards from my mum's place in Bellshill. I was so chuffed – it had a nice lounge downstairs with a balcony bedroom overlooking it, but there were two reasons why it wasn't absolutely ideal.

1. It really only became a weekend bolthole, with the rest of the time being spent with my folks, getting my meals made and my clothes washed.

2. Whenever I did stay there, Barry would be at Mum and Dad's front window like a wee spy, reporting back on whoever went in and out.

That little house would also become proof of my absolute lack of brains when it comes to business. I'd seen a fantastic flat in a converted church in Hamilton and right away decided to go for it – though, again, it would turn into more of a weekend retreat. So the first place I ever owned went on the market and the idea should have been to make enough profit to get myself ahead of the game when I moved up the property ladder.

Not me. The first viewer was a Rangers fan who was about to get married and the combination was enough for me to let him buy the house for exactly the same as I'd paid for it. It's nice to be nice.

Soon after that, with the Hearts deal done, Carol and I got together.

I remember seeing her around for maybe two or three weeks but never having the bottle to go over and talk to her – and she didn't come near me because she thought I was a nutter.

She was blonde, a real cracker, but she had no time for me or my crowd. Eventually I took a bravery pill and chased her and we got talking and I asked her for a run home. She never gets fed up telling me that I was so drunk I gabbed all the way back and then, outside my house, I rolled about on the bonnet of her car yelling that I wanted to have her babies!

In the end the only way she could escape was to give me her phone number and after that I just persevered until she gave in. She was the first girl I ever went to the movies with or took for a meal and the only one there will ever be.

The best thing about her was that we became great mates. Even when I was going out with the boys, I'd meet up with Carol first and have a laugh. She was good-looking, she was funny, she was perfect.

Plus, she didn't have a clue about football and didn't care that I had played for Rangers. For years I could be half an hour in the house some Saturday nights before she even remembered to ask how we'd got on.

Now she's got three boys in the house who all sit and watch football, go out and play football, who live for football and it must drive her daft.

We went out for maybe nine months then decided she'd move into the flat in the church, which didn't please her folks. Danny and Millie are devout Catholics, so we decided to do the right thing.

We waited until they went on holiday and sneaked her stuff round to mine.

They didn't speak to me for weeks, but eventually came round. They could see how much I loved Carol. I'd known from the start that I wanted to marry her, even if she wasn't so sure, and proposed on holiday in Barbados in June 1991. We got engaged officially back home and were married on 4 June the following year.

What a brilliant day that was. We had the whole thing at the Bothwell Bridge Hotel, with 140 there during the day and buckets more at night. We were gutted when it came the traditional time for the bride and groom to leave – the singing was just getting started.

We went back to our wee flat, Carol still in her wedding dress, then flew out to California to stay with her brother Danny the next day. Then we had a few days in Las Vegas, where Carol's sister Joanne shared a room with us and I spent most of the day dropping hints for her to go for a wander somewhere else.

We must have got some time alone, though, because Carol reckons that's where she got pregnant.

Carol and I had great times in our little church flat. It had a ghost, we were absolutely certain of it – we just could never agree where it hung out. I used to get up in the middle of the night for a drink of milk from the fridge and could swear I saw something down by the front steps. Carol, though, would see our lodger sitting on an armchair in the living room.

So life was pretty good, despite all my reservations about switching clubs. My fitness improved dramatically, the style of football was better for me, even the journeys there and back every day made you feel good.

In training, the games were always East v. West and they had a real edge, believe me. Yet for a while they were as near as I got to competitive football, because Doddie wouldn't pick me regularly until I got myself up to the fitness standards the rest were already at. I wasn't happy – who is when they're left out? – but there's no doubt he was right.

For two or three months after Doddie signed me, I'd rarely gone over the door at nights or weekends. I've never been one to go out for a quick shandy or sit in the pub drinking orange juice. I like to enjoy myself and, to be honest, I had to get myself out of harm's way until I'd done what he was demanding.

The gym was manky, like something out of a *Rocky* movie – nothing like the magnificent facilities they have now. Our Darren's privileged to be able to use them every week as part of Stevie Fulton's Under-12 side.

We did loads of circuit work and sprints under the beady eye of conditioning coaches George McNeill and Bert Logan. George is a fantastically funny guy, a big player on the after-dinner scene, while Bert's known as The Bookie From Tranent. They were a brilliant double act who also knew their stuff like few I've known in the game.

I used to tell them all their ideas were bollocks, but it was just a wind-up, because I took it all in. Anyone who didn't must have been off their head.

George and Bert asked me to come in Mondays, Wednesdays and Fridays during the summer so they could work with me. I said no, but asked for the programme so I could do it on my own.

Those two got me into Creatine and tablets to help build muscle and aid recovery. If I'd been on them at Rangers, who knows? But then again, surely someone like Graeme Souness should have known about all that stuff and told us daft boys about them?

I don't know if George and Bert realise the influence they had on me. Their training was hard, but it was tremendous.

I never realised how good it would feel to be really strong and fit. Sure, I'd thought I was in good shape. But I was kidding myself. All these years on, that feeling is still an addiction with me.

Hearts didn't just run you or have you playing small-sided games. They seemed years ahead of their time in improving your core fitness – working on the band of muscles round the centre of your body that make everything else work efficiently.

At Rangers, for instance, there always seemed to be a lot of hamstring and stomach injuries. At Hearts, they were very rare.

These days, bright young managers like Craig Brewster have latched onto the benefits of keeping their players together longer each day, though not just to batter them. They do conventional training in the mornings, feed them well at lunchtime, then work on the core stuff.

Craig took his players at Caley Thistle for spinning classes on static bikes, for aquarobics, for boxing training, and he carried all that on when he moved to Dundee United. It's worked wonders for both teams and Doddie and then Joe Jordan were doing the same for the Hearts boys more than 15 years ago.

Rangers? They left you to your own devices come noon. If you went to the gym, you were on your own. More often, the boys would go into Glasgow for pizzas or a game of snooker.

I loved working with Joe and with his assistant Frank Connor – a mini Jock Wallace, right out of the old school and a joy to be around. When we were doing hurdling work, Frank used to whack me with a stick to get me to jump higher. It worked, too, but just imagine if a coach tried that technique today – you'd have young players demanding charges were brought for assault and raging headlines in the papers.

For me, it wasn't bullying. It was just the way men of his generation were with each other. Jock had been an army man and Frank was from the same generation, an era when you took your knocks and didn't complain.

Joe? He was a monster in training who could run all day with the best of them and who was still in fantastic physical shape. He definitely made me want to look after myself and stay in the game as long as I possibly could.

He'd set up the doggies – shuttle runs that had you changing direction as you went from a starting point to markers at various yardages away and back – then do the run himself. Whatever he clocked, we had to do maybe three in the same time. And he wasn't slow.

One night we played Everton at Tynecastle in a pre-season game and they had the full squad out, the Neville Southalls and Kevin Ratcliffes, all the stars who'd made them the most feared team in England.

Joe fancied a run out, so he put himself on the bench and just before half-time he disappeared to do a warm-up. We'd been in the dressing-room for a few minutes when he appeared, glistening with sweat. When he took off his T-shirt, his body was rippling with muscles, not an extra ounce on him.

He wasn't massive, not like you imagined when you watched

him on TV in his World Cup days. But he was toned, wiry and solid as a rock.

He pulled on his shirt. And then he took out his front teeth and suddenly the centre-forward they called Jaws was back.

And when I say he was back, I *mean* he was back.

First decent cross into the box, up he went with Southall and Ratcliffe, went right through both of them and we were 1–0 up. Away he ran, fist clenched, expression fixed somewhere between a toothless grin and a terrifying snarl.

From then on, he gave a striking masterclass, running his socks off to shut down defenders and fighting like hell to win every ball in the air and on the deck. He scored again and we'd beaten a really top-class side 2–0. That performance from Joe will always live with me.

I can only imagine what he must have been like to play with and against at his peak. God knows what he did to the opposition, but he sure as hell terrified me.

Not much in life makes me jealous, but the ability to score goals regularly is one. It's maybe the one bit of my game that was lacking, those dozen strikes a season from the middle of the park.

One in every 30 league games, that's my career record.

I didn't work hard enough on my shooting and Barry's had the same accusation. It's too late for me, but he still has time.

Not that finishing practice at training does you much good. For me, the idea of a ball being rolled in front of you is too fake. Watch a Steven Gerrard or old footage of Bobby Charlton and you'll see how they dig shots out from every angle – from the side, from behind.

But anyway, no, it's not hard to pick out my best-ever. But the truth is that even if I'd netted a hundred, the answer would still be the same.

4 November 1986. Estadio do Bessa, Porto. UEFA Cup, second round, second leg.

Coop comes in from the right, I'm pretty central about 22 yards out and his pass bounces up nicely for me to hammer a shot past the goalkeeper.

Only goal of the night. Three–one to us on aggregate.

What a buzz to have made such a vital contribution to a Rangers game in Europe.

I remember just bursting with excitement when the ball hit the net – but after that what sticks in my mind is flying home from Portugal and trying to stay away from the limelight.

I've never been one for talking about myself to the press. It's not that I don't like them, just that it makes me uncomfortable. I'd have been happier that night if someone else had told them how well I had done. Again, that maybe goes back to when I was a boy and I knew I had played well when my dad said nothing to me.

It's never been a problem for me to talk about Barry or anyone else who's due some credit – but I just like to blend into the background when it comes to my own game. It's an ancient cliché, but the talking's done on the pitch.

The kids were asking me the other day if I had ever scored against Celtic and I'd really like to have been able to say yes for their sakes. They'd be so chuffed.

Unfortunately, the nearest I came in an Old Firm game was hitting the post, though I set up a good few goals and that means just as much to me as scoring would have. Don't think the boys feel the same, though.

While we were talking about it, Carol walked in and said: 'No, your dad *didn't* score against Celtic – but he *did* score against Rangers!'

You should have seen their faces.

Mind you, I'd love to see a picture of my own expression after it happened. It was the first time I'd come back to Ibrox since Souness got rid of me and I was a big bag of mixed-up emotions.

Of course, what mattered most was trying to get three points for my club, Hearts. But there was no doubt I also had a personal point to prove, while at the same time knowing how strange it would be to try and turn them over.

I just remember picking the ball up wide on the right, driving inside, hitting the shot early from the edge of the box and seeing it flash past Chris Woods. It was a bizarre moment.

As I'm writing this, I've been watching the highlights from an FA Cup replay between Everton and Millwall where Tim Cahill scored the winner. He'd moved to Goodison from the London club and it was obvious from his reaction that while he was delighted, he also didn't want to rub Millwall's noses in it. That's exactly how it was for me that day against Rangers.

I definitely held myself back out of respect for my former club, for my friends in the Copland Road stand. That may not please some Hearts supporters, but it's real life. You don't sneer at your mates.

All the same, I'd have loved my goal to be the winner rather than ultimately a consolation in our 2–1 defeat.

My dad was there that day – I think Carol's dad Danny was too, because he went to a lot of my games then – and he was delighted for me. My dad's a Rangers man through and through, but he's proud of his sons above everything else.

As for the rest of my time with Hearts, one of the things *I'm* proudest of is never being on the losing side against Hibs. Three wins and a draw the first season, a win and three draws the second, two wins, two draws and four clean sheets the third. Not a bad record, unless your spiritual home's Easter Road.

Those capital clashes were terrific; not quite the same buzz as I'd have in Glasgow derbies, but you didn't dare forget that they meant just as much to the locals as Old Firm games did to Rangers and Celtic diehards. You knew they'd either be going to work on the Monday with their chest puffed out or their heads hung low. Which one was down to you.

Same goes for Hamilton against Airdrie, Ross County and Caley Thistle, Raith against East Fife. They're all the biggest showdowns in the business to those involved in them. In pre-season with the Rovers, we went to New Bayview and got pelters from our fans because we went in at half-time two down. I was left in no doubt what was expected after the break and we came back to win 4–2 and send them back up the road happy.

I also had a crack at a Dundee–Dundee United game in my short-lived Dens loan spell and would have loved a Sunderland–Newcastle game, but we were in different divisions then.

Overall, it was a great time on the park. In my first season, we finished fifth. The next, we started as well as they did under George Burley in 2005 – unbeaten in our first 12, the whole country talking about our chances of winning the title.

In the end, we couldn't quite make it. But we did split the Old Firm and that was a big achievement. I loved it and the same went when the following campaign began. I was right in there where I wanted to be, pulling the strings for a team winning more than it lost and pushing for Europe.

But then something was to happen that put everything about football in perspective.

EIGHT

LAUREN

A butterfly lights beside us,
Like a sunbeam,
And for a brief moment,
Its glory and beauty,
Belong to our world.
But then it flies on again,
And though we wish it could have stayed,
We feel so lucky,
To have seen it . . .

The saddest words in all the world.

The words on our precious daughter's headstone.

Lauren Ferguson came into the world on 15 February 1993 and – just like that butterfly – left it again all too soon.

Seven weeks, two days. Every minute spent in pain. If I could have suffered in her place, I would have done it without a murmur.

Instead, all Carol and I could do was sit with her and pray for her and cry for her. Two helpless young parents, confused and angry and desperate all at the same time, living a nightmare that would never end.

If there's one positive out of what happened to Lauren, it's that an experience proven to smash marriages into tiny pieces actually pulled the two of us closer together, made our relationship stronger.

And boy, it needed to be strong. Because as if it wasn't bad enough having to bury our baby, seven years later we'd have to do it all again.

We'd braced ourselves for the birth of our first child being a toughie. Carol had a problem called placenta previa, which meant the afterbirth would come out first in a normal delivery and put the baby in danger. She would need a Caesarean section and the chances were it would be well before her due date.

Early in February, six or seven weeks before she was due, Carol suffered bleeding and was taken into Bellshill Maternity. A week later she was still there, which meant our first Valentine's Day as a married couple was a cosy one spent among the monitors and the drips.

When I arrived, she was propped up in bed wearing new silk pyjamas – they were bursting at the seams, but she looked great. I brought in a lasagne Carol's mum had made, non-alcoholic wine, fancy glasses, chocolate cake and roses and we sat on the bed and had a romantic picnic.

Well, romantic until Carol got up to cut the cake and all hell broke loose downstairs.

We thought at first her waters had broken, but suddenly there was blood everywhere. She was in a room by herself and ran into the corridor shouting for help. The nurse told her to get back on the bed, to get off her feet.

Now, don't ask me why, but at this point I started stripping. I had on a denim shirt with a T-shirt underneath that had a picture of Carol's head on a supermodel's body. I think my idea was that it'd get really hot in the delivery room and I didn't want to be standing there in the T-shirt, so I'd take it off and put the shirt back on.

But to get the shirt off I had to unbutton my trousers, so I'm standing there naked from the waist up with my flies undone – and Carol's on the bed taking her pyjama bottoms off. It must have looked like we were at it.

We never did get to eat that chocolate cake.

Poirot was on the telly in the labour room. Don't ask me why I remember something as stupid as that. I stayed with Carol into the night, until one of the midwives sent me home. In the morning, I rang the hospital and they said there was no panic, so I headed into training.

Then, about half-ten, I was in the gym when they called and said the baby was coming, and I was off like a shot. Showered, dressed, in the car, offski. A big Fergie-shaped hole left behind me. At the hospital, I didn't even bother to park, just bumped up onto the pavement and ran out leaving the door open. It was like something out of *The Sweeney*.

I battered through the front door and hared along the corridors. And when I got to the labour room? It had all been for nothing. Carol had already been taken through, and they wouldn't let me in.

So back I trudged and straightened the car up, locked it, and when I came back in it was over. Lauren had been born at 11.27 a.m.

They let me see her right away and I took a picture to show Carol. She was a lovely wee thing, all curled up in her cot with a little smile on her face. I wonder what she was thinking about?

Years later, we got a drawing made of that photo and it hangs in our front room. She still looks as gorgeous as she did that first morning. Not much hair on top, but loads down the back. We nicknamed her Danny DeVito.

Carol thought she was my double.

Soon after, they took her to the Special Care Unit because she was so premature, nothing else. The only thing I'd noticed was that her legs were sort of blue-ish, but we were told that wasn't a big deal.

Everything seemed fine. Carol was knackered but OK, Lauren was being looked after, so that afternoon I went with two proud grandpas to a pub in Bellshill, chuffed to bits at being a dad, not a care in the world.

Through the night, they told Carol her baby had breathing difficulties and was on oxygen. Carol was on too much morphine to take it in, so she just told them to do what they had to do.

Next day, though, she got taken down in a wheelchair to pick Lauren up for the first time and bring her back to the ward, but when she got to Special Care everyone was panicking.

She remembers them looking kind of embarrassed when she came in and being left in a wee room on her own, worried sick. When she finally saw Lauren, the wee thing was crying in pain and the bit right under her ribs was going up and down like mad.

That's when they broke the news that they thought she had a heart defect.

It was only later that we found out those first 24 hours would eventually be what killed her, that her heart had already been so badly damaged by the time the problem was spotted that it had worn itself out.

When we eventually got her records, they told us she had suffered Cardiac Respiratory Collapse at around 9 p.m. the night she was born. There wasn't another note in the file until 9 a.m. the next morning.

Had they seen what was wrong earlier, they would have ventilated her and the stress would have been taken off her heart and . . . well, who knows?

All we *do* know is that her problem shouldn't have been

fatal. Arnie Schwarzenegger had it, thousands of others have it and survive it, an aortic valve that is too small and needs to be replaced. But so early in a baby's life, even letting it go unchecked for a few short hours is far too long.

She was about 30 hours old when she was rushed to Yorkhill by ambulance, me following in the car. When we got there, you could clearly hear the noise from across the water at Ibrox, where Rangers were playing.

I'd never felt further away from football.

I went in with her and then when they asked me to wait outside in the corridor I punched a solid wall and nearly broke my hand. The frustration and anger were overwhelming.

The specialist, Mr Pollock, went into her chest and stretched the valve rather than replacing it, but although he seemed to be successful, the joy was temporary.

Mr Pollock was a lovely man with great big goalkeeper's hands. Every time I met him I'd just keep looking at them, wondering how he did all that intricate work on such tiny bodies. Yet he did, and his talent was amazing.

Once Lauren was settled, they moved Carol to the adjoining Queen Mother's Maternity, though what a performance that was. She got taken in one of those ambulances that's more of a taxi and they had so many other patients to drop off that after an hour and forty minutes she still wasn't in Glasgow.

How terrible is that, when a young mum's baby is lying critically ill?

She had another week in hospital and every day I'd push her in a wheelchair to see Lauren. She moaned that I used to batter her off every doorframe on the way. After she got out, she still spent the night at Yorkhill whenever they had a room available – thankfully, these days they have a designated block for parents.

I have so much admiration for the time Carol spent in that hospital. Being there non-stop would have broken me.

Instead, I had the release of training and playing, getting a sweat up, being with the boys and doing what I do best. When we finished every day, I'd be showered and changed in a flash and back through to Hamilton, where Carol would be grabbing a few hours' kip. Sleep was *her* escape and after Lauren died she'd close her eyes as often as she could. I suppose it was a form of depression.

I think I held myself together pretty well during it all, until one day in training it all boiled over. I went in a bit high in the tackle on big Graeme Hogg, there was a bit of pushing and shoving and next thing we were rolling about. I'll never forget how Joe Jordan handled that flashpoint.

There was no shouting and bawling, no dragging me away. He just calmly whistled for the boys to gather round, told them what a good shift they were putting in and sent them all for a drink and a stretch. Then he quietly said to me that I'd done enough for the day and to go and get a shower.

I was still fired up and wasn't having it, but he put his arm round me and said it was for the best. He was absolutely right, of course, and that was what made him such a great guy.

In that moment when I flew in on Hoggy, I was angry at the world and Joe defused the ticking timebomb. By the time I was changed, the other boys were back in and everything was fine again. They all knew my situation and they were fantastic with me.

You can definitely say the same for Joe and wee Frank Connor. One day, they turned up at the hospital unannounced with flowers for Carol and that meant the world to her. They told me if it was getting too much I was to take all the time off that I needed. Joe asked if I wanted to play on Saturdays and I said yes.

Some people might think I was an idiot for even thinking about the game while my daughter was lying there desperately ill. But there was this stupid idea in my head that if I played well, Lauren would get better.

And sometimes, it even seemed to work – I'd have a good game, then get to the hospital and find out she'd had a good day. There were times when she really did look as if she was getting over the worst – but that, sadly, was before we realised the significance of those first 24 hours when the valve damage wasn't spotted.

A football dressing-room is a great place to be when you're in turmoil. It's good to go somewhere and hear laughter, even if you don't feel like joining in with the joke.

Players are insensitive. If your marriage is on the rocks or if you lose your licence, they don't comfort you, they slaughter you. There's never any time to feel sorry for yourself or mump in a corner. You have to be strong for the time you are in there and being with the boys stopped me going over the edge when Lauren was ill, no doubt about that.

Some days I'd drive in with Tosh McKinlay, a guy who dressed better for training than I did to go to a wedding.

When I knocked on his door in the morning I'd be like a burst couch. Unshaven, hair all over the place and wearing a tracky. Tosh would appear in an expensive suit, perfectly ironed shirt, silk tie and not a hair out of place.

I used to think that after training he went off to run a business or something, but all he did was go back home the same as the rest of us. He was just more comfortable looking smart and that has never changed.

Carol got close with Tosh's wife Yvonne while Lauren was ill. Yvonne was pregnant with their second baby at the time and went to visit Lauren's grave with Carol soon after the funeral.

We were made up for them when little Jordan was born, but nine months later he took ill and died and is buried in a grave next to Lauren's.

It was a horrible time for them and we knew exactly what they were going through. We felt their pain and you would not wish the experience on your worst enemy.

During those weeks when Lauren's life hung in the balance, Carol would stay in bed sleeping while I was out. When I got home, I'd wake her up and we'd go into the hospital together. We'd stay as long as they'd let us, eat together in the canteen, then she'd stay the night if she could while I went home for some shut-eye before it started all over again the next day.

At four weeks, they did an angioplasty – an operation using a cable passed up through her body – to stretch the valve again. For a few days after that, Lauren was breathing on her own and looking great. Then the valve shrank again and she went a horrible grey colour.

You felt so sorry for her, lying there with tubes from the ventilator up her nose, leads from the monitors attached to her tummy and chest with red and yellow and black clips, tape everywhere holding it all down. She even had a line going into her little tiny foot. It broke your heart.

One regret we have now is that we didn't take photos for a while when she had all that stuff on her. We thought she'd be out soon enough and didn't want to remember her looking like that. Eventually, though, we decided to get the camera out again and we're both so glad we did.

We've a stack of pictures in her own little album, and in quite a few of them she's wearing our favourite sleepsuit, one with a little star on the front. All the boys have worn it since.

As the tubes and clips became fewer and fewer over the weeks, she looked more and more lovely. At times she radiated happiness. Then, at others, she'd look at you as if to say: 'I've had enough.'

She had one big scar on her chest and, as time went by, it was healing up nicely. Then they had to go and open it up again.

By six and a bit weeks, they said they had to operate or she'd die and even then her chances were no better than 50–50.

On 7 April, her day of destiny came.

That day, Carol was at Yorkhill with her mum until about half-one in the afternoon, then came back to the house to get me. We had an argument about whether to go through before the op or not. I wanted to stay and go later, but Carol insisted we saw Lauren before they took her to theatre.

Thank God I listened to her or I'd never have seen the wee soul alive again.

As they wheeled her away, I had a horrible feeling in the pit of my stomach that this was it. Later, Carol told me she'd also been sure Lauren was going to die. She actually said 'Goodbye' to her, not 'See you later'.

When Darren was about a year and a half old, he stuck the head on Carol's nose while she was trying to get him to sleep. She eventually needed surgery and told me she had exactly the same feeling of doom that day. It must have been terrifying for her.

Carol looked like the Lion King after her nose op. She had two strips of rubber up her nose with ribbon tied round her face. Darren was too scared to look at her.

The wait for news on Lauren that day seemed like an eternity and words can't describe the feeling of helplessness as the seconds dragged. Yet when the time came, it came all too soon.

Out came Mr Pollock, this giant man with the Pat Jennings hands, the tears rolling down his face telling us everything before he said a word.

It was a surreal, awful moment.

He told us he'd replaced the valve and the operation had been a success. But when they'd tried to get her off bypass, her wee heart wouldn't start.

They'd lost her.

We'd lost her.

Lauren had been 6 lb 7 oz when she was born. She was 8 lb 7 oz when she died. Everything about her was normal, except for that tiny little valve. It all seemed so bloody unfair.

The staff at Yorkhill could not have been kinder or more caring to us throughout it all. One of the nurses, Louise, is Lewis's godmother and every year on Lauren's birthday she sends us a card with a butterfly on it.

In fact, there's only one person there I wouldn't shake warmly by the hand. This one, I'd grab round the neck and never let go – the ratbag who leaked the news of Lauren's death the *Scottish Sun* before we'd told the family. Can you believe a reporter was on the phone to my mum for a reaction before Carol and I had even been told?

It was a disgusting thing for anyone to do to a grieving family. I didn't realise then that newspapers had people in hospitals and morgues and police stations, and pretty much every other public building, and they slipped them cash in return for tip-offs.

I hope every penny brings every one of these gossips nothing but misery.

In the days and weeks and months that followed Lauren's death, we cried a lot. We laughed a lot. Talking about it a lot definitely helped.

The experience definitely made me a lot more emotional – even today, certain songs that were around at the time set me off bubbling. Or who knows, maybe I was due to mature anyway. Whatever, success wasn't the be-all and end-all once we lost her.

To this day I can't watch kids in hospitals on TV, they make me well up. Carol sits and watches all these baby programmes or gory hospital dramas, but I need to go out of the room.

What was I writing earlier on? That as a young guy, you think you're invincible?

Well, now I knew different for absolutely certain.

Carol's also a massive part of the change in me. She made me a better person, no doubt about it. Being single and rich might have been fine, but you need someone to share your life with, the good and the bad.

Staying at Rangers *and* having Carol? Now *that* would have been something. They'd have seen the best of me then. But what use are if onlys?

Neither of us ever dreamed we'd have had the strength to beat something like this. But together, that strength was double.

One thing was for sure right away – we wanted another baby. We had so much love inside that we hadn't been able to give to Lauren. Now, with three great boys, our family is terrific. But with Lauren around as their big sister, we'd have had everything.

Then again, she'd have needed so much treatment had she lived that maybe her life would have been miserable. Maybe it'd have put a huge strain on us all. Again, what use is there in wondering?

The week she died, I offered to play against Dundee at Tynecastle on the Saturday. I needed an escape hatch again, but Joe said that, although he appreciated the sentiment, he wouldn't pick me.

Barry, meanwhile, was down in Greenock with the Scotland Under-15s. My aunt Angela and and her husband Brian went down to bring him back the night Lauren died and found him playing pool with his mates. He said he wasn't coming and they left without him.

Carrying Lauren's little white coffin down to the front at the Co-op funeral parlour in Bellshill was the hardest thing I've ever had to do.

I got out the car, they handed her to me, and I thought my legs were going to give way. It all suddenly seemed so real, so final.

I know the whole Hearts team were there. When I saw Nicky

Walker he burst into tears. But who else was in the congregation? I can't remember, so much of it's a blur.

Carol's brother Jim had been there when Lauren died and it devastated him. He read the eulogy and we keep his typewritten sheet in Lauren's photo album. He spoke simply about what she'd been through and it was a lovely tribute. Lying there in the coffin, she looked more beautiful than ever. You'd have thought she was fast asleep. When Jim came into the parlour to see her, he fell to his knees, roaring and crying. A big man brought down by the death of someone so tiny.

Afterwards, she was buried at Bothwell Park Cemetery by Father Jim Morris, the priest who'd married us. I tried to be strong, but there was no chance. Carol was the same – the thing that sticks in her mind is apologising to the priest for crying, saying over and over that she was being selfish.

Afterwards, I took a couple of weeks off, and pretty soon it was the end of the season. Carol and I went on holiday for two weeks, then came back and had another fortnight away. We'd booked two breaks deliberately, thinking that we'd be away from it all. But you'd see a kid playing in the pool or hear a baby cry and realise that it was always, always going to be there.

When we got home, the news broke that Joe Jordan was leaving and Sandy Clark would be the new gaffer, but by then I'd made a massive decision.

I was ready to get away from Scotland.

Hearts had been great for me on the pitch and great to me off it, but it was everywhere else that was the problem. The bottom line was that I just couldn't bear being asked about Lauren any more. How were we coping? How did we feel? Poor you, sorry to hear the news – all of it sympathetic and heartfelt, but pretty soon it became like a buzz in your head that you had to shut out any way you could. There was just so much confusion and frustration at that time.

Carol's religious – and that's great for her, she needs her faith – but I really started to question whether God exists. Over the years we've had long, deep conversations that always circle around that one old chestnut: if he really is up there, why do babies die? Why did 9/11 happen? The Tsunami? Aids? Why is there so much hunger and sadness in the world?

But it's a reflective thing now, not a barney. As a boy I played angry, wanted to fight the world. These days I'm still driven, but I want to win more for the other guys than for myself. It's nice to see part-time guys get a few bob in their pockets. It's a feel-good thing.

My church is the gym, the training pitch, the open spaces of Strathclyde Park. That's where I get the same feeling religious people get during worship.

As time's gone on, I've got my spark back, my sense of fun. But for a while after Lauren, nothing seemed to matter hellish much.

How can it when you realise you've played football right through your child's lifetime?

When you've lost a child, nothing ever erases the memories. But the very least you can expect is that over time you can be allowed to unlock them when you choose, not when someone else forces you to. Carol and I were denied that right by news so appalling I still can't get my head around it.

Seven years on from Lauren's funeral, stories started to appear about organs being taken from children who'd died at Yorkhill. They seemed too far-fetched to be true. Or maybe we just didn't want to believe they were. Carol, though, needed to know and wrote to Yorkhill. They wrote back confirming our worst fears.

And all our hurt came bubbling back to the surface again. They'd taken her heart, her lungs and even her brain. The first two we managed to get back from them, but her brain had been sent to the Southern General Hospital and – I can still hardly write the words – it was burned. Like a piece of rubbish.

We were sick to our stomachs. And what got to us most of all was that in the hours after Lauren's death we had actually *offered* her organs to Yorkhill to help other children. After all, she had been given one last chance of life thanks to a heart valve taken from a dead baby, so how could we deny another family that one glimmer of hope we'd had?

The hospital, though, said no thanks, that it was too late for her organs to be of any use. They sat there and spun us their story and then they went and took so much of her little body away.

We'd been promised her post-mortem would be a simple one, that they would only re-open her existing scar. But when we finally got the record of that examination – and that took a fight, because they originally told us it was missing – they had taken every part of her that they could.

It was like she was taken apart for scrap. The way they treated her, you'd think she'd been found dead in a park and they didn't know what had killed her.

That's what stings so badly about what they did, the deceit of it all. We can't criticise all the staff who we know were as shocked as us by what went on behind closed doors. But a lot of people at Yorkhill knew an awful lot about what was going on and we will never forgive them.

And so, on 2 November 2000, seven years and seven months on from the funeral, the priest came and Lauren's grave was opened up and her heart and lungs were finally laid to rest on top of her little coffin.

After that, I began to resent Yorkhill. We'd done a lot of fundraising for them, helped set up a fund in the *Scottish Sun* and gave thousands from my wages. We had an accumulative bonus system at Hearts, and after a really good run of results we handed over the whole amount. The rest of the team all gave up a win bonus. Money flooded in.

After what happened to Lauren, though, I was left thinking it was all taken under false pretences. We'd trusted these people and they'd let us down. But just because some people at one point did something so terrible doesn't mean other children should suffer. No one should *ever* have to go through what we and so many other parents have.

In fact, I look at the football industry today and believe we don't do nearly enough for places like Yorkhill. I was on Rangers TV last Christmas when they showed a piece with the players taking presents to the kids and it struck me how little clubs do to help those in need.

An organised visit like that shouldn't be a once-a-year thing. Players should be giving up their time regularly as a team to visit children in hospital, because half an hour with their heroes will stay with those children all their lives. We can make a real difference.

We talk about role models, but clubs definitely don't do enough to promote a positive image of their stars. I'd have them visiting the homeless and the elderly, as well as kids, three or four players to one person, so they could really get the patter going.

It's taken me time to get back to that way of thinking, though. Back then, the people who'd asked us for financial help filled us with nothing but anger and disgust. A few months after the second funeral, I went to Glasgow University for a meeting of all the parents affected by what happened at Yorkhill and it was a truly horrible experience.

We were advised to sue, but that was where we drew the line – because what would have been the point? What good would money have done us? How could anyone put a price on a baby's life?

And one day, we would once again have reason to thank Yorkhill. If Lauren's life and death is still as fresh in our minds as it was at the time, what our middle son Ross went through still seems to have happened to someone else.

He was still a newborn when we took him to the doctor with

a high temperature only to be told that he probably just had indigestion. But as the hours went by, he was making a noise that I can only describe as sounding like a whale in pain and we rushed him to hospital. Freakily, when we got there, we heard the noise of Rangers playing at Ibrox, just as they had been the night Lauren was taken in. Thankfully, our third child came back out in good health.

He went through brain scans and hearing tests and we were so relieved when it turned out that although he had meningitis it was viral and not the far more dangerous bacterial form. It was a scary time, yet somehow something inside me said he'd be OK and thank God that's how it turned out. He's been left with no ill effects, though his little oddity is that he has two webbed toes on either foot. That's a tiny price for him to pay when you think what might have been. Losing two kids? Would his mum and I have been strong enough to cope with that?

It's just such a relief we never had to find out.

When I was writing down notes for the opening pages of this book, Carol looked over my shoulder and told me I was wrong, that I hadn't been as selfish during it all as I was making out. She says she'd never have left me, even though I'd scribbled down that she'd have had every right. She actually says I was quite attentive, that we were always in it together. That means an awful lot to me.

I couldn't live without her. And I also carry around a little reminder of our daughter with me, a tattoo of an angel at the top of my right arm with the inscription: 'Lauren – Always In My Heart'.

Yet part of me constantly wants to be even closer to her, no matter how nonsensical that sounds.

Every time I've gone for surgery since she died, I've hoped to float away under the anaesthetic and see her.

Every time, I've woken up gutted.

But it doesn't stop me hoping.

NINE

REID IT AND WEEP

So this is where we came in. Sunderland. The car crash. Life just as mangled as the front end of the Astra.

So much went on in my first year down there – the night of the accident, Carol was convinced she was pregnant. The next morning, after I got out of the cells, we were devastated to find out she wasn't.

Then, within weeks, she was. And suddenly we were ecstatic, terrified, confused, you name it.

By the end of November, Terry Butcher had been punted. I went to court in the March. By the start of May, we had Darren.

I went through a time when I wasn't enjoying life. That little bit in your make-up that you take onto the park and sparks you off, that was missing. I didn't get it back even when I came back to Scotland. Maybe I've never had it back.

When I speak to Carol about it now, she says I'm wrong, that I wasn't as bad and as selfish as I make out. But that's still how I see it.

The lads weren't good with me after the crash. They all had

agents and they got together and were going to sue me. My insurance would have covered it, but it would probably have meant me never getting to drive again.

Sometimes the bad feeling boiled over into training. I remember having a flare-up with Phil and trying to do Ian one time. Andy was a big laid-back guy and he was a bit better with me.

I thought it was a bit of a 'F**k you' by them and it was all a bit frosty. But the rest of the dressing-room were fine – none of them had known the four of us before we arrived, so they didn't take sides.

Thankfully, nothing came of the legal action thing – maybe Terry or somebody explained the pressure I'd been under – but things were never the same. I've never spoken to any of them since.

Andy did really well for himself, captaining Fulham and Crystal Palace, as well as playing for Wales. I liked Phil. His nickname was Tippy and he was a typical Northern Ireland boy, full of life. I don't blame them if they fell out with me, because I could have mangled them. I can't even expect them to understand now if they read the reasons. None of what happened to me and Carol and little Lauren should have left them fearing for their own lives.

But you never realise these things at the time. You're too lost in your own little world. Sometimes it takes something as major as what we all went through that night to bring everything to a head and get you going on the right track again.

The odd thing is that I was rooming with Phil on away trips to start with – and that can't possibly work when there's an atmosphere hanging over the two of you.

So we sorted it out the football way.

One day in training we niggled at each other until it turned into a shoving match, then handbags, then a proper rumble.

Then we got back to the room and talked everything out. The tension was broken and after that we were fine.

The fact that big Tel only lasted a few months after I went down there was no real surprise, because the feel of the place wasn't right from the off. Five or six of the lads, local boys, didn't fancy him. They were on a downer because they'd been told the previous season they weren't needed, but hadn't got themselves moves. When Terry was then forced through injuries to try and fit them back into the plans, they clearly didn't give a shit for him.

I think the world of Terry. There's been no better captain in modern football. But if even one or two guys in a dressing-room don't feel the same, if they don't have a bond with the gaffer, then he's in trouble.

Five or six?

That's a nightmare.

His assistant, Ian Atkins, was gutted when he didn't get the job after Terry was punted. Instead, it went to Mick Buxton, a bloke right out of the old school. Maybe I have fond memories of him because he played me regularly – because, at the end of the day, that's the best quality a manager can have – but he was a genuinely good thing for us. We were a happy team under him and never more so than on our journeys to and from away games.

We'd leave on Friday mornings, check into the hotel, train late afternoons, dinner, team talk, early night. After the game, check the results in the players' lounge, then offski. More often than not we'd have four or five hours in front of us. We had slogs to the likes of Oxford, Charlton, Millwall, Luton, Southend, Portsmouth. Suddenly, Aberdeen seemed like a stroll to the shops.

We did a hell of a lot of miles together and when you're in a confined space that long with your mates it becomes your social life. The team bus is your local on wheels.

There was a fridge at the front and another halfway up, and after every away game there would be food on the tables as well as a few beers. Then, an hour into the drive back – win, lose or draw – the music would go on and the cans came out for real and the party started.

I always sat with big Gary Bennett, a monster on the park and a diamond off it, and we had an absolute ball. I loved it when he danced – he's the only black man alive who has no sense of rhythm. We're still in touch and that means a lot to me.

If there was boxing on the telly, we'd stop at a pub on the way back. Then we'd always have another stop at Wetherby for chips. By then we'd be dancing in the aisle. It was midnight before we got back sometimes, our wives waiting in the car park with the engines running. We'd fall off the bus and they'd be well impressed.

Some clubs you go to, they organise a team night out once every six months. At Sunderland we had one every time we left the city.

I loved the people down there, both at the club and in streets. We had Kevin Ball as captain, a man in the Butcher mould – a hardcase on the pitch, social convenor off it. He was a natural leader and a terrible loser.

First few training sessions I had there, we'd warm up with a game of Toro – everyone in a circle, one in the middle, the rest keeping the ball off him – and it was competitive, but a laugh.

Except when Bally was in there.

He'd hammer in, studs up, put you in the air – then pick you up and smile at you. Then you'd try to give him one back when it was your turn. You soon learned.

Bally had great habits, ate well, slept plenty, trained hard as hell. But when the work was done, he got stuck into the fun with the rest of the boys.

The disappointment for me is that I never got a chance to

play for Sunderland in really good times. We were stuck in what's now the Championship when I joined and were middle-of-the-table, middle-of-the-road all the way. Yet Roker Park was still a bear-pit of noise, fantastically partisan, with a good pitch to play on.

Away from the club, Carol and I moved to a lovely house at Chester-le-Street in County Durham. I'd have stayed at the County Hotel as long as I could, mind – the staff were great, the leisure facilities were top class and so was the food.

I loved the idea of coming back from training, having a swim, getting coffee sent up, all that stuff. But when I was away, Carol was stuck in a little room for hours on end, pregnant, fed up and far from home.

The one mistake we made with the house – story of my life, chapter 94 – is that we rented instead of buying. We'd actually have been cheaper with a mortgage, we just didn't think about it. If we had, we'd have had an investment for the future, but there you go.

It was a gorgeous place, though. If we could have picked it up and taken it home to Hamilton, we'd have been in heaven.

But that was the problem for Carol. It wasn't Hamilton and she was missing home more and more.

She didn't come with me when the court case over the crash came up. I'd wanted to plead guilty, but the lawyer said no and she felt sitting through a trial would have been too stressful at seven months gone.

When the day came, the moment I walked through the door I knew for certain that pleading not guilty was wrong. I didn't want to be there, didn't want to hear the lawyer trying to get me off. The crash had been my fault and that was the end of it. Anything else that was said felt like a lie.

It got to me most of all when the Prosecution produced a plan of the crash scene, a diagram of my car and the roundabout and the car coming the other way. It was horrible. Something that had been the result of so much personal trauma, reduced to a few squiggles on a piece of cardboard.

I wanted to stand up and shout for them to stop, to call it all off, just give me my punishment and let me get away.

But all you can do is sit there and listen and wait until it comes time for the inevitable verdict. In the end, the fine and ban was probably heavier than it would have been had I just held my hands up.

A year's ban, £2,300 plus £300 costs and ordered to re-sit my test.

Still, a small price to pay considering what might have been that late, crazy August night.

Don Goodman lived not far away from us at the time and he used to drive me to training and back most days.

Though I say *drive* – the word *race* is more appropriate.

He was a top man, but a nutter behind the wheel. He'd scream along the roads, cutting in and out of traffic, everything absolutely hyper.

Funny, but the 15-minute walk down to where he used to pick me up took me right back to being a Rangers kid getting a lift into Ibrox from Stan Anderson, my old reserve-team coach.

Both times I sat in the passenger seat too scared to speak . . .

When the ban was up, I thought I'd only need a couple of refresher lessons before putting in for the test. But then, most idiots who've got themselves into that position probably do. And most likely then found it took nearer half a dozen. You learn a lot of bad habits down the years and you have to unlearn them again sharpish.

Come the big day, it went fine and as he handed me the pass slip, the examiner said: 'You've driven before, haven't you?'

That was when I told him my story. I was so relieved to get

my licence back, but embarrassed to be admitting the reason I needed to.

It was a chapter I was only too happy to see closed.

However, a much happier one opened when Darren was born. What a joy that was for us after everything we'd gone through with Lauren.

I think becoming a dad to a healthy, happy little boy was the moment when my spark started to reignite. Nothing could ever replace the daughter we'd lost, but this wee fella was a wonderful gift.

The doctors were fantastic – as soon as they knew about Lauren they never seemed to stop scanning Carol to put our minds at rest. They even scanned the heart itself inside the womb.

All we wanted was a healthy baby and when that happened . . . well, it's hard to describe the feeling. He's our little Englishman, though don't dare tell him that. He's so patriotic and gets quite upset if we wind him up about being One Of Them.

Carol spent fortunes on Darren when he was born and I never interfered. He had a new outfit every second day, but I know why. She was getting all that pent-up love out in any way she knew how. And anyway, Sunderland was the only place where we ever felt rich.

Like all our kids, Darren arrived early. He wouldn't open his eyes when he was born and Carol said to the midwife: 'Does he have eyes? Because I can handle it if he doesn't, just as long as he's alive.'

I had the full Dr Kildare rig-out that day – the mask, the blue hat, the clogs. For Ross's birth, they gave me the plastic overshoes, but I wore them over my bare feet. I must have looked a state. There were a few complications when Lewis was born, but he's a wee fighter and came through with no ill-effects.

* * *

Anyway, in the midst of our domestic joy, Mick Buxton had gone after less than a year and with seven games to go of 1994–95 and us well down the First Division table, in came Peter Reid.

There was a terrific buzz when he arrived and Roker was bouncing when we beat Sheffield United in his first game. Me? I wasn't bouncing, I was writhing. Because that bloody shoulder of mine went again.

It wasn't my fault, but it was still the worst possible start any player could have under a new manager. Though, to be honest, when I look back I reckon if it hadn't been that it'd have been something else. He just didn't seem to like my face, full stop.

We all knew he was Celtic daft, so I wondered if maybe my background was the problem. Nah, no manager would cut his nose off to spite his face like that. Then I starting thinking back to him playing for Everton when Rangers beat them in the Dubai Cup that time. Did he hold a grudge about that? Or were the rumours right and he just hated Jocks, full stop?

Whatever the reasons, it didn't happen between us.

And within days of his arrival, our relationship hit the buffers when he refused to let me come up the road for David Cooper's funeral.

That really hurt me. OK, so he didn't fancy me from the off, but surely stopping someone paying their last respects to someone who was not only their friend but their hero was beyond a joke.

You think sometimes you're over things, but when I was sitting at home watching George Best's funeral on telly in late 2005 the resentment I felt towards Reid came flooding back.

I heard myself hiss: *'Bastard . . .'*

Carol and her mum and dad turned round to look at me. I felt embarrassed, but they understood when I told them what was going through my mind.

The service they had for Best really moved me – it was a proper celebration of life – and brought back so many memories of Coop at the same time. I'd gone to his grave not long before, just to say hello. Walking between the headstones, it struck me that there were people in there who I knew, who I'd grown up with, but who I didn't even know were dead.

Coop was a Hamilton boy and today his statue stands in God's country, Strathclyde Park. I've run there at the crack of dawn, in the height of the afternoon heat, at sundown. Whatever time of day you go is always the right time. When I'm pounding away and look up and suddenly see Davie Cooper looking down on me, I'm in heaven.

Whenever I've felt sorry for myself, I go and see him and everything comes into perspective. What a guy. I watched him weave his magic when I was a kid, then had the privilege of playing in the same team as him, then mourned him.

I've never gone for any footballers' fads down the years – coloured boots, breathing strips across the nose, all that nonsense. The only wee thing I ever had was wearing one of Coop's old tie-ups round my calf.

I found it on the dressing-room floor after a game when I was 16 and just thought: 'It's Coop's, it'll bring me luck.'

So I tied it on and wore it non-stop, even when I wasn't playing. It got washed in the bath, still on me. One day the other players grabbed me and tried to cut it off and we ended up fighting. It stayed on for about a year until it just withered away.

The funeral of my old coach Stan Anderson really got to me. He was a tough man – when he talked, you listened. He used to pick me up and drive me into training. I'd be standing there in the rain, Safeway poly bag on my head, and he'd pull up and I'd get in and I'd sit there and be too scared to speak.

Me and my pal Mark seemed to be the only two at his funeral who weren't men – you know, *big* men. When they sang, the hairs on the back of my neck stood up. Then they went for a drink and swapped stories about his life and all the characters he'd known, and for so many people that's how the grieving process turns into something they can smile about.

Carol doesn't like to see drink at funerals, but I've told her when I go, everyone's to get hammered. She's not having it, but it'll be written into my will. Not that I should be alive today, if you ask my dad. He's always sworn it ran in the family that I'd die when I was 39. Cheerful soul, eh?

We're different, Carol and I. But that's why we work together so well. She's the best thing that ever happened to me and I couldn't be without her. You know what football's like; you virtually live in each other's pockets and you know the gamblers and the drinkers and the womanisers. Well, I don't bet, I did my big drinking years back – and as for women? No chance, no matter the temptations.

After what Carol and I have been through together, I could never even think of cheating on her. Apart from anything else, she'd know as soon as I walked back in the house – I've got the guiltiest face on the planet.

Anyway, it seemed to me that Reid had decided right away that he wasn't keeping me, and what probably sealed the deal was me going to Scott Nisbet's testimonial at Ibrox at the start of May, despite being injured.

Well, I say 'going to'. I actually mean 'playing in'.

What made me think for a second that Reid wouldn't find out? Who knows, maybe somewhere deep down I didn't really care.

Whatever, I was just back in training after a good few weeks out and asked if I could go up for the game. He said yes, but never expected to hear that I'd put the boots on. But that's me, I can never resist a kick at the ball. And I can never just sit back and stay on the fringes of the action for my own good.

So it's Rangers against ex-Rangers and the old guys want to show the new guys who's boss. Which means leaving the foot in. After about five minutes I ploughed somebody – Alex Cleland, I think, they all look the same when they're flying through the air – and that turned it from a kickabout into a game of football. The crowd loved it, we loved it, so everyone was a winner.

I didn't regret playing at the time, I didn't regret it the next morning or when I had to face Reid the day after that and I don't regret it now. I'd grown up with Nizzy, come through the ranks from Under-12s to big team with him and he was due the respect of his mates being stripped and ready for his big night.

Plus, it was a right good chance for a night out – and what a night it turned into. Back at the Moat House Hotel, it was me, Coisty, Durranty, Johnny Watson from *Only An Excuse?* and Graeme Clark from Wet Wet Wet, and if I'd laughed any harder I'd have wet wet wet my pants.

Clarky's a top man – we got to know him and the band when they got a few of the Rangers boys passes for a show they did at Glasgow Green.

What struck me before the gig was how much it was like the last hour before a football match. In one room, the trumpet players were warming up by doing their scales. In another, the guitarists were battering out riffs. And in another, the Wets themselves were exercising their vocal chords with cans of lager.

But wherever you looked, everyone was geeing each other up, just like we do. They don't want to fail, the same as us. Their minds are focused in on the first note of the first song, just as we'll be thinking of the first kick after the first whistle.

Marti Pellow signed a T-shirt for my mum that night and she was over the moon – she loved him.

As the night wore on, wee Johnny was in magnificent form with the impressions, and Coisty and Ian were like a double act who'd been polishing their material for years. I just sat there listening and cracking up. That's me, I love being entertained.

There was so much entertainment that we didn't even notice it getting light . . .

The good news was, I didn't have to be back at Sunderland that day. The bad news was, by the time I turned up for training the day after, Reid already knew the score. The grapevine had done its stuff.

He pulled me in and said – rightly – that I was out of order turning out in a testimonial when I hadn't been playing for him. The shoulder had gone in his first game after taking over, so he'd never had a chance to make up his mind about how I fitted into the team.

Now he knew for sure. I didn't. In just over a month, he'd seen me carted off, we'd fallen out over Coop's funeral, I'd been stuck on the treatment table when he had a relegation battle to fight and then I went behind his back over Nizzy's game. By the next pre-season, Carol was back up the road and I was in a B&B on Sunderland seafront. The glamour, eh? The word was Falkirk wanted me and Bill McMurdo was trying to sort something out there, but meantime I just soldiered on. Our keeper Alec Chamberlain took pity on me and I moved in with him, then after a week the Falkirk deal went through.

To be honest, by then I just wanted home, but going to Brockville appealed – especially as Mo Johnston was there and I'd have played in the same team as him any day of the week.

So that was me and Sunderland finished. Except, of course, that the chapter wouldn't be complete without another sorry tale from the Ferguson School of Financial Mis-Management.

188

I walked away from Sunderland without a penny. But only because I'd knocked back the two-year contract extension Mick Buxton had offered me not long before he got the tin tack . . .

TEN

A KNEE WHERE IT HURTS

We bumped across the pot-holed car park, picked our way across the puddles on the blaes, squeezed through the front door and found ourselves almost straight out onto the pitch.

Then I took my wee brother into the centre circle and told him: 'Look around – and never stop appreciating what you have.'

I'd been in and around Ibrox from when I was 12 until my early 20s. He'd been there from even younger, right back to his primary school days.

Now, this was my way of telling him that there was a big, scary world out there where not everything was laid on a plate for you.

This was Brockville.

And believe me, after Rangers, Hearts and Sunderland, I was only just getting used to being around the place myself.

Falkirk's beloved old home was football in the raw, a proper, crumbly ground with floodlights run by an asthmatic hamster on a rusty wheel and dressing-rooms so small you'd think you had cramp, then look down and realise you were putting your socks on someone else's leg.

It was always one of the places I'd loved coming to play, a tight, exciting little hotspot where the locals roared the place down and you never, ever got it easy. Ask big Joe Jordan about that – his fate as Hearts boss had been sealed by a 6–0 hounding we suffered there in the spring of 1993.

But bracing yourself for a couple of visits a season's different from turning up there day in, day out to do your stuff – and it *was* day in, day out, because we trained there, either on the pitch or on the astroturf behind the main stand.

When I arrived in September 1995, they were coming off the back of a season that so nearly ended in European qualification, but which in fact came to a horrible anticlimax for players and punters alike as manager Jim Jefferies jumped ship to replace wee Tam McLean at Hearts.

The choice of John Lambie as Jim's replacement didn't go down well from day one and after a few bad results the natives, as they say, were revolting.

I didn't realise just how down the place was until I got myself in the door, but even then the challenge was an exciting one. I had a two-and-a-half-year deal in my back pocket and was ready to give it a real go.

What a bad joke that turned out to be.

I was there for a couple of months short of three years and only started a measly 31 games. What started out as a simple block tackle turned into a major op that snowballed into an 18-month hell of tears and frustration and anger.

Until my right knee went under the full weight of a Kenny Brannigan tackle, things had been going great guns. After it, I was never able to straighten the leg again.

In between times, I found that I wasn't bad at kung-fu.

Not that my bosses were particularly impressed.

We were coming back from Aberdeen after the last game of my first season and for some reason decided to see who could karate chop the big wooden club crest that sat in the back window of the bus. We had it across the aisle between two seats and took it in turns to see who could smash it in two with the side of their hand.

Gerry Collins was in charge by then and he was sitting up there with us, laughing his head off, which is all the more reason why it didn't make sense that I ended up in trouble for what happened next.

After a right few goes from all the boys, I gave it a particular tasty Hong-Kong Phooey job and – SNAP! – it collapsed on the floor in bits with the kind of noise I wouldn't hear again until the knee graft went. We were dancing about and giving it high-fives and it seemed like just another daft away-day stunt.

But come the Monday, a shock. They handed me a letter saying I was being fined two weeks' wages. I went to see George Fulston, apologised and offered to replace the crest – and I'd have got them a better one as well because, to be honest, it wasn't exactly five star. He wasn't having it. When I look back, it seems to me they were just trying to claw some money back. But the PFA then confirmed what I thought, which was that the club didn't have a leg to stand on. I never paid them a penny, but the incident left a sour taste.

Falkirk was also the only club where I ever played alongside anyone I actively disliked and that was wee Albert Craig. For a start, he seemed to spend more time in with the gaffer than he did with the boys and that's not my scene. Quite often he'd walk in for training and ignore you. That wasn't for me either – even if it's a general 'Good morning' to the whole place, you have to say something to the rest of them.

Albert was gloomy, a bit of a loner. And what really set me off with him was the day he put it about that I was swinging the lead. Nobody says that about Derek Ferguson.

We'd been having a game on the astroturf next to the main stand, a surface I never liked. An old knee injury was bothering me, so I played wide right where I could run up and down in straight lines rather than turning and twisting in the middle. Then, going home in the car, Paul McGrillen – Mowgli to the boys – says to me that Albert's been moaning that I was hiding. Red rag.

Not saying it to my face at the time, that's what got to me most. I'd soon put that right. Next morning, I waited for him in the car park, asked him straight about what he'd said, he hummed and hahed, I lost the rag and demanded a square go. It all calmed down, because in the end just facing him up was enough to sort it and after that we were fine. Later, we'd play together again at Thistle and become pals.

There's no doubt the good old scrap is how so many problems get sorted out in our world. There's no time for sulks. Festering fallouts do nothing for team spirit. So you swing a few handbags, clear the air and usually end up better mates than you were before. Honestly, one day at Brockville I watched Brian Hamilton and Ally Graham have an argument, start poking each other in the chest then hit the deck rolling around, scratching each other's eyes out – and ten minutes later the two of them are in the car home with me and Mowgli. The four of us travelled together every day, changed together in that pokey room, fought on the same side every week. We'd have been odd kind of people if that never bred a moment's tension.

Especially with big Ally's patter. He'd give an aspirin a headache.

When we came back up the road from Sunderland, I'd wanted to move to Quarter, a lovely wee village up the hill from the centre of Hamilton, where we now live in a smashing bungalow at the end of a safe cul-de-sac.

Back then, though, we looked around and couldn't find

anything suitable, so we settled for a house on a new estate in Bothwell and lived with my mum and dad while it was being built. Once we moved in, Craig Moore and Charlie Miller went round the corner from us and it was a really nice area, but I never really settled and 18 months later the house in Quarter became available.

By then, one Ferguson tradition had already been upheld. The manager who bought me had been binned. On 16 March 1996, John Lambie's unhappy spell ended – and six months after that, it was time for another regular occurrence.

The career-threatening injury.

On 5 September, two days after the first anniversary of my move from Sunderland, little Ross was born. Nine days after that, we were playing Clydebank. I went to hit a volley and right as I caught it flush, big KB – not a man you want hitting you at 30 mph – hit me at 30 mph.

Nighty-night.

The impact knackered the cruciate in my right knee and I went into Bon Secour Hospital in Glasgow, where the surgeon Gavin Tait said he was going to take four strips from one of my hamstrings and make them into a replacement set of ligaments. He was confident I'd soon be fighting fit again in no time.

Timing? Don't talk to me about timing. A week earlier, I'd had the chance to talk to Dundee United, but I was enjoying myself and said thanks but no thanks.

Fate's an utter bastard sometimes.

With a cruciate, 'no time' should mean six to nine months of rest, rehab and training. You need to get your movement back, but before that you have to work really hard to rebuild strength.

Falkirk didn't have the facilities I needed, so they sent me to St John's Hospital in Livingston, where I did circuits and worked on my quads and hamstrings on a machine called the King Kong.

But six months came and went and I was no nearer running, never mind kicking a ball. Then it was nine. And suddenly, a whole season came and went without any real improvement. I questioned myself about it every day, wondered if I wasn't working hard enough or was doing the wrong kind of exercises. It was doing my head in.

Then one day I was on a treatment table at the hospital with a physio manipulating the knee to break down scar tissue. It was bite the bullet time, an incredibly painful but equally necessary part of your recovery.

And suddenly – **BANG!** – we got the fright of our lives. There was this almighty noise like a plank of wood cracking in two. An old bloke called Russell at the next bench nearly jumped out of his skin. None of us had a Scooby what had happened. For a few horrible seconds I thought the cruciate had gone again, but the searing pain never came. The leg bent. I felt no different than I had before the crack – and, in fact, come next morning I had more movement in the knee than for a long time. It looked like whatever the bang had been, it had been good news.

But then the knee started to swell up without warning, and for four or five months I didn't know how it'd be from day to day. Sometimes I could do anything, run and jump, others I could barely get out of bed.

I was at my wit's end, wondering why guys with exactly the same injury had been back playing for yonks. The more I busted a gut, the less progress I seemed to make.

And what made it all the more frustrating was that the knee kept me out of the team's incredible run to the Scottish Cup final.

It was an adventure that would put the whole town on a massive high. But one which began just a few weeks after the dressing-room was on a terrible low thanks to the sacking of a man-manager I had endless respect for.

I'd known Eamonn Bannon, who replaced Gerry Collins in the manager's chair, from our days together at Hearts and he was a guy whose training methods were right up my street. Loads of gym work, quick feet sessions, short runs on the track. It was just like old Tynecastle times.

Sadly, he was gone all too soon. And through little fault of his own.

The week after I was crocked, wee Mowgli scored the only goal at Love Street with a 90th minute penalty. But it turned out that big John Clark, who'd just signed and had come on as a sub, wasn't registered properly and when the case came up at the SFA the club got hammered. There must have been a whole bunch of fingerprints on the paperwork – or lack of it – that led to the blunder. But guess who was left holding it when the music stopped?

Correct. Eamonn.

Bye-bye, boss.

You want an insight into how a football dressing-room works? Well, here you go.

The boys were just getting on the bus to go on our Christmas night out when we heard the news. It felt like a smack in the face. A guy we all liked and respected had been binned for something that couldn't possibly be all down to him and the talk there and then was about doing something to help him. We wouldn't take this lying down, no way. We'd get behind the gaffer. Definitely. As soon as we got back to training.

Did we? *No.* Why? *Because we all wanted to play.*

See, you're full of indignation and 'Up the workers!' at the time, but the bottom line is that, come Monday, someone else is in charge and they're the man you've got to impress if you want a shirt on Saturday. So we said nothing, got our heads down, grafted away and when Alex Totten was unveiled as Eamonn's replacement we shook his hand and vowed to give our all for him.

Horrible, isn't it?

Eamonn had given his lot to Falkirk and was a good coach who was liked by his squad. Maybe someone behind the scenes just didn't fancy him, though. Maybe he took the fall for someone else's cock-up. Maybe it was all a neat way to get Totts in, I don't know. And when it comes down to it, I can't afford to care.

Sit there with your face tripping you because a gaffer you admired's been shafted and by the time you look up somebody else'll have your number on his back. That can't happen, not even if that guy's your best mate in the whole world and desperately needs the appearance money to pay his phone bill.

Whoever's in charge, it's your job to keep him happy and get a game in front of all comers. They're your buddies on the training pitch, on the bus and in the boozer. But when it's time for the sheet to go up on the board, they're your rivals. Forget that and you're finished. There was a time when I honestly thought that feeling would change, that as I matured I'd find it easier to accept being left out. What a load of old bollocks that turned out to be.

When that sheet's pinned up and your name's missing, the emotions go through you in four waves.

1. You're embarrassed.

2. You're furious.

3. You remember that it's a team game and you wish the lads all the best.

4. You watch the guy who's in your place pull his boots on and hope they give him terminal corns.

Then you're thinking back to training. That time he went through you, was he trying to do you in? Did the gaffer think you were soft letting him away with it? Did you laugh at the wrong time, take too many touches, walk on the cracks in the pavement, what? Why? How long till the next session so you can make it all OK again?

In my case, it would be a long time – a whole lot longer than I'd expected when big KB ploughed me into the earth's core that September day at Brockville.

Watching the boys march through the cup was brilliant. The run started with a draw at home to Berwick, not exactly Hampden form. But they held their nerve to win the replay 2–1 and were off and running. Brockville was bouncing for a 2–1 fourth-round victory over Dunfermline, with wee Crunchie McAllister and Davie Hagen scoring. Raith were beaten 2–0 at home in the last eight.

And then out came the draw for the semis.

Falkirk . . . . will play . . . . Celtic.

At Ibrox.

How much would I have loved to play in that game? Or the replay that followed? Or the final, which was back at my spiritual home?

So much it hurt, maybe even more than that bloody knee did.

Fair play to the Bairns, they couldn't have been better with me – or my fellow crocks Brian Hamilton and Ally Graham – throughout the run. Totts included us in everything, even took us away when the team stayed overnight before ties.

I roomed with Hammy, who'd broken his leg. When everyone turned in at night, we'd sit up with a glass of red and talk, talk, talk for hours. Deep guy, Hammy, wanted to get right into the heart of football – and to his own performances. I mean, we all obsess at times, but he took it to extremes. Before games, he'd analyse every single little thing he wanted to do and afterwards he'd pick it all apart again, down to tiny little segments.

Nothing was ever off the cuff with him, he really, *really* cared. I always thought he'd make a good coach and sure enough he's now working for the SFA's community department in Renfrewshire. He'll be brilliant at it.

A great guy, Hammy. Never hid on the park, even when things were going against him – and you can't say that for everyone around you. And fantastic on a night out, a real magnet. You'd be sitting there at a bar and suddenly – ping! – a woman just appears at his side and I'd be left reading the beer mats.

Being injured during that run definitely brought him, me and big Ally closer together. I can't imagine what it would have been like to be the lone odd man out in a squad pumped up with cup fever.

Though, actually, that's a lie. Because we *all* knew what it felt like. We knew as soon as the light went out at night and we were left praying to wake up and find it had all been a horrible nightmare and we were about to pull the boots on and go out there and get rattled in.

It's fine at training, you're in and about it all with the rest of them. It's a laugh at dinner back in the hotel. You go in for the team talks and watch the videos of the opposition and play snooker or join in the quizzes or whatever else passes the time on those nervy Friday nights. Matchday breakfast's good, reading the papers and winding each other up. Even on the bus to the game you're still close enough to it all to get that excitement in the pit of your stomach.

It's only when the team gets read out. That's when your guts collapse. That's when you don't want to be around them and they don't want you around. Once the team's announced, the dressing-room's theirs, no one else's. That's when it's time to escape.

On the day of the semi, Hammy and I got out of the dressing-room, went along the corridor to the gym and battered ourselves, the same way I'd released my frustrations at not playing under Souness. Then, when the others were out warming up, we showered and got our suits back on and went out for a look at the stadium. I stood at the touchline, watching Paolo Di Canio go through his paces and he was a class apart, a real pro. You looked at him and thought: athlete.

But the nearer it got to kick-off, the more like spare pricks we felt. We wished the boys luck. We went up to the stand and took our seats. We watched the teams come out. We saw our mates make it through to half-time unscathed.

And then we did a runner.

Down the stairs, out the door, up to the subway, off at Buchanan Street, down to Princes Square, into Buzzy Ware's.

We'd had deep conversations before, but as we sucked on our beers in the basement of that glitzy shopping centre, this one came right up from the soles of our feet. No two guys ever felt sorrier for themselves.

The bar staff shouted to us that Celtic had scored and we felt momentarily guilty. Then, after another beer or two, they shouted that big Kevin James had earned the Bairns a replay. It didn't turn into a session – I was on a train heading back to Hamilton by seven – but it had been enough to take the edge off the hurt we both felt at missing such a big game in our careers.

Brian had won the cup with St Mirren as a teenager ten years before and the League Cup with Hibs in 1992. I had my League Cup medals. But neither of us had been in enough semis and finals to feel anything but gutted right then. No matter how close Totts had tried to keep us to it all, the truth was we felt a million miles away. Although by the time the replay came round, I was *literally* thousands of miles from the action.

Carol and I flew out to Torrance in California to stay with her brother Danny and the first thing I asked when we landed was: 'Where can I see the game?'

He sorted me out no bother. And then the local Celtic fans nearly did too.

Weird, isn't it? All those years in Glasgow, right in the middle of the Old Firm mayhem, and not a problem. Got on great with the other side. Then you cross the Atlantic and they want to kick your head in.

Danny was going to work, but he organised for a pal to take me to the local Celtic Club – so there we were at 7.30 on a Wednesday morning, heading down to see the game over a few beers. A bizarre feeling. Almost as bizarre as what happened next.

The minute we walked through the door, I knew I was in the wrong place. It was packed with 200 Celtic-daft expats and only two people spoke to me the whole time I was there. The other 198 just glared.

Nervous? I had nine bottles of Miller in half an hour, so that at least if someone battered me I wouldn't feel any pain. It was like being back at Dens Park, playing Celtic during my short-lived loan spell with Dundee. That day, the halfwit who spat on me didn't see a Dundee player, only a Rangers player, and it was exactly the same again now. What made it worse for them was that 19 minutes in, wee Mowgli put us ahead and, try as they might, their team just couldn't do what we had in the first game and level it.

When the ball went in the net, I just remember taking a big slug of my beer and screaming for joy inside – while the Celtic punters were all charging up to the screen going mental. By the end, they were all howling drunk, I was well gone and Danny's mate had the job of getting me away safely. He must have wondered why he'd volunteered for the job, but he did it well.

We laughed about it all the way back to his place, where we sat in his back garden for a few more beers before going to a place called The Fort and ending up absolutely bladdered. The Bairns boys themselves couldn't have had a better celebration than their wounded mate.

The final itself? I'll be honest, it's a blur. After being dropped by Souness in 1989, here I was sidelined again and knowing that third time lucky was highly unlikely. My mind just seems to have blocked it all out. I watched from the back of the dugout as Paul Wright scored for Killie and Neil Oliver had what we thought was an equaliser ruled out. The game seemed to come and go in a flash. And when it was over and the rest went back through the town in an open-topped bus to a reception at Callander Park, I went up the road. Just didn't feel part of it.

That summer was more slog for little reward, pre-season was the same, the action got going again without me being close to a return. It was only once Barry suggested that I go and see Paul Jackson, then the youth-team doc at Rangers, that things started happening. And I got *really* angry.

Paul put me onto some good tablets for the pain and sorted me out with top physios. But still the knee was blowing up. I was running like I was on a skateboard, right leg bent and the left straight.

Even once I was finally sorted and got back in the saddle, I watched a tape of a game of me playing for Dunfermline against Rangers – the first time Barry and I had been on opposite sides – and my movement was terrible. Today, when I lie down, I can get my left leg flat to the floor, but my right sits up at about a 30 degree angle.

More than once back then, the pain got so bad I was ready to chuck it altogether. I even walked off the training pitch one day in tears. It was soul-destroying. I'd been back to see the surgeon time and again after the op and he just kept calling my problems 'unfortunate' and to keep working away.

For the first time in my life, though, I simply couldn't face the slog any more. It had been a wasted year, the last thing I needed just when life was coming together again after losing Lauren.

That's where Carol came in. She told me to give it one last shot, to go and see the Hearts doctor, Malcolm McNicholl, and see what he said. He wasn't happy with the state of the knee, not one bit, and suggested a second op. I was so desperate we said 'Yes' on the spot and paid the £1,800 ourselves.

After it was over, Mr McNicholl came in and said he had good news and bad news. The good? I'd play again. The bad?

The first op might not have been what it at first appeared.

Mr McNicholl wasn't able to say for sure, but my theory now is that far from using the hamstring tissue to replace my damaged cruciate, the surgoen had in fact put in a synthetic graft, the kind that had already been found in the cases of Durranty and Craig Levein to give way under stress.

For me, that's what the noise had been that day, the graft smashing into bits and showering shrapnel everywhere inside the knee. There was so much debris I needed another hoover out six months later, though by then so much damage had been done the leg was never the same again.

We tried to get my records from Bon Secour, but they were missing. I was shocked – OK, so it wasn't an omission on the scale of Yorkhill, but it still freaked me out that you could be told a surgeon had carried out one procedure then be left wondering if he'd in fact done a completely different one.

Yet, if I hadn't taken Carol's advice, I'd have packed the game in thinking that I really *had* just been unfortunate. Going to see Mr McNicholl put seven or eight years on my career. Maybe that's why I've appreciated these past few seasons so much, no matter the surroundings. And it's why when Paul Jackson told me to chuck it after my last op I dug in and vowed to give it one last go.

Paul said that if I'd been three or four years younger I might have been OK to carry on – but as far as I'm concerned, I'm as fit in every other department apart from the knee as I was at 34.

One thing's for sure. If I'd had the money back in the Falkirk days, we'd have gone to the law about that graft operation. But it was too much of a financial risk for us and the club didn't have the dosh to get behind me.

As for our Players Union? They didn't seem to have the resources or the structure in place to help. They're tiny compared to the English PFA, a body with real money and real clout.

Just after I signed for Hamilton, I did my knee a bit of damage playing in the Masters five-a-sides down south. The old West Ham and Spurs player Paul Allen, who works for the union, was there. We had a chat and next thing they were paying for treatment. No messing, no argument. I was on their list from playing down there, so they did the business. That really impressed me.

Then I see boys up here in the lower leagues who only need a quick scope, a half-hour's clean-up, but they don't have the insurance and their clubs can't afford to pay, so they struggle on and struggle on and the injury gets steadily worse and their day job suffers as well. That's where I wish the union could help.

By March 1998, things were going badly wrong for the Bairns as a club. Out of the blue, the day before a game at Love Street, we went into administration. Overnight, chairman George Fulston became Public Enemy No. 1, as the fans asked where the money from the cup final run had gone.

But amidst all the barneys, those fans also rallied round the players and eventually their 'Back The Bairns' campaign would pull the club through. They had whip-rounds to pay the wages and turned up in terrific numbers to start making a dent in the debts.

I'd just made it back into the plans then, coming on after 66 minutes of a 1–0 Brockville defeat to Raith Rovers on 14 March – though the comeback would have been six weeks earlier had some arsehole not stolen my *insoles*.

The first day I was back training with the boys I'd told myself to stay away from 50–50s, just to ease myself in. But within 30 seconds, Marino Keith had ploughed me. I lay there on the deck waiting for the knee to scream SOS. The feeling when it didn't was brilliant. In that moment, my confidence was back. I owe Marino for that.

Pretty soon, I felt ready to go. But once again, fate stepped in. It was a Saturday night and we'd gone to a séance, of all things. Carol wanted to get in contact with Lauren, and although I wasn't sure about the whole thing, I went along.

It was eerie, this woman asking if there was a Margaret in the room, because so-and-so wanted to let them know such-and-such. Powerful stuff if you believe in it all, a bit disturbing if you're unsure. And when we came out at the end, I was left asking why they hadn't been able to tell me that while we were in there someone was screwing my motor.

The window had been panned, the stereo was gone and so were two pairs of boots – one of which had the orthopaedic inserts I'd had specially made after a foot injury a few years earlier. I tried to train without them on the Monday, but it was really uncomfortable. You get so used to having them that even now they're the first thing I look for in the morning whatever footwear I'm putting on.

When I rang the guy who'd made them, he said it would take a week to mould a replacement pair and three weeks to break them in. So suddenly, on top of the year and a bit the knee had sidelined me, I was looking at another month without football. All thanks to some sneak thief. It was one thing after another. The whole move had been one long jinx.

Once the new insoles arrived, though, I was raring to get in the side. But Totts seemed reluctant to play me. After six or seven weeks champing at the bit, I chapped his door and asked if I was on the way out. He said far from it, he was actually going to offer me a new deal in the summer. He didn't know what wages would be on offer, but that wasn't an issue for me anyway. Only being there mattered.

His reason for leaving me out was plausible enough. They'd only lost one in fourteen and he didn't want to break up a winning side, but I knew I could improve that side even more. When in the end the contract never materialised, my fear was that clubs would look at the situation and reckon I couldn't have been fit after all. But I was raring to go and the whole business was getting me down.

My 30s were well under way. I'd been through personal hell, suffered two serious spells of injury. Things were drifting. But I'm a great believer that something good's always just around the corner – and so it was proved when the Premier League came calling again a few weeks after I said goodbye to the Bairns.

Bert Paton took me to Dunfermline and the chance to get back in among the big boys was the perfect lift. As was the chance to work with possibly the most enthusiastic coaching team on the planet.

Bert. His No. 2 Dick Campbell. Their right-hand man John McVeigh. An absolutely magnificent trio of motivators who cared so much about the game it hurt. I'm not saying their training was always how I'd like it to have been done, but they put their heart and souls into it.

You only have to look at the number of players who've gone from club to club with all of them to know how highly thought of they are. They inspire loyalty and commitment, and that's a rare quality.

You just can't keep Dick down. Some days down at Pitreavie, the public park where we trained, he'd have us doing crossing and finishing in 90 mph winds. McVeigh? He was passionate to the point of smothering you. He expects so much of his players.

I remember one day we had a right bust-up. We were on the track at East End Park and it was solid under foot, so I asked if I could run down the edge of the pitch to protect my knee. He wasn't having it, because he won't have anybody even *looking* as if they're pulling a sicky. I tried to tell him I wasn't, that I'd be doing the same work as everyone else, but he wouldn't listen. So we were like:

'C'mon, John, I'll be working just as hard as anyone.'

'Naw!'

'But I'm only a couple of feet away from them, it's just a better surface for me.'

'Naw!'

'Look, all I'm trying to do is protect the knee, give myself the best chance of playing for longer.'

'NAW!'

And in the end, naw it was. Because in the end, just as with Souness and in the aftermath of Eamonn's sacking, you do what you're told. After the session was over, I went to see John and asked him about it again. It turned into another argument and, naturally, it finished up 2–0 to him.

Everybody has their own coaching methods. Big Jock Wallace and his lieutenants Joe Mason and Stan Anderson ran you until you threw up. Souness wrapped his stars in cotton wool. Hearts were all about science. And at Falkirk, the one and only Lambie made it up as he went along. You'd be standing there ready to go and he'd think for a minute then shout: 'Run up to that tree and back again!'

That was his way of buying time so he and Gerry could think what to do next. If you were back too quick, he'd send you to a tree further away. He was a constant cabaret act whose main aim every day was to see his entire squad come in from a session utterly bollocksed. His work with the ball was unbelievable – he'd set you up in a shape then start pointing all over the pitch, going: 'Hit it there, there, there and there, then put it in the net.'

We'd all go: *'What?'*

And he'd yell: 'Just f*****' dae it!'

It's funny, but he was a totally different guy when I went back to work with him at Partick Thistle. Training under him there was a real pleasure. He was at home there and it showed.

Training's magic and anyone who doesn't take it seriously shouldn't be in the game. I can't stand guys farting about with the ball before the session starts, trying to hit the crossbar or playing keepy-uppy. You warm up first. You need good habits, standards that come as second nature. Save your tricks and flicks for after the graft's done. Never understood players who skip training, either – and you find them at every club. The ones who nurse wee twinges when there's a big game of running on the go, then give it Lazarus when it's five-a-side time.

You should be *desperate* to train, rain or shine. Or snow, for that matter. There's nothing like a sliding tackle in the snow. Some boys get away with murder. They don't want to warm up, don't fancy the sweaty sessions, seem to suit themselves all week. If only you could get inside their heads and give their brains a tweak.

You can put up with dafties, as long as they have those good habits and do their work. But eventually dressing-rooms react against anyone who continually swings the lead. You're all there to win together, to earn your wages. Everyone has off days in training or bad games on a Saturday, but there's no excuse for hiding.

The old pros behind the scenes can spot the hiders in a heartbeat, though. Bert, Dick, Doddie, Lambie, Big Jock, wee Frank Connor. Cut them all and Wintergreen flows from their veins. Football's everything to them. My worry is that we're breeding a generation who simply don't share that passion and that the game's suffering because of it.

We need people who are football to the core. And at Falkirk, I worked with one of the most devoted of them all.

Through the worst of my injury nightmare, the man who kept me sane was club physio Bob McCallum – though physio was only his official title. Fact is, he was more than a sponge man, so much more. Some days he also had to be my shrink, my social worker and my surrogate dad. He was magnificent.

The day he died broke me up.

He'd let me off early from a rehab session so he could take some of the players for a run along the side of the canal. Bob loved a run, was fit as a fiddle. Never had a day off, never cut corners. A true, utterly dedicated pro. So I said cheerio, that I'd see him tomorrow, then headed up the road. I felt good, like I always did after an hour in his company.

By the time I got to Hamilton, someone had already phoned to say he was gone.

Came back from the run, sat down on the dressing-room bench beside Andy Seaton and just keeled over. Poor Andy, left holding a dead man in his arms. God knows how he got over that one.

God knows where football goes when the last of the Bob McCallums are gone.

ELEVEN

DOLE NOT GOAL

From the Premier League to the dole queue to Northern Ireland to Maryhill to Australia to Dingwall.

One hell of an end to the old Millennium, that.

One week you're fighting for £500 win bonuses, the next you're paying the milkman with DSS tokens.

Then you're getting your wages in cash. Through the post. In an envelope.

Checking in for a foreign flight on your own for the first time in your life. Sitting in your trunks by the pool watching Santa go by on a fire engine.

And shopping for health food in Tesco with your male flatmate.

If you're getting the vague idea that my career wasn't quite going to plan by now, give yourself a chocolate medal.

When the season with Dunfermline drifted towards relegation and then the inevitability of a free, I experienced a horrible feeling for the first time in my life.

The fear of the phone not ringing.

From 16, I'd always been wanted, never once had to go actively looking for a club. But now, in the summer of 1999, and a few weeks off my 32nd birthday, I wasn't signing on the dotted line for a new manager.

I was just signing on.

The thought of it doesn't embarrass me. My family needed feeding, the mortgage was due and we didn't have a big comfy pillow full of cash to fall back on.

So the rock'n'roll it was.

Bert Paton had quit as Dunfermline manager in January 1999 – mainly so as not to spoil my record – and try as he might, his old assistant Dick Campbell couldn't keep us in the Premier League.

I felt useless for most of the time. I was doing all the training and was playing here and there, but there was something missing and it really disappointed me that I couldn't get in there and do my bit.

So come the May we shook hands and went our separate ways and I waited for something to happen. And waited. And got a bit impatient waiting.

And realised that, for the first time in my career, the phone wasn't going to ring. The offers not only weren't flooding in, there wasn't so much as a trickle. And I started to panic.

Ever since I'd left Rangers I got the feeling a lot of people would have like to see me fall on my face. It's human nature, though it's not mine – I like to see folk getting on. But I wish I had a quid for everyone who's come up to me in a bar and told me what I *could* have been. They've never been able to see that I was still playing and that was what mattered, what made me happy.

Now, though, those people would no doubt have been delighted to know that I was toiling. I had a wife and kids to look after – Lewis was born on 23 August – and I wanted to do for them what my mum and dad had done for me.

They'd always worked their socks off to make sure I got what I needed and a little bit more. Dad used to come in from working up on those roofs, knackered, have his dinner put down in front of him and literally fall asleep in it. I've actually seen that happen.

Being on the dole was no way to emulate that kind of work ethic. But right then, it was the only option.

I was so nervous about going into the DSS office in Hamilton. Didn't know what to do, didn't know how other punters would react to me. Certainly didn't realise how sniffy some of the staff would be about someone well-known claiming benefits.

I was sitting in the queue and guys were looking across, giving me the double-take then going: 'Awright, Derek?'

Then they'd look away and seem to realise where they were and look back as if they were thinking: 'What the f*** are *you* doin' here?'

I felt like saying: 'Same as you, chief.'

There was one guy, a Motherwell fan, who was brand new. He was chatting away and telling me it was all no problem. But you could tell others were desperate to get out and tell their mates about the ex-Rangers star who'd hit Skid Row.

It was one of the most uncomfortable feelings I've had in my life.

Even worse, when my turn came to shuffle up to the desk, the woman on the other side gave me exactly the same look and sniffed: 'Well, we don't have to ask *your* name, do we?'

Now that *was* the most uncomfortable moment of my life.

She made me feel like I was doing something wrong, trying to get something on the sly. I felt like yelling: 'LOOK, I'VE GOT NO JOB – WHAT'S YOUR BLOODY PROBLEM?'

So she hands me this bundle of forms and tells me to go and fill them in.

Me? Forms? The day wasn't getting any better.

I went and sat at a wee table and picked up a pen. Every time I glanced up, the woman was staring across. I'd look back at her, then down at the pile of paper, then back at her. I was churning up inside.

After a couple of minutes, I couldn't take it any more. Picked the forms up and walked out, with her going: *'Excu-'*

But the door was already banging.

Who knows, maybe the woman was actually being friendly with me, but she just had an unfortunate manner. Or maybe she was just being rotten. But whatever, she was the final straw for me and I shot up the road and left all the pen-pushing to Carol. As per usual.

In the end, I went back and bit the bullet and signed on for about six weeks. We got £120 a week, which didn't even cover the mortgage. It wasn't a great time.

When your milk got delivered, you handed over tokens instead of money. Luckily I knew the milkman and he was fine about it – he still got his tip!

So John Lambie will always have my undying gratitude for giving me the chance to get away from reality and back into football.

He came on the blower, said he knew someone at Portadown in Northern Ireland and that I could go there. Brian Hamilton came as well and it all started fine; they put us up in a lovely hotel, we played Waterford down in the south, we did OK and they offered us both a month. Brian didn't take them up, but any kind of game would have done me at the time.

So back over I went, ready to give it a go. Except that when I got there the second time, on the Friday night before the game, it wasn't the same hotel.

It was . . . well, I don't like being rude, but it was a doss house.

Tiny room. One tiny window away up high on the wall. Cardboard furniture. But everything's worse at night, isn't it? Nothing's as bad as it seems at first, is it? So I think, I'll be fine, I'll go for a walk and feel better about things.

Sure.

I couldn't get into the town centre because the Army still had barriers up in case of terrorist attacks. All you could hear in the distance were flutes. The place was eerie.

Still, they were paying me cash, so get a kip, get up and earn your money. How bad could it be?

Very.

It was hammer-thrower stuff, the ball lumped up and down all day, no chance to get it down and try and play a bit. It wasn't me, and but for the fact that the club had been great, paying all my flights and being really hospitable – that hotel excepted – I'd have binned it right away.

But instead I hung around for a few games until eventually the chance came to go to Partick Thistle and we called it a day. Before my last game, one of the directors came over and said: 'Derek, listen, we didn't have time to get your money together, so it is OK if we send it over to you?'

I said yes, but never thought I'd see a penny. Went home, forgot all about it. Then, weeks later, in plops an ordinary envelope with a second-class stamp on it . . . and a wedge of notes in it. No letter, no compliments slip, nothing.

Fair play to my postman for honesty.

Thistle? A breath of fresh air. I had six or seven games under Lambie and loved it. The boys were terrific, the training was always up-beat and – though I probably shouldn't mention this – the wages were in readies again.

Even better, we went on a wee run. Don't think we lost while I was there. It was the team with the likes of Kenny Arthur,

Alan Archibald, Allan Moore, Des McKeown, Robert Dunn and Tommy Callaghan in it – great guys who went on to win the Second Division title.

But just when I was settling, the old Dundee player Albert Kidd came on the blower from Down Under and, to be honest, what he was talking about sounded too good to ignore.

Instead, it turned out too good to be true.

Believe it or not, the day I flew out was the first time I'd ever flown abroad on my own. I was 33 and the furthest I'd been without a football team or Carol or my mates was London.

I was bad enough checking in at Glasgow. I still had to get to London and then have a stop-over in Kuala Lumpur before getting to Adelaide.

Naïve? I thought a Kuala Lumpur was a wee guy who worked for Willie Wonka.

As it turned out, though, it was a brilliant place. The airport had a wee hotel you could book by the hour, so I checked in, used the gym, had a shower and got changed. Quite proud of myself for that, I was.

The deal when I got to Oz was to be that I'd see if I fancied it, they'd help me find a house, then we'd send for Carol, Darren, Ross and Lewis and a new life would begin.

Yes, we had reservations about moving away from our families, all the usual stuff anyone gets when they're faced with uprooting. In the end, though, we accepted that it was only a couple of years at most and the experience would surely outweigh the hardships.

Plus, Carol's sister lives in Melbourne, so she reckoned that would be enough to attract her mum and dad out either on holiday or for good.

It wasn't the first offer I'd had from abroad. At Rangers, there was talk of interest from Italy and Spain, though it never came to more than that. But had a far more concrete proposal come off, I'm certain we'd have no financial worries today.

It was when I was at Falkirk and it came from South Korea, through Bill McMurdo. The offer? Just your £250,000 for a two-year contract.

The Koreans had the World Cup coming and were desperate for foreign players to give their own league a bit more profile. They plainly had money to throw about and, apart from that, I'd have been tall enough over there to play centre-half.

It would have been one hell of an adventure. And, to be blunt, the one time in my life when I'd have done it for the money.

A quarter of a mill? For two years? Tax free? We *would* have been cruising.

It's the story of my life that the word 'Yippee' was forming on my lips when the Big Man crashed through me in that bloody game with the Bankies and left my knee in bits. End of cushy number before it even started.

Funny, though, when you look back. That's a decade ago now and they were putting up £125,000 a year, yet now there are journeymen at the arse end of the SPL earning that much no problem. That can't go on.

Australia was never going to be that lucrative, but the sunshine and the lifestyle really appealed, the healthy outdoor stuff and everything else you read about them doing over there.

Fancy a barbie after training? Bonzer, I'll get the tinnies in. All that caper.

Albie said they were talking $700 (approx. £300) a week, and that over there that was a good wage. They'd pay for the digs and a car and were happy to get the family over, so I took the chance. And regretted it almost immediately.

First up, they were *actually* paying me $500 (£200). Then, after a week or two, they still hadn't shown me around any houses and it became clear that it wasn't happening. Suddenly, two years seemed a long time.

Which is why it ended up being two *weeks*.

I fronted them up about the broken promises, they hummed and hahed, so I said I wanted my ticket home. They looked at me like: 'What ticket home?'

I played one more game, went to see the chairman and they reluctantly agreed to get me a flight back in three or four days. After that, I chilled and enjoyed myself and maybe got even more fed up that it hadn't worked out.

They'd put me up in a drive-in motel and at night I'd sit by the pool and look across at guys playing cricket in the park. It was really cool, the kind of set-up you could easily have got used to.

Then, a couple of nights before I went home, I was sitting out there with a beer and suddenly you could hear Jingle Bells. When I looked over to the park, there was Santa, surrounded by kids, doing all the pre-Christmas stuff we do back here, except in blistering heat.

There was me, in my shorts and shades, looking at weans with excited faces being handed presents and that was my mind made up. I needed my family.

Carol was upset that it never panned out, because the whole idea had really excited her. From me being on the dole to us living in that environment would have been rags to riches stuff the way she was feeling.

Plus, it'd have been great for the kids, brilliant weather and a population obsessed with sports and health.

Still, Dingwall wasn't a bad alternative.

Ross County chairman Roy McGregor had been on the phone to Carol while I was on my wee Aussie holiday and she really took to him – and little wonder, as he's one of the nicest men you'll ever meet. A wealthy bloke, but a Christian and plays it by the book.

He told her there was a deal waiting for me if I came back and to phone him whenever I was ready. That meant a lot to me, and I was happy to go and play for my old Rangers mate Neale Cooper.

I'd go up on Tuesday for home games and come back after the match, and when we were playing away I'd go on a Monday then come home on the Friday and meet the boys wherever we were playing on the Saturday.

They put me up in a flat with our big striker Derek Holmes and I ended up being his minder – although his only enemy was himself.

He ate an absolute load of crap and needed to learn some good habits, so I'd take him to the supermarket in Inverness and show him how to shop for decent food. He never ate breakfast for a start, and that had to change.

It was only after a while that it occurred to me how it looked to be pushing a trolley round Tesco together, arguing over vegetables. Homer was always on your shoulder, all day and all night, but he was a good lad.

They were long days at Ross County. We'd be back in the flat at three in the afternoon after soup and sandwiches at the ground and Derek was climbing the walls – but as I kept reminding him, we weren't there to live the daft single life, we were there to play football.

Changed days, eh?

TWELVE

PART-TIME LOVER

No ground, no fans, no future. No way to start your managerial career.

Especially when you're not even sure you *have* started it – or even if you particularly want to.

When I'd gone to Clydebank as a player in August 2000, Tommy Coyne was in charge. Then, near the end of November, the curse of Fergie struck again. He fell out with the owners and left.

Mick Oliver and I were asked to look after things and, to me, the obvious set-up was Mick as gaffer and me as player-coach. That would have suited me down to the ground. But Mick said: 'Well, you'll be winding down as a player, eh? So this is a great chance for you . . . '

Winding down? Why does everyone keep saying that to me? I'd just turned 33. I'd just turned *down* a three-year deal at Ross County because Darren had started school and I didn't want to uproot the family. Yet, in Mick's eyes, I was on my last legs. So when the Scottish League yearbook came out, there I was, listed as boss. And there he was, down as Player Liaison/Consultant. Whatever that meant.

To say the Bankies were in a mess was an understatement. They'd sold Kilbowie Park – a fantastic wee ground – when they had nowhere to go, shared at first with Dumbarton at the old Boghead, then moved to Cappielow.

The Steedman family, who'd taken the club from the juniors to the Premier League, had sold up to . . . well, to be honest, only a real diehard would have managed to keep up with the shadowy figures joking in and out over their last couple of years in business. There were plans for a new ground in the town. Then for a joint one with Dumbarton halfway between the towns. Then a crazy plan to move them to Dublin.

We were in the Second Division when Mick and I took the reins and finished halfway up the table, but I had high hopes of a real promotion push come the following August.

Before that, though, came the most glamorous fixture of my life. Barry's wedding on the sun-kissed island of St Lucia.

A few weeks after the end of the season, he flew the whole family over for the do. It must have cost him a fortune to do it in that much style, so fair play to him. It was one hell of a trip – though not as funny as the one he *didn't* plan. And which put him on the treatment table just when his married life was about to kick off.

On the morning of the ceremony, we went down the beach and these Rasta guys were playing heady football. After they finished, we went on the court – me, our cousin Kevin and Uncle Brian against Barry, his mate Ian and his father-in-law-to-be. It started out as a laugh. Then, of course, the two of us got competitive. We were throwing ourselves all over the place, and when Kevin dinked one over the net, Barry dived to get it back and landed right on one of the pegs. I was killing myself, but then we realised he was in agony. We rushed him down to the water to take the sting out, but it was more than just a wee knock.

By coincidence, a guy who used to be the St Mirren physio was there on holiday and he had a look at the wound. He said it needed an ice pack, pronto. So there we were, a couple of hours before the biggest moment of my brother's life, packing ice round his throbbing leg and cracking the beers open. All we could do was laugh.

I was his best man and after the wedding and the meal, then he and I went out on the balcony, put our arms around each other's shoulders and stood there singing Rangers songs – even though 80 per cent of the guests inside were Celtic daft.

It was a terrific night. Next morning, Michael Jackson's dad was in the restaurant for breakfast.

The only downside for a guy like me counting the pennies was that it was £6 a beer, so me and Barry's father-in-law walked half a mile to a supermarket and came back pushing a trolley filled to the brim with local brew. We had ground-floor rooms, so we filled one of the baths with ice, carried the sofas out onto the patio and sat back drinking. Barry and some of the others were looking across the pool, shaking their heads at us for being so mean – but why go ten yards further away and spend a fortune?

Every night I'd go out and watch the sun go down, and eventually it became a ritual for everyone. Then we'd have torch-lit dinners on the sand. It was magnificent. The hotel also had a fantastic gym, so every morning – no matter what we'd got up to the night before – I'd go in there and do my bit. It made me feel better about spending the rest of the day sinking a bathful of beer.

But all too soon we left paradise behind. And it was back to the reality of what turned out to be my last-ever season of full-time football.

The Bankies squad took shape nicely – Henry Smith in goal,

Mark McNally and Neil McGowan at the back, boys like Eric Paton and Brian McColligan alongside Brian Hamilton and myself in midfield, Alex Burke, big Ally Graham and wee Mowgli up front. Then Rab McKinnon arrived and took over as captain, we got wee Joe Miller for a while later in the season and things were really motoring.

We had a nice blend, loads of experience and in boys like Alan Gow – spotted by the kitman and now in the SPL with Falkirk – we had really bright young talents.

I even started to think the job might turn out to be fun after all.

That'll teach me to think . . .

In the September, a guy called David McGhee bought out Dr John Hall as owner and it was announced that Barry's agent John Viola would be coming in as sponsor. It all smelled a bit odd from the off. It's also typical of me and Barry that we've never talked about what was going on. Still, we won five of our first seven in the league and after an in-and-out spell, a 1–0 home win over Alloa almost exactly a year after I'd taken over sent us to the top of the league.

Come Christmas, we were still there – and we'd stay there until well into February. But by then, things were already going badly wrong. I could see the slide coming and I knew exactly how to prevent it.

Unfortunately, our future was taken out of my hands by the people upstairs.

Well, I say upstairs. We had no upstairs. Or downstairs. No home, that was the problem. All correspondence went to an address in Glasgow, we trained at the Ferguslie Park complex in Paisley, we went to Greenock every second Saturday to be greeted by fewer and fewer punters.

One day early in the season, against Cowdenbeath, the attendance was 154. It's a real credit to the boys that they were professional enough to go out and get the job done with that little support and virtually no infrastructure. We were a bag of balls, a set of strips and a whole load of love for the game. Yet it looked like being enough to win us the title until agents decided they knew better.

At the start of December, wee John said he was bringing in some of his clients to give us that final push. He was giving us Billy McKinlay, Darren Jackson and the former Northern Ireland winger Michael O'Neill.

I told him thanks, but we didn't need them. The balance of a team is what matters most, not how many caps the players have – and we had that balance just about bang-on. If we needed anyone, I'd rather have gone for a Billy McDonald type, a lower-league midfield battler who'd been there and done it all his life.

The Mowglis and Grahams and McNallys had my utmost trust. Plus, we had guys in that dressing-room on £100 a week full-time. What were *they* going to think when superstars starting swanning in? Don't get me wrong. When I was at Rangers it didn't bother me how much more than me the Butchers or Goughies or whoever were on. It wasn't an issue, it was between them and the club – and with the effort and performances they put in, they were due every penny they got.

But this was different. This was quite clearly nothing more than a shop window for out-of-contract players, no matter how John dressed it up. And it cost not only the league, but in the end it finished a proud little club.

Michael scored two or three when he first arrived, then Darren chipped in with a couple, but the wins got fewer and further apart. At the start of March, we lost at 'home' to Queen of the South and slipped to second. We would never get that top slot back.

Viola's clients were definitely not giving it everything. For the rest of us, this was a championship drive. For them, it was a fitness exercise until something better came along. Sometimes they weren't even at training, and the boys were raging at that. For them, this was real life – more so than ever as stories began to filter through that if we didn't go up, we'd go under.

It was all falling apart and I felt like the piggy in the middle. There's no doubt the senior boys – guys I'd brought in as mates as well as good pros – thought I knew more about the situation than I was letting on, but I swear to God I didn't. Viola and his men were telling me next to nothing. It was all tearing the team apart.

One win in our next four left us going to Cowdenbeath on 23 March – I'm not great with dates and times, but I'll never forget that one – desperately needing three points to stay in the promotion race.

Just before half-time, Ian Mauchlan put them ahead. Just after, our big defender Simon Vella put one in his own net. Mowgli got one back with 25 to go, but it was too little, too late.

When it was all over and reality bit, I couldn't even go into the dressing-room. I walked to one of the corner flags and sat down, lost in misery. I felt responsible, even though looking back now that's plainly nonsense.

What I did know by then was that the rumours were true. No First Division football, no football full stop.

Now, I don't know what the Bankies fans thought of me then or think of me now. I doubt if it's very complimentary. But I hope they realise that in those final six weeks of the season after Cowdenbeath, after all was lost, I stayed put and so did the players who'd got us to the top of the league. Which is more than you can say for those who were meant to be running the club.

They never came near us. The last month's wages never arrived. The squad would have been within their rights to down tools and quit. These were professionals, though, right down to the bitter end.

Our last win was at home to Forfar on 13 April in front of 166 diehards. The bitter end itself was a 2–1 home defeat to Berwick Rangers, when Murray McDowell had already scored two for them before Eric Paton pulled one back.

The final goal in the 37-year senior history of Clydebank Football Club – and the rest *is* history. Airdrie United took their place in the Scottish League, Gretna came on the scene and the outfit who'd produced Davie Cooper were no more.

I hadn't wanted to be their manager in the first place. Player-coach, that was the job. Good cop. Not bad bastard. And the fact is, only a *true* bastard can be a successful manager, and I don't know if I've got that quality in me.

You get the odd gentleman, the Craig Brewsters of the world, but nine out of ten who reach the top have a ruthlessness and a selfishness that would chill your blood. They have to look guys in the eye and tell them they're dropped, they're fined, they're freed, then turn on their heel and get on with the job.

But hey, at least all we lost was our jobs. For pretty much all of us, another one would come along somewhere. The fans – not just the ones who followed us to the end, but those who'd been driven away by rotten owners – lost their club.

Though maybe not for ever.

It's great to see that fans have re-formed the club and they are coming up through the junior ranks fast and hopefully, one day, they'll be back where they belong. Playing real football, with real football people in charge.

Mind you, I say all I lost was a job, but that's not quite true. Because what happened at the Bankies also cost me the trust of some good friends. I'm no longer as close to the likes of big Ally and wee Mowgli, we're not on and off the phone any more. And

227

that saddens me more than most things that have happened to me in football.

So no, management's no picnic. But coaching? That's when I'm happiest. Give me a football pitch, a bag of balls and some people willing to listen, work hard and learn, and I'm in my element.

I'll coach anyone to do anything – I even had a go at golf, despite never having played a full eighteen holes in my life. I get as far as nine, chuck it in and go and find a pool table.

Souness took us up to the Highlands once and had the whole squad out on the course for an afternoon. Now, at every football club you get guys who take the game seriously. And then you get guys like me and Durranty.

Back then we got bored really easily. It must have been like being around overgrown schoolboys – if we played a half-decent shot we'd be chasing after it to see where it landed. We were shouting and bawling. We'd dump clubs after we'd used them and leave the guys coming behind us to pick them up.

So why anyone would ask me to show anyone else – especially children – how to play the game is a mystery. But there we were, former Hibs player Graham Mitchell and myself, standing in a school playground in Ayr with a couple of dozen first-years waiting for us to show them how it was done.

Mitch is panicking because he reckons he couldn't hit a golf ball to save himself. So he hands me the club and suddenly all eyes are on me. There's a target across the playground, so I take a swing, catch the ball nicely and somehow put it where it's meant to go. The kids are impressed – then one of them says: 'Can the other coach show us too?'

What does Mitch do? He pretends he's done his shoulder in . . .

We were working together for the British Heart Foundation, taking coaching sessions to get kids active. It's all the quick feet stuff again – you don't need amazing facilities for it, you can set up exercises in the tiniest spaces.

It was brilliant fun – as was the project that Paul McStay got us involved in back in 2003. He called it Soccericulum and he asked me, Mitch, Tommy Coyne, Robert Prytz, Paul Wright and Tosh McKinlay to work with him on it, coaching Glasgow schoolkids in football and general PE.

Here's a another good example of what footballers are like when they're taken away from the protection of the dressing-room and forced to stand on their own two feet.

When Paul got us together, we had to take it in turns to stand in front of the rest and practise giving presentations using slideshows so we could handle ourselves when faced with a class full of kids. But when you're in that dressing-room, it's only ever the gaffer or the coach who stands up and does the talking, so we were hopeless at it. We couldn't talk for laughing – it should have taken us half an hour each to get the hang of it, but I think we were at it about three days.

Tell a lie, Paul was excellent, a natural. And Mitch wasn't too bad. But the rest of us were an embarrassment. You'd need a shrink to work out why a bunch of guys who'd all played in front of massive, angry crowds without batting an eyelid couldn't hold themselves together in front of five or six mates, but that's the kind of people football produces.

Of course, once we got out there doing what we knew best, we were fine. I loved setting up the exercises and telling the kids that this was how they'd be doing it if they were pros. I know if someone who used to play for Rangers or Celtic had come to coach me when I was 12, I'd have been desperate to do the best I could and I wanted these children to feel the same way.

All the boys tried to put the same feeling into their sessions with the kids, and the response we got was fantastic. I thought Paul's whole idea was a winner, right down to his brainwave of putting ex-Rangers men like me and Prytzy into Roman Catholic schools and himself, Tosh and Tommy into the non-denominationals, so youngsters learned early on that the two sides could mix no bother.

I even went to one school just round the corner from Parkhead, and I have to admit I was worried about what reaction I'd get. But kids aren't like grown-ups, they take you for who you are, not *what* you are.

Same went for Paul – we had lunch with all the boys from the coaching scheme one day, and as this one and that one drifted away, it ended up with the two of us going round a few boozers in the middle of Glasgow for the afternoon. You should have seen the looks we got. It was like: 'What's *he* doing wi' *him?*'

I loved that, the fact that some small-minded people couldn't get their heads round a Rangers man and a Celtic man having a beer and a laugh together.

We were all having the time of our lives around each other. When sessions were flying the teachers joined in, we joined in – it was incredible fun and just so satisfying. We did a whole summer up in Drumchapel and we really felt like a team. For a while, we even hoped Socericulum would lead to a new career for all of us, but sadly the one thing Paul didn't think of was to copyright it.

And next thing, guess what? It was hijacked by Rangers and Celtic. Whatever Paul charged schools, those two giant clubs were easily able to undercut the price and that was him pretty much finished.

Didn't I tell you our generation weren't cut out for business?

So let's see where we all ended up. Mitch now works for Scottish Power. Tommy's a joiner. Paul Wright's a driving instuctor. Tosh builds kit houses to sell them. How can football let talent like these guys – and scores more like them – just slip away unnoticed?

I mean, take someone like Jimmy Johnstone. People mourned him in their hundreds of thousands, stood silent or broke into rapturous applause before matches the week he died. Players from all over the world queued to pay tribute to him. Fans were urged to send a song he'd made to Number One.

This was a man so loved, so admired, so idolised he was as close to a religious icon as you can get without being ordained. So how come he was allowed to drift away from the game the way he did?

OK, so he worked with the youths at Celtic at one time, but he should have been used at a much higher level. What kid wouldn't pay 110 per cent attention when a genius like Jinky was telling him what was what? Who wouldn't want to impress someone so talented?

Unfortunately, though, it seems he wasn't the right type to fit into the coaching set-up. Like Paul McStay himself, a wonderful footballer found that ability wasn't enough to get through the right doors.

It's football's loss.

No disrespect to everyone else out there who likes coaching and has studied for their badges, but there's surely a good chance that someone with experience within a workplace is going to have a better chance of passing on the skills required to make it than someone who only knows the theory?

I mean, if I was coaching the Under-12s at Rangers right now, I'd not only be able to work on their shooting and passing and movement, I'd be able to tell them what they have to do if they want to stay at the club right through to first-team level. I've been there. I've been *them*. I've made it into the marble hallway – and I've managed to find my way back out onto the street again.

All over Scotland, all over the world, there are guys with the same story to tell. They worked their backsides off to make it, they took the knocks, they gave their all and then, when their time was up, the game simply asked them to shut the door on their way out.

Is that a sensible way to run an industry? To overlook its own skilled workers for jobs as instructors and give them instead to people who've only read the manuals?

If it is, the game's knackered.

As for me, after Soccericulum ended, Glasgow Council offered me some work through the McDonald's coaching scheme in schools and I did the same kind of thing with South Lanarkshire Council. Work like that was perfect for me once I was part-time, because I could plan my day round eating properly and getting ready for training at night. And because I was taking part in the school sessions – half the fun of coaching is taking part – I was also keeping myself sharp.

All my adult life I'd been up early doors, having my toast and banana and whatever else, driving into training, being with the boys, all the wind-ups in the dressing-room while we got changed. The running, the ballwork, the team-talks. The crack in the physio's room where the slackers hung out. Hanging around for ages afterwards, having lunch, playing heady tennis, messing around in the gym.

Some days we'd just stay there for the sake of it, we just loved the place so much. It was our second home. Either that or a bunch of us would head into town for a pizza or go shopping. We were always together. Now, I was alone.

Carol at the shop. Kids at school or nursery. Long, long days. Go to the gym? Good idea – but you can only spend so much time there. See your mates? How? They work normal hours, you graft at night. Suddenly I could see why some guys never even considered going part-time. Tosh was one, he just didn't fancy it and I understand why – but it still disappoints me. He always asked me why I put myself through it. All I could offer was: 'Why not?'

The money's not the same, that's for sure. But it's still the identical buzz, you still wake up high as a kite on Saturday mornings, still get the tingle walking into the dressing-room, going out to warm up, hearing the clack of studs on the stone floor as five to three arrives. That's my Saturday – and that's why I was so impressed with Roy Keane when he came to Celtic and answered questions about how he'd handle playing at small grounds with small crowds after years of Old Trafford and Anfield and Highbury.

'Listen,' he said, 'whether there's 100 people there or 50,000, it's still the same thrill every single time.'

There's a football man for you.

Plus, if anyone thinks it gets easier the lower you go, think again. Everyone you come up against sees a Big-Time Charlie in front of them and fancies their chances. You're a target, especially for the young guns. But that's the best bit, because what I want then is to show *them* I can take a hit *and* give one back. It fires them up, it fires me up, so it fires the game up. Competitiveness is either ingrained in you or it's not. I need to compete.

If there's a downer, it's the feeling you get when the season's over and you realise you're basically out of a job. Since the Bankies folded, only Hamilton have given me more than a one-year deal, so a few days after the final league game, you shake hands with everyone and say see you later. You have your holiday, then you come home and you beat yourself up as every day passes with nothing sorted for pre-season.

You have to try and think positive. Yes, security's great. But I turned it into an exercise in proving myself time and again. I like proving myself.

Just as well, really.

By the time I'd turned 30, I'd had 18 months of knee problems which had pretty much stopped me kicking a ball. But once I was over them, I could easily have played Premier League. The chance just never came again. Ability? It wasn't an issue. Neither was fitness. Even by the time I was 34 and with Clydebank I was no less a player than I'd ever been, and I was actually more of an athlete – but by then, you're out of the loop, some people even forget that you're still playing.

See, I love football, but I don't choose to play it. Somebody needs to want you.

After Clydebank folded, I was willing to go on trials if the phone didn't ring. That thing Clyde did the other year, the Football Idol business? I'd have put myself through that, although a lot of others wouldn't have touched it with a bargepole.

Luckily, though, the phone did ring and on the other end was Terry Christie, offering me a year's deal to go to Alloa. He wasn't a hard man to deal with – my only haggle in the wage talks was over an extra tenner a week for petrol and it turned out they paid us that anyway. They were a good club who looked after players properly, always prompt with your money and no quibbles over peanuts.

I liked working with Terry – even if his team talks lasted longer than some games. You don't have to like each other to be successful, just to have a working relationship, but with Terry I had both.

I've known managers who've let their personal feelings influence selection, but if I was in charge of a team I'd pick anyone who'd help us win games. You can't surround yourself with pals, you need people who benefit the squad.

And Terry had more of a potential conflict of interests than most, because his son was in the dressing-room. Max is a bubbly boy who took a great corner and hammered away for all he was worth in midfield, but it must be murder for the son of a gaffer. Some fans simply won't accept he's in the team for any other reason than his mammy will be annoyed if he's not.

He'd started full-time with Hearts and then Dundee, but then went off and trained as a financial adviser when injuries forced him out of the full-time scene. Smart boy. But dear me, did they argue in that dressing-room. It got to the stage where we couldn't work out if it was about football or his bedroom being untidy.

But if it wasn't the manager barneying with his boy, it'd be someone else having a pop at someone else about something else. That's just the dressing-room, a hotbed of moaning and laughter and wind-ups.

I've been in plenty and they're all the same – not the décor, not the size. But the feel, the smell, the mess, the noise. And whether it was Cliftonhill or the Nou Camp, I'd need the same space to get ready in. Hate being stuck in a corner, it makes me uncomfortable.

There aren't any grounds in football that I really dislike, but there are plenty that I love. Tynecastle's fantastic, Broomfield and Brockville were the same before progress caught up with them. Cappielow survives in pretty much its original form and it's another great place to play. Real cauldrons, all of them, even two-thirds full. And Parkhead? Magic. When I first went there as a 17 year old, the Jungle was still there, so when you ran out of the tunnel the whole place looked so much smaller than it does now. I remember Souness deliberately warming up right in front of it, just to noise their fans up. He fed off all that animosity.

Now, of course, you come out the tunnel and the North Stand's hanging over you. It's massive and holds every decibel of noise in. It's an incredible feeling and an incredible sight – one you'd hope every footballer gets to experience at least once in his career. Even guys from Barcelona, your real world superstars like Ronaldinho, must have stepped into the lights and the din and felt a shiver running down their spine.

Hampden, on the flip side, is a disappointment for me. The

old stadium was absolutely magnificent, this massive wall of noise and colour. The old terraces seemed to go up and up for miles, right into the sky, like you could touch the clouds from the top step. But I can't help thinking they blundered when they rebuilt it. For all the millions spent, all they seemed to achieve was the loss of the world-famous roar, when they should have made it even louder than ever. Those big arcs behind the goals have had their day; most of the great stadiums have the fans right on top of the players; the Nou Camp, the Bernabeu, Old Trafford, all the real theatres. Hampden could have been right up there.

And the old Wembley wasn't what I thought it would be, even though it's still fantastic to say you played there. I went down with Scotland Under-15s and the first thing I thought was: 'It's smaller than it looks on telly.'

Even the pitch wasn't as big as I imagined it – you always read about players coming down with terrible cramp because of the turf they had to cover, but it just wasn't that way. Just didn't bowl me over the way I thought it would.

These days, of course, I get to see the complete opposite end of the scale. Alloa's ground, Recreation Park, has a neat little main stand, but the rest of the place is right out of the 1930s, all railway-sleeper terrace steps packed with dirt, a wee rickety shed on the slope on the far side.

Hamilton's new stadium has great facilities but only two stands, and it's never great to have huge open spaces staring at you when you're running out the tunnel.

When I went to Raith, it gave me the chance to play at Stark's Park, another of those great old traditional homes of Scottish football. It's hard to fathom out how they managed to build it on the flat, even though you need to rope yourselves together to get up the street to it.

It's a funny jumble of different kinds of stands. You come out the tunnel by one corner, with the main stand ending halfway down the touchline; on the opposite side there's a low, fairly recent stand with the railway running behind it. And behind each goal they've put up really nice modern ones, but totally out of keeping with the character of the ground as it was.

But it's been brilliant getting to play more often at some of the really special lower-league grounds. Glebe Park in Brechin's great, with that hedge running down one touchline and separating the ground from a graveyard. Then there's Gayfield in Arbroath, where if it's not bad enough that the wind always sweeps you off your feet, the locals also do their best to make your stay as inhospitable as possible.

And that, by the way, isn't a criticism. I actually like their style.

The first time I went there it was freezing in the away dressing-room and although they'd given us one tiny little electric heater, they'd also forgotten to close the window, so it was like an icebox in there. There was one single toilet, so if two of you needed to go at the same time, the other one had to pee in the shower. Primitive? Course it is. But why *should* the home club make the visitors feel comfortable? If it was down to me, I wouldn't even give them a ball to kick about in the warm-up.

Yes, treat them like royalty when the game's finished. I've no time for clubs who make the sandwiches disappear when they've lost, that's just bad sportsmanship. Win or lose, you should make your guests feel welcome for as long as they want to stay.

Before then, though, it's all about winning. And if making their players feel crap right up to kick-off gives you an advantage, fair play to you. So much of football is about mind games – not just about playing them, but being able to cope with them.

You're lucky as a full-time player with a family, because you can get home every day in plenty time to play a bigger part in normal domestic life than the average working bloke.

237

And most definitely more time than the average part-time footballer.

I feel so sorry for those guys, out early doors to work in a shop or an office or a factory, on the roads or up on the roofs, then grabbing a quick bite somewhere before rushing to training two or three times a week.

You see them coming into the dressing-room, still black from their shift, big working boots caked in mud. And there's me, nice and fresh from eating right and resting right and planning everything around that night's session. It doesn't seem fair. It most definitely opens your eyes to who the real grafters are in the game.

Not that I understood this right away. The first few months at Alloa were frustrating, because I couldn't get my head round why we did so little in training. It just didn't get through to me, someone who's never worked, how hard life was for the other boys during the day.

The gaffer simply *couldn't* push them too hard, they just didn't have it in them. That sometimes, if their touch wasn't right, it was because they were mentally tired.

Mind you, I still think we could have got more quality out of the squad, though it's hard to argue with Terry's record over the years at Meadowbank and Stenhousemuir, and then taking Alloa up to the First Division. He'd obviously earned his success using tried and tested methods on and off the park.

On Tuesdays, we'd do a 20- to 30-minute warm-up, then six runs down one side of the pitch and across the back of the goals. We had to do them in 25 seconds. After that, it was a wee game and up the road. Come Thursdays, we worked with the ball, especially on set-pieces – amazingly in this day and age, not something enough managers do.

We toiled for the first half of the season, as you'd expect of a part-time side in a mainly full-time league. We lost a lot of goals before Christmas, including a couple of sixes in front of our own fans.

But once Terry let us off the leash a bit, let us play outside his traditional, tight system, we were one of the form teams as the run-in came. Gareth Evans also replaced Graeme as No. 2 and brought some fresh training ideas and all round the mood was terrific.

Unfortunately, despite four wins in our last five games, we ran out of time and were relegated on goal difference. It was the third time in seven years I'd taken the drop and, added to what had happened at the Bankies, it was a period that tried my devotion to the game.

But you're part of these failures, so you take your share of the blame and you take your medicine and you come back fighting.

So when Terry offered me a second year, I was up for it. Sure, the money would be reduced because we'd gone down, but that was only fair. I told him he could definitely count me in.

But then came the chance to sign for the Accies, and as soon as I knew they were keen, so was I. At the same time, though, I was torn because I've never been one to go back on my word. That's just not my style.

Some might have found it easy to give some wee part-time club the Dear John phone call. Not me. For days I was all over the shop; yes, I wanted a crack with my hometown club, always had. But letting Terry down didn't appeal, not after he'd been there for me when the Bankies went under.

Now, maybe he'll read this and know different, but when I got round to breaking the news he was superb about it. He wasn't happy, not by any means. But he understood what the Accies meant to me and he told me to go and sign with his blessing.

George Fairley had rung to find out if I was interested in going to New Douglas Park and then asked if he could come over to the house. When I said yes, he was at the door within half an hour and, before I knew it, pen was on paper.

Signing for Hamilton was a big deal for me, the only *other* club I'd ever wanted to play for. OK, so it wasn't Douglas Park, but it was right across the road. It was still my home turf, even if it wasn't *real* turf. They gave me a two-year deal and the minute it was signed I had hopes of extending it and maybe even finishing my senior career there. Pre-season was great, I played in the first game of the season and was right up for it.

But remember Sunderland? That wee trip to Nizzy's benefit game and all the fallout from it? Well, it all went and happened again. This time, the Accies agreed to let me go and pull on a Rangers shirt. But the outcome was still the same.

Me on the sidelines.

I played in the Masters five-a-sides at Braehead Arena and took a bang on my left knee. The next day we trained at Strathy and it felt not too bad, but the day after that it blew up and I was in trouble. It was the first time that leg had ever bothered me and I suppose it was the beginning of the end.

Malcolm McNicholl did the op again, but two weeks later I had an internal bleed and heard him say those three little words that so many others have uttered: *'You've been unfortunate . . .'*

He stuck a giant needle in and drew off blood and all sorts of other fluid and told me I'd need six weeks off. Motherwell physio John Porteous worked with me after that and just before Christmas I was playing in bounce games.

Freaky thing was, just as I was coming back, Barry picked up the terrible knee injury seen by millions on telly. It was three days after Christmas, and Blackburn were at Newcastle, when he went into a nothing tackle – just him and Gary Speed coming together in a muddy centre circle. The kind of run-of-the-mill challenge I'd always told my wee brother not to hold back from. Only this time, he didn't get back up from it.

I didn't see the game live, I was at Strathy watching Darren play, but while he was getting changed afterwards I went to the car and switched on the radio and they were talking about how Barry Ferguson had been stretchered off.

When I rang Mum, she told me what had happened and after that it was just a case of trying and trying until he answered his phone. God knows how many times they showed the clip on *Sky Sports News* while I was trying to get through.

When I finally spoke to him, he was surprisingly upbeat. The kneecap was broken in three places and needed wiring up, but he was sure he'd be fine. It didn't sound like him, because normally Barry with an injury gets himself really down.

The last time he'd been out long-term, a pelvic injury under Dick Advocaat at Rangers, he'd toiled to cope. But he'd been a boy then. He was a man now. He needed four or five months in rehab and was home a lot when he wasn't working with Phil Boersma. We were on and off the phone a lot and he really did handle the whole thing better than I expected.

They say every footballer gets one serious injury and I hope Barry's had his now – especially when you think of how 'nothing' the challenge was that caused it.

My own latest wait for action ended in January 2004 when I finally made my competitive return in a Scottish Cup tie at home to Cowdenbeath. I only lasted an hour before Jim Sherry, who'd also been out long-term, replaced me – but it was a start. For the next couple of months I was in and out – an hour here then off, or the last half-hour as sub there – sometimes sitting on the bench for whole games.

Two minutes before the hour mark in a 3–0 defeat at Airdrie on 2 March, my number went up and I wasn't involved again that season. There's no doubt they weren't happy about how little action they'd had from me in that first season, and to add to that, George was grumpy about me not travelling to away games.

You know me, I see sitting in a stand eating pies as a waste of time, I'd rather be training. So when the boys were away, that's what I'd do. I actually offered to take the others who weren't involved in the first team for Saturday-morning sessions, which I reckoned was a pretty good use of everybody's time. The club, though, didn't take me up on it and for me that was daft. I mean, what else would any self-respecting footballer want to do with his Saturday than play or train?

It was the end of the season before I sat down with George to discuss the situation and it was obvious he didn't want me around. He said: 'I suppose you'll be thinking of moving on.'

I said no way, I had another year and wanted to make it a far better one. By the following August, I was desperate to make them see I was worth the money. But that, of course, was when my bottom decided to haemorrhage.

After I came back from that, the appearances were pretty in and out – which was a pity, because we'd signed a Spanish full-back called Paquito from Raith and he was great to play with, really on my wavelength. On 23 April, we won at Stark's Park to guarantee First Division football for another season – and come the start of the week, they told me I was free to go. Soon after, Gordon Dalziel phoned and asked if I fancied going to Raith, which made me wonder if something had been said up there on the Saturday.

I was disappointed to be leaving the Accies, but at least I'd played there. And if there was a consolation, it was that it wasn't just me who didn't settle. The dressing-room had needed a revolving door for my two years there. Players were coming and going after two or three games.

It was a baffling set-up, on and off the pitch. Allan Maitland was the manager, but everybody knew George picked the team. So at half-time, we'd be in the dressing-room waiting for Allan to finish talking to George so he could come in and tell us what to do next. We'd sit there thinking: 'Why don't you just tell us yourself, George?'

If I was a full-time manager, this would be our training week:

MONDAY: Out for an hour of walking, jogging, running in the fresh air. Somewhere with a view. Maybe back for some ballwork, then lunch and into the pool for the afternoon to relax the legs. A rubdown if any of them fancied one.

TUESDAY: Fitness day – but not a pummelling, no pushing them until they vomited. A weights circuit, concentrating on the upper body. A spinning class on the bikes, Boxercise, something different like that. Maybe bring in instructors from outside to take the sessions. We'd always train twice on Tuesdays.

Show a player a 300-metre run on the track and he'll groan. Give him the same work disguised with a ball or a few hurdles or a rope ladder and he'll do it with a smile on his face. And probably get more benefit from it. Coaching isn't rocket science – if you're setting up a passing and shooting exercise, you don't need 15 passes first. You can leave players cross-eyed with some of the routines that I've been involved in.

WEDNESDAY: The traditional footballer's day off, but I'd use it for something better than bevvying or golf. Gauge how the guys are, how the schedule is. Even if you just get them in for a sauna, they're spending time together and the more they're in the one place, the better the bond on the pitch. It could be the day when we discuss the next game, get some pasta and soup in and watch videos of the opposition. Too often, managers wait until Friday and Saturday to prepare the players.

THURSDAY: Always my favourite day, the one when you get the best mix of all the disciplines. There'd be some running, some shooting, a few skills, shape up for the game, walk through a few moves. Name the team if possible, give them time to take in their jobs for the weekend. Have a game, get the tempo sharp. And none of this business of sending all the ones who won't be involved away to train on their own. No them-and-us. They all have to know the drills in case things change.

FRIDAY: A walk, a jog, a stretch. Take it down to nothing at all, keep it in the legs for tomorrow. A game of heady-football, maybe, a possession box at the very most. As a player, Friday always used to be the day for sprints, but that stuff should be done earlier in the week.

SATURDAY: Matchday begins the moment you open your eyes, and until you realise that, you'll never be 100 per cent focused on the job. Carol and the kids can't talk to me when I'm getting ready to play, my head's too tuned in.

Other guys might be more relaxed, try and keep their minds off playing for as long as possible. But it doesn't matter, as long as when Saturday comes everything points towards kick-off time, as long as all these guys with all these different little idiosyncrasies come together as a well-knit unit at three o'clock.

I'd get them in before 12, away from all the distractions of home. Have a laugh together, eat together. Get comps organised and on the door hours before kick-off. Game heads on. Let them watch telly, read the paper, have a kip even. Everyone's preparation is different. All that matters is that the preparation's right.

It's your business day, what everything else that week has been about. Ideally, I'd have them bringing all the bits and bobs I did as a part-timer, because if the honey and the water and the massage oil and whatever else makes them feel good also makes them last even one minute longer at full pace, that's 11 collective extra minutes that could make all the difference between winning and losing.

If I was a part-time manager? Different story. You'd only have two nights, maybe three if you're lucky, to work with the squad – and even then, it's a squad who've already done a day's work. I'd tell the boys how I wanted them to prepare, what their responsibilities were away from training. Get them into good habits, because once you've got them they never leave you.

At Rangers, everything was laid on for you. Snap your fingers and someone would bring you tie-ups or tape or an extra shirt. There was always someone there to give you a rubdown. Not long ago I went to meet Barry at Ibrox and he was in a meeting about getting a coffee machine in the dressing-room so the foreign lads could get their wee jag of espresso whenever they felt like it. Once you've had treatment like that, there's only two ways you can be. You can whine about everywhere else being sub-standard – or make sure you're properly equipped when you turn up.

Enter the Big Nike Holdall.

Ever since Hearts, I've carried it around with me, packed with everything I could possibly need before, during and after games. And then a few extras, just in case. I used to take my match boots, just in case they didn't get packed in the kit hamper. Then I started carrying my match boots AND my training mouldies. There's a wet top for the warm-up, a T-shirt in case it's cold. My own pair of slips – never forgot those share-and-share-alike early days at Ibrox – and a pair of ankle socks. Isotonic drinks for rehydration. Water for before and after the game. A tuna sandwich to refuel at time-up. Some Jelly Babies for instant energy. A little jar of honey for the same reason – Mo got me into that one. On long away trips, I even bring a cheeky wee bottle of red for the bus home.

The boys used to look at me dipping into the bag and pulling more and more stuff out like Mary Poppins and think I was mental. But I'll look at some of them coming in with nothing more than a bottle of shampoo and some aftershave in a toilet bag and *know* they were daft. Then they come and ask me for some water and I almost feel like telling them to sling their hook.

But the further down the leagues you go, the less they give you. It's usually put down to finance, but how much does it cost for a big gallon bottle of water or a cash-and-carry box of sweeties?

And so, even if I didn't know it at the time, I went to Kirkcaldy and signed my last-ever contract as a footballer.

The one-year deal Gordon Dalziel gave me was eventually torn up early in the New Year thanks to that damn knee, but at least the memories of the laughs I had with the boys will always be with me.

The minibus to training twice a week was magic, especially in the light nights. Mark Crilly drove a lot of the time and he handled this old rust-bucket the way he did his own BMW. He was hurling it round corners, but the indicators didn't work, so he spent half the time with his arm out the window.

It was Scott Wilson, Emilio Jaconelli, Toddy Lumsden, Eddie Annand, me and Don Lennox the physio, having a laugh and hanging on for dear life, if it's possible to do both at the same time.

Then we'd get to the sliproad leading to the Forth Road Bridge. And the fun would *really* start. We'd be carrying a lot of the training gear, so we'd slide open the door and each grab one of those long slalom poles – and have a competition to see who could pick up the most litter off the road.

We kept all the best bits and stuck them up around the inside of the bus, like trophies.

I sat nearest the door and when Crilly picked up speed it would slide open. Rattling along the motorway at 80, nothing between you and disaster, is actually quite stimulating.

Some nights I'd get home and just be thankful the papers

weren't preparing the front page headline: RAITH ROVERS STARS FOUND IN FIELD.

It was a relief when Don decided to drive instead. He's a far more sensible guy all round – well, except when it comes to his training, because you've never seen anyone run as far as he does.

Some people do marathons and I've so much admiration for them. But 26 miles is Don's warm-up. He does 42-milers and 8-hour runs – the last thing he was planning for was 95 miles up the West Highland Way. There's not an ounce of fat on him, a real fitness machine. Yet eat? He never stops. You take him in a big cake and he won't have a slice, he'll munch the lot. Then get on the treadmill and be gutted that it cuts out at two hours.

The boys on the bus were the only part-timers at the club, so it must have been odd for the full-timers to have to wait until night-time to train on Tuesdays and Thursdays. It was an odd mix. Though probably not any odder than the nonsense we got up to sometimes.

One night, when all the scare stories were going around about bird flu, Scott Crabbe was taking the warm-up when I spotted a seagull by the side of the pitch. It was very big. And very dead. So I broke off from the pack, picked it up, sneaked up behind the wee man and put it round in front of his face. He freaked out and I was chasing him round the touchline, waving the thing at him. Then I had it on my shoulder, talking. Later on, I scored a screamer and celebrated with it. The young boys wouldn't go near it, they thought it would infect them.

We discussed putting it on the front of the bus as a mascot, but they bottled out in the end.

They were good boys. Pre-season, we went over to Ireland and Daz gave us a night off on the Saturday. Of course, they were all out like a shot, but I was happy to sit in the lobby with a glass of red. I remember when I was a boy at Rangers and the older guys sat in at nights and I called them boring old farts. Now, it was me slaughtered by the kids.

On that trip, Daz handed me the captain's armband and didn't understand why I wanted to throw it right back at him. It's not that it wasn't an honour. It's just that I'm not skipper material, because a good one has to come away from the players at times and I couldn't do that.

I like to blend in – *off* the park, that is. On it, I want to shine. That's where I come alive, where I'm cocky and self-assured. Often you get boys in the dressing-room who seem completely full of themselves, but the second they cross that white line they go into their shell. I revel in the pressure of matchday and Barry's the same.

Accies wanted me to be captain and we ended up having a fall-out over it. I got a temporary break from them going on at me when I got injured and Steven Thomson took over, but when I was fit I told them they'd be better giving it full-time to someone who enjoyed inspiring the team with their words, because I prefer to do it with actions on the park. It didn't go down very well.

One reason why captaincy is not for me is that when I prepare for games, I like to do my own thing. When you're the leader or the dressing-room joker, you're always the centre of things. I prefer to live in my own space.

First, I give myself a rubdown with a little massage oil. I sort of lose myself for a few minutes and it gives me time to get my head right for the game. Between two and half-past I try and tune out from the banter altogether and disappear into my own little world. If I need a quiet place to be, I go into the showers. Just stand there and think about the first pass I want to make, the first header, the first tackle. You're going out to perform for people soon and your preparation is no less important that it is for an actor to learn his lines before walking out on stage.

As captain, I couldn't guarantee I'd carry out those preparations to the highest level and that's why I've always said no to the role – it might seem odd to keep turning down the honour of leading the team out, but I'd rather do that than not do myself justice on the park.

But if you think people always expect the captain to be on top form – and just ask Barry about that one – how do you think it is if you're the gaffer AND you're in the team, as happened to me at the Bankies? I had to be fitter than anyone else and playing better than anyone else simply for the fans to accept me being out there. You could hear them going: 'How can he criticise anyone else when he just gave the ball away?'

Being captain would really have put the tin lid on it there, so Rab McKinnon took the job and did it superbly. Captain's an important selection to get right, and managers generally do – put it this way, I've never had a skipper who spoke to the dressing-room and left you feeling worse than you were before. But for me, once the game starts you need 11 captains, 11 guys willing to take responsibility on their shoulders and see the team through.

Even in pre-season, there were signs that we could have pushed for promotion to the First Division – and with a bit more ambition, we could have. There was a lot of football in the team. The trouble was, Daz wanted to play it into the channels all the time and have strikers like Paul McManus running their arses off. Now and again we'd get it down and pass it and look the part, but not often enough to even push for the play-offs.

My own season started to fall apart as early as August. I went into a tackle in a CIS Cup tie against Airdrie and came out the other side hobbling. It settled down enough for me to get through a 2–0 win, but soon it started locking up and I'd have to shoogle it about to get moving again.

Going out for a bounce game against Dunfermline one day, Daz shouted to me: 'Are you limping?'

'No.'

'Yes, you are . . . '

And he was right, I was. From then on, the pain got progressively worse until it was taking me 20 minutes of struggle to get the leg going before training and games. Sometimes it would stop me in my tracks, really take my breath away.

On 5 November, we drew 1–1 at home to Partick Thistle and I was really struggling. I was out for a week. Then they wanted me back to play Peterhead at home but I wasn't up to it and got the operation the following Tuesday. And that was that.

The feeling in the tunnel at five to three never changed from my first game at Rangers to my last with Raith Rovers.

I played in Old Firm games where the noise would deafen you and in front of less than 100 people at Cappielow in the final days of Clydebank – and it was always exactly the same.

Game time. Job to do. A happy Saturday or a miserable weekend lying in wait.

Football's 100 per cent emotion. The cracking feeling of victory makes your night. If the punters go away happy, it's job done. They're nicer to the wife when they get home, slip the weans some extra pocket money, the dog doesn't get kicked. They're happier about being forced to cut the grass next morning when they'd rather be sleeping on the couch. The weans aren't ashamed to wear the strip out playing with their mates.

That's what we can bring to so many lives. Football might not be more important than life and death – I know that from bitter experience – but it *can* be the difference between the family getting treated to a Saturday night takeaway or having to stay out of the way of a grumpy dad.

Then, next week, you lose. And this time there's no music

on the team bus home, only the sound of ifs and buts in your head. You force down your meal, still mentally replaying all the mistakes. And come Sunday, as with a killer hangover, you get that five seconds of bliss before it registers. We lost. Shit.

For me, even playing well but losing's a rotten feeling. It's not how *I* did that counts, it's how *we* did. You can't look into the eye of a gutted supporter and say: 'Hey, never mind, I had a blinder!'

When you lose, you let everyone down. The doorman, the secretary, the tealady. Their happiness depends on you.

Your own happiness?

The older you get, the less time the feelgood factor lasts.

When I was a kid, half the time I couldn't even have told you who we were playing the next week. You're too busy enjoying the ride.

In your mid-20s, you discover marriage and bills and responsibilities, but you still never think it's all going to end one day.

Then, in your 30s, you start to see the bigger picture. Just playing each week becomes a little victory in itself. And the high from good results starts wearing off a little earlier and a little earlier . . .

How are the legs? Is that just cramp or a strain? That bruise's hanging around, eh? Hope he picks me . . .

Then it's: 'So, Forfar away. That means meeting up at X. So I have to have my rice pudding by Y. And who's driving anyway?'

As long as the answer's not Mark Crilly, you should be OK.

THIRTEEN

THE PERFECT GAME

Many times, way past two or three in the morning, I've sat on the couch with the telly on in the background and a glass of milk in my hand, running a game over and over in my head.

Big clubs these days have a thing called ProZone, a video analysis of collective and individual performances designed to work on mistakes and improve on strengths.

But every player already has his own personal ProZone in his head. The loop recording of every move, every touch, every pass and tackle and shot. The glorious moments, the disastrous mistakes and everything in between. And when that recording's running, sleep's an impossibility.

That's why I used to laugh when we were criticised for being out on the town after midweek games. We weren't being unprofessional the way some people think – we just knew we wouldn't be able to rest if we went home straight after the game. Football makes your head buzz. You come off at full-time physically drained but never more mentally alive. Your legs need rest, but your nut has energy to burn. So you burn it.

On a Wednesday night, that means going out for a meal or hitting a club where there's music and laughter and a few beers to finally tire you out. It only needs a few hours and then you can finally get the head down – which is why Saturdays are more of a problem. When you're a kid, you can go out and still be at it the next day. But as you get older – and hopefully a tiny bit wiser – the yeehah gets shorter and the yawns earlier. Zeds, though, are still hard to come by.

So after your couple of drinks and a Chinese, and whatever else the night brings, Carol goes off to bed and I'm still there, wide-eyed but not legless. Could I have played that pass earlier? Was my positioning right? Should I have tracked that run better? How did I lose that 50–50?

You have this idea in your head that one day there won't be any ifs and buts, that you'll go out there and have the perfect performance. You're kidding yourself, though. It'll never happen. Not even the world's greatest players give perfect performances, not in their own eyes at least. The fans might have been wowed, the reporters might have given them ten out of ten in the Man-by-Man ratings – but I'll bet any money that they themselves had one moment in their mind when they could have made it even better, improved on genius.

Hard as I tried, I've never got close to that level. The nearest I've come?

A game just a few days before the loss of our baby.

It was 3 April 1993, a Scottish Cup semi for Hearts against Rangers at Parkhead. Remember I wrote earlier about this thing going round and round in my head about how, if I played well, Lauren would get better? Well, this was the culmination of all my fervent prayers for her to recover.

Everything inside me that day made me hurl myself into the game. The prize at stake, the venue, the opposition, the fact that my little girl was about go in for a make-or-break heart operation. I was simply flying, played out of my skin. Everything I tried came off, every pass I saw found its man, every tackle was won. I dominated my area of the pitch. It was just one of those afternoons when it all came together.

The downer? We lost. But no matter how well you play, unless you *are* a Maradona or a Coop, the result is something you need to rely on others to help make happen. But I don't remember ever coming off the pitch feeling more like the footballer I'd always wanted to be.

I didn't last the full game. About ten minutes from time, cramp set in and that was me done, no more left to give.

The physio helped me off on the far side from the tunnel and we had to walk round past the bulk of the Rangers fans. My head was swimming – anyone who's ever had cramp knows that feeling – but through the haze, I suddenly became aware that they were giving me dog's abuse. Really slaughtering me.

What a weird experience that was. Part of me was delighted, because if you get the opposition support's back up then you know you've done your job. But another part was broken up – because these were my people, my mates. I'd stood in among them so many times. And now they hated me.

Very, very strange.

It was the worst abuse I'd ever taken at a game – though years later, some stick thrown at me by St Mirren fans when I was playing for Alloa at Love Street was far more savage.

I went over to take a corner right in front of the home fans and I swear they were running down to the front to scream at me. I was a dirty Orange bastard, a piece of scum, a Hun wanker. It was all I could do to hold myself back from going over the barrier and taking them on. They were horrible people.

There's no doubt that over the past 20 years, the language and stick that comes down from the terraces and stands has got steadily nastier. Fewer and fewer songs are in support of your own team and more and more are slaughtering the opposition. The humour's gone out of it, everyone just wants to be abusive.

After that semi-final at Parkhead, my big mate Johnny Bayne – Beano – told me he'd nearly got into a scrap defending me against the punters round about him. That's friendship – and I've been lucky when it comes to that commodity.

When I was going about with Ian we had a crowd of 11 or 12 and there were definitely hangers-on among them. It all definitely got out of hand sometimes because there were boys just there for the ride.

But before then, and for all the years since, I've had three really good mates: Mark Paterson, Robert McGregor and Jim Gillespie. I met Robert and Jim when I was about 16 and I was in school with Mark.

Barry sometimes has a beer with Mark, Robert and Jim as well. They're great boys to be around, guys you know you're safe with. There's not a lot I need to write about them, because they know what they mean to me.

It's enough to say that when it comes right down to it, you can claim to have as many pals as you like, but how many people would be there in a real crisis? How many would be there if you desperately needed a quid?

Mark, Robert and Jim would give you their last penny and that'll do for me.

What does nothing for me, as you know by now, is sitting watching from the stand. Never once in my career was I anything but restless as a bored teenager when stuck in the stand instead of playing.

No, wait. That's a lie.

There was *one* night when I was glued to my seat, had no notion to disappear and get up a sweat in the gym, felt cheated that it only lasted 90 minutes.

The nearest thing to a perfect game I've ever seen in the flesh. Rangers v. Ilves Tampere. First European tie of the Souness era.

The record books show it as a regulation 4–0 win over a team of Finnish part-timers, a Robert Fleck hat-trick and one from Coisty, nothing more or less than the gaffer and the fans would have expected.

But stats in black and white don't come close to describing the magic that went into producing that result.

It was Davie Cooper's night.

I've been lucky to share a football pitch with a lot of tremendous players – Terry Butcher, Ray Wilkins, Trevor Francis, Coisty, Durranty, John Robertson, Mo Johnston and a whole lot more – but I hope they don't mind if I put Coop on a pedestal higher even than theirs. He *was* simply the best.

In training, in games, even just absent-mindedly keeping a ball up in the tunnel, I could have watched him all day. He was so talented it made your jaw drop. And never, ever, did that talent come flooding out more than that September evening in 1986 when he tampered with Tampere until they must have felt like breaking down and crying.

The only word I can use to sum up his performance is phenomenal – and it's no exaggeration. Now, I always liked taking people on. Running at them, selling them the dummy, sweeping past, seeing the pass and picking it out. It's a fantastic feeling of power and achievement.

Coop must have felt like some kind of God that night.

He didn't just beat the Finns. He destroyed them. Then he went back and he did it again and again and again. I don't believe in humiliating guys for the sake of it, but that's not what Coop was doing. He was just in the zone and wanted to entertain the fans to the absolute maximum.

He fed off the adulation from the stands. He went round defenders, through defenders, over and under defenders. He twisted them, turned them, flipped them like pancakes, folded them up to make paper aeroplanes. The only trick he didn't do was pulling a bunch of flowers out from his sleeve.

And when he'd had enough of each session of teasing and tormenting, he always seemed to find the defence-splitting pass that no one expected. It was a masterclass from the master. Simple as that.

It's the biggest privilege of my career that I got to tread the same turf as him. But if there's one other man on the planet I'd have given anything to be in the same team as just once, it's Diego Maradona, quite simply the most exciting player of all time.

I was about 12 and playing for Gartcosh when he burst on the scene and I'd never seen anything like him – the control at pace, the strength on the ball, the clinical finishing ability at the end of his mazy runs.

And to think I was growing up in an era when Rangers wanted two-touch football or else. Oh, to be Argentinian back then. The nearest I got was having the kit. Every time they changed theirs back then, I got it.

Football strips were just about the only present I ever asked for at birthdays and Christmas. I'd get five or six every year, picked up on trips into Greaves Sports in Glasgow – and the more unusual the better. One of my favourites was a green, white and gold Paris St Germain top with the sponsor's logo in velvet on the front. The other was Coventry's chocolate-brown away strip made by Admiral. I had the sky-blue home top, too, but the brown one was a classic of the '70s.

The Rangers strip I wore most as a kid was from about 1981, the one with the big, flappy red, white and blue collar. Right out of Coop's golden era. Once I was playing for them, however, it had to be the one from Souness's first season, with the little stand-up neck and the tiny squares all over it. We looked great in that.

Luckily, we also played some great stuff in it – though nothing like Maradona and Argentina. Their style of football was everything I was about, committing men, charging at defenders, getting in the box and having a dig.

I know the wee fella never played in the 1978 World Cup in his own country, but every time I hear the BBC's theme tune for the tournament – Argentinian Melody – it's him I see. The following year, I was one of the lucky 70,000-odd at Hampden when he tore us to bits almost single-handed. He was extraordinary, unique, and I don't think our boys had ever faced such an incredible talent.

I was so disappointed in 1982 when it all petered out for him with a red card against Brazil in those daft three-team second group stages. But 1986 was just magnificent. A lot of people will never forgive or forget the handball against England. However, it shouldn't be allowed to be the overriding memory of a tournament he made his absolute own.

The second goal was out of this world, that slaloming run from halfway, leaving my wee pal Peter Reid blowing out of his backside then making big Tel pay to get back in before drawing Shilton and scoring. No one who loves the game could do anything but appreciate that goal. If you'd been watching your very first football match, you'd have been hooked for life. But it's fair to say that unless you've played the game it's hard to truly appreciate how hard it is to produce something so wonderful in that heat, under that pressure, at that level of competition.

And it wasn't even as if it was a one-off, the kind of moment some players don't realise they have in them until suddenly it all goes right for a few magical seconds. No, Maradona went on and did it all over again in the semis. Twice. His two solo goals against Belgium were mesmerising and it was his teasing and passing that opened up the West Germans in a classic final.

He's been given such a hard time in the past decade or so for his lifestyle, for the drugs and the guns and whatever else. But the weight of expectation on his broad shoulders in his great years was so much greater even than the weight he carried that helped knacker his knee joints.

Old Firm players think they live in a goldfish bowl, and there's no doubt that life's pretty intense for them. But in Latin America, where temperaments and temperatures are so much hotter, someone like Maradona must have felt like he was being suffocated sometimes. By the time of the 1994 World Cup he was a scary mess. That pop-eyed scream into the camera after he scored against Greece? I don't know why they still needed the formality of the dope test before he was sent home afterwards.

At the time of writing, he seems to have got himself together and I hope he keeps it that way. He's given the world far too much to go down in history as someone who threw it all away.

For every dream game, though, football throws up a nightmare. And my biggest one came on a day when I could least afford it.

My debut for Sunderland.

Pre-season had gone really well – car crash apart – and we really fancied ourselves to hit the ground running when the league season kicked off away to Derby. Thirty-five minutes in, I was left wondering if going down there had been the biggest mistake of my life. From the off, it was a different game altogether from back home. Miles more physical, so little time on the ball. Derby had huge, big defenders and midfielders and quick, nippy strikers and that was what you needed in the First Division.

They ended up in the play-off final at Wembley while we finished 12th in the league and that opening 90 minutes was a pretty good guide that it was all going that way. A big guy called Paul Williams, a massive, muscular black guy, called me a Scottish bastard the first time he put me on the deck. Welcome to England.

Then Marco Gabbiadini and Paul Kitson started taking us to bits at the back and it just never got any better. And just after the half-hour, it got far worse for me when my thigh muscle went. What a way to start such a crucial phase of your career. When they took a look at it back in the dressing-room, the physio reckoned it wasn't too bad, just a two or three week job. But that was two or three weeks too long for me.

I was flattened and the journey home, with my leg stretched out across the back seat, was a killer. But the worst feeling was thinking I'd let big Tel down. That really hurt, because he was a manager I wanted to do so well for.

The best manager I ever worked under? I think I've dropped plenty hints already, but it has to be Joe Jordan.

For his fitness, for the quality of his training sessions, for the way he led by example, he was top quality. Good managers don't need to be everybody's pal and Joe certainly wasn't – but he got respect, no doubt about that. Add to that the human side he showed throughout the time Lauren was in hospital and you have a real man. I was sorry to see him leave Tynecastle and hope one day he'll be back in charge at a big club.

You see managers who've made it young and you realise they must have been planning ahead all their playing career. Look at Billy Davies – he was building up a dossier of training routines from when he was a kid at Rangers. No wonder he's done so well with Preston and is in demand from far bigger clubs. He plainly had it all sussed out while most of us were toiling to see past the next game.

And for all my problems with Souness – I may have mentioned something along the way – there's no doubt he took Rangers onto a new level, brought a new arrogance and belief to the club.

Our whole image changed almost overnight, from dusty old Establishment to a football version of the Yuppie culture growing up in society under Maggie Thatcher – who actually visited him at the stadium. You wonder if David Murray would have come in had Souness not been there, if Butcher and Woods and Wilkins and all the other huge names would have bought into it all without such a big-name gaffer doing the selling.

Souness's one failing – and for me, it was a big one – was his inexperience as a manager. He leaned on Walter Smith an awful lot, but he should have done more than that. He should have *learned* from someone who was in a different league when it came to handling people.

My favourite coach? I've worked with plenty and most have already been documented – though one I've missed until now is Gordon Chisholm, who was No. 2 to Neale Cooper in my time at Ross County.

Chis made you work really hard, but it was always enjoyable. His knowledge of the game is excellent and it was rotten to see him dumped by Dundee United after taking over as boss from Ian McCall. He should be right up there at a high level, as an assistant at least, and surely some smart chairman will realise that soon.

There's one guy, though, who I think has a real chance of going right to the top – and that's not just me bumming him up because he's been good to me.

Jim Chapman has terrific talent as a coach *and* a manager, great football *and* people skills: all of them tested to the max when he was handed the reins at Albion Rovers in the summer of 2005.

It has to be one of the toughest shifts in the game, yet after six months or so you could see the improvement he'd made in a bunch of boys virtually dragged in off the street. He made them into a team and that's the bottom line of coaching.

He didn't just do that by knowing where to put the cones and how to organise a set-piece. It's maybe even more about knowing how to treat the players, how to speak to each of them in a way that gets the best from them, not just smother them in a big blanket of shouting. Chappy's one of that rare breed who you could easily see going to the very top if he gets the right breaks – and staying there.

Of course, no coach can make it work without the co-operation of his players and I've shared a dressing-room with every kind under the sun, from the fitness freaks to . . . well, to the freaks.

The longer I've gone on in the game, the more I've prided myself on making the absolute most of my fitness, But I've never had anything on the monster of a man who was my Sunderland skipper – Kevin Ball.

He was so naturally fit it made you sick, but he still kept on top of it every single day. He worked his socks off and he really, really wanted it. Every player coming into the game should be given a video of him at work so they know how it should be done.

Bally could run all day and that was always something I loved too. I ran everywhere as a kid and even got into the Scottish Cross-Country Championships – the only sporting thing Carol and I have in common. She reckons she might even have been at Heriot-Watt in Edinburgh for the races at the same time as I was.

I ran there four years in a row and remember being on the starting line in my football strip and mouldies – I felt like a complete pauper, but I finished 33rd out of 500, which wasn't bad.

You judge players differently at part-time level than full-time. With the restrictions on the time you have them all together and the graft they put into their day jobs, it's more attitude and commitment that makes the best ones stand out. And for me, the best of the best are Billy McDonald and Steven Thomson.

I played in the same midfield with Billy for a while at Alloa, until he fell out with Terry Christie and drifted away. But he was a terrific partner, a real fighter suited perfectly to the lower leagues. You knew exactly what you were getting out of him, week in, week out.

When he went to Stranraer, I then found out what it was like to have him in your face. It was as tough a challenge as anything I'd faced in the full-time, big-time game. Great wee operator.

Stevie? He's not blessed with the greatest natural talent, but there's no better competitor at that level. We were together at Alloa, and again at Hamilton, and we both wanted to win so much we were willing to scrap with each other.

One day at Alloa we yelled at each other over who should have picked someone up when we lost a goal and when it all settled down and we were getting ready for the kick-off, I ran past and gave him a dunt in the ribs. I kept waiting for him to jump on me, but he didn't take the bait.

Then in a pre-season game at Hamilton I made a mess of something and he gave me probably the biggest bollocking I've had in my career. It was a hell of a rant and it made me realise more than ever how much he cared about the game.

Meanwhile, I hope he doesn't get too umpty about me saying it, but few guys I've worked with need to see the Kevin Ball Training Video more than another old Hamilton mate, Brian Carrigan – Carrots. He has all the ability in the world, enough to take him all the way. His control is terrific, he's got the pace, his delivery from corners and free-kicks matches that of anyone around. But the application? It just isn't there. I took Carrots to Clydebank in that fateful final season then played with him again at New Douglas Park and he simply never seems to change. Won't go that extra mile that matters.

Thing is, he's not a kid any more. He was picking up awards in his teenage days at Clyde, but he's past his mid-20s now and is in danger of missing the boat. All for the want of pushing himself through a few barriers.

Compare that to the desire showed by his fellow ex-Bankie, striker Alan Gow, to play at as high a level as he can. One performance he gave – against Cowdenbeath, I think it was – was maybe the best I've ever seen outside the top flight. He had everything; pace, power, skill, cheek.

You could tell then he'd make it if he wanted it enough, and it seems he does. When we folded, he joined Airdrie and since then has won a move to the SPL with Falkirk, where for me he always seems to change games when they let him loose. And he can go higher still. He can play at the highest level. He can be every bit as good as the likes of Derek Riordan.

You can tell how much he's maturing. For instance, he's been plagued with hamstring problems, but he took it on himself to go for specialised Thai stretching sessions that seem to be helping. He doesn't drink, he works his socks off, and once he comes out of his shell more and really expresses himself he'll be a star.

Toughest guy I ever played with? Bally's up there and so's my other Sunderland pal Gary Bennett, a fantastic competitor. Stick the two of them together, though, and John Brown would still run through them. Smiling.

Bomber's hard as nails, but what makes him a great player was that he could also *play*. Some guys can tackle, some guys can pass, some can score goals. He's one of the few of my generation who were equally good at all three.

How he made it to retirement without a Scotland cap is one of football's most baffling mysteries.

He once scored a hat-trick from full-back with Hamilton. Scored another three at Ibrox for Dundee and earned himself his big move to Rangers. He made himself into a cult hero with the fans – and has gone on to make a name for himself as reserve coach alongside Durranty.

When he hit that ball, it stayed hit. His passes had real whip about them. And his 50–50s? Nine out of ten turned into 90–10 in his favour through sheer will to win – the same quality that kept him ploughing on when Mother Nature was screaming at the top of her lungs for him to quit. You start out in the game with four cartilages in each knee. By the time Bomber was at his peak, I think he had one left between the pair. He was hanging together by a thread yet he never hung back, treated every game as if it was his last. Not to mention every night out.

Bomber's a social legend – but then, these last 23 years have been full of them. Durranty's stamina was scary, he was still giving it pelters long after I'd wimped out and hit the sack. Wayne Foster at Hearts was another one who'd go on all night, though usually taking a break halfway through to get the boxing gloves on.

But there surely has never been a machine to match Stuart Munro. My mate Jim's known as the Quiet Man, but Stuarty made him look like he spent his life running around hollering through a megaphone.

He blended into the background so well you'd forget he was around. Maybe that was his trick under Souness because, no matter what superstars came and went, the boy signed from Alloa just kept on chugging away at left-back. He actually outlasted the gaffer who got rid of me and played 179 games, 60-odd more than me in the same 7-year period – and his no-fuss style carried itself on into nights out. First to the bar, last man standing, first in for training next morning. Sir, I salute you.

Football's full of madmen, and I've been a magnet for them from the word go. It's been one of the best things about being in the game. To list them all would take a book in itself. So I've narrowed the wide-boy list down to two.

Gerry Britton and John Kay. Each more mental than the other, but in such different ways.

I was at Dunfermline with Gerry and still do some coaching work with him for an anti-racism charity round schools in Glasgow. He's never changed a bit. Still incredibly intelligent – he's been studying law for years now – and still fantastically funny. He's a natural-born clown. We walked into a gym in Govan one day, he booted a ball up in the air, it came off the ceiling at a mad angle, whacked him on the head and knocked him flying. You'd have sworn he meant it.

He's perfect for working with today's schoolkids, a really bright guy with a laid-back attitude. He definitely copes with some of their behaviour better than I do, because these kids shock me sometimes. We've had first-years openly smoking and swearing and quite clearly having no respect for authority. One wee guy was effing and blinding when I was talking to them, so I sent him to the side. I wasn't having him spoil it for anyone else who was there to learn something. Gerry deals with it differently, gets their wandering minds occupied by being hyper. He makes people learn without them realising it.

It scares me that Darren's going to high school in an era when there's so little discipline about. Kids aren't kept under close enough check at home, their teachers aren't allowed to belt them and they all know their rights when it comes to trouble with the police. They're lawless. And that spells trouble for our future.

When I'm coaching kids, they don't ask if I'm Derek Ferguson who used to play for Rangers. They ask if I'm Barry Ferguson's brother and can I get them his autograph. I wasn't sure how I'd get on working with kids at first, not when I'd been so used to the language and the aggression with dressing-rooms full of men.

But it's been great – and I'm really interested now in coaching girls, because everybody I know who's done it tells me they're far more attentive than boys, take things in quicker, work really hard.

The best player in the street when I was wee was a girl. Katie, her name was, a real tomboy who ran rings round the lot of us. Back then, of course, the street was the one place she could kick a ball. No mixed football in schools, no teams for girls. Definitely no professional game when she grew up, no Women's World Cup.

Last summer I was doing some coaching with Glasgow Council, up in Shettleston, and there was this skinny, wiry girl who was head and shoulders above all the boys, and it all came rushing back, the times when we all wanted to be in Katie's team. Wonder what happened to her?

I'm not sure about women in the dressing-room in the men's game, though. Take female physios – for me, they're a distraction for young guys. It's not the fault of the women, it's just that the guys try and show off to her, and when they do that, their minds aren't 100 per cent on the job. When you're in that dressing-room, all that matters is the game. Nothing else should be in your head. But once you start thinking about impressing a girl, you're not focused properly. Or maybe I'm just old-fashioned. I don't even like swearing in front of women. It's a carry-over from the values your parents brought you up to believe in.

Anyway, end of sermon.

Gerry's big pal was always wee Geordie Shaw, and the two of them couldn't be more different. Geordie's always immaculate and is the tidiest man I've ever met. I've been round his house and he's got the Marigolds on, scrubbing work surfaces. He's almost obsessively clean. Gerry's a shambles, floppy hair and studenty clothes, a running style that goes in about nine directions at once.

He also has the ability to keep a straight face when doing things that make others crack up, as I found out on a brilliant team night out in those Pars days.

We went to Hamilton Palace for a meal and a few beers that turned into many, many, *many* beers. At one point I got up from the table, weaved my way to the toilet then lost my bearings on the way back and went up a flight of stairs to where the various different nightclub rooms are. It was about nine o'clock and I was too drunk to realise it was too early for them to be open, but just sober enough to realise there were lights on in one and music playing somewhere and that I should really get myself on that dance floor.

So there I am, all alone in a disco, throwing some shapes all on my own and feeling no pain – when I look up and see Gerry. Pushing a shopping trolley.

He walks past me without a flicker, nods and goes: 'Evening, Fergie . . . '

If I remember rightly, later on he was drinking beer out of his shoe and ended the night by doing back-flips off the bar.

And then there's big John Kay, a different kind of mad altogether. Scary mad. He was a smoker who never used ashtrays – not because he threw his dogends on the floor, but because he had his own special place to stub them out.

His body.

Seriously, he'd take his last puff and grind it out on his arm, his leg, his stomach. You were backing away going: 'Riiiighhhtt . . .'

He must have cost pubs a fortune in pint tumblers, too. Thanks to his cute little habit of finishing his drink and crunching the glass as a wee snack. Truly bonkers.

And the great thing is that everybody reading this, no matter what job they do, will know someone like him or Gerry. Guys who make you laugh until your guts hurt and the tears run down your cheeks. They're the people who make you realise life's too short to go round with a torn face on.

May they have many sons who keep pulling the same ridiculous stunts.

I've had my ill-fated stint as a manager. Whether it's enough to put me off having another go remains to be seen, because the truth is that no one else has asked me to give it a go yet.

But what if somebody, somewhere, was daft enough to put me in charge of the game of football itself for a week? What damage could I cause? What improvements could I make?

In truth, not many. But mostly because not an awful lot needs done to football. Just a few tweaks here and there and we could stop so many people moaning and get them roaring again.

We'd start off by moving the season to the summer. Shut down for the whole of December, January and February and at least give ourselves the chance of getting the sun on our backs now and again.

I remember going to a question-and-answer thing at the Burnbank Masonic in Hamilton years ago and suggesting summer football and all the old blokes glared at me and went: *'Whit? Whit did he say? Summer fitba'? Away and take a flyin'...'*

Why not, though? We've tried everything else to get fans back through the gates and put a smile back on the game's face, so why not experiment with playing at a different time of the year?

My little spell in Australia showed me the benefits to football of good weather. Families would come out for games, set up barbecues in the car park, have a couple of beers, turn it into a full day out.

We hide in the pub for as long as possible then sprint through the rain to huddle in and try to enjoy seeing the ball being blown about by the gales. Surely it's worth even considering playing from April to November and getting the best of the year?

Next, I'd cut admission prices. I couldn't afford to take the three boys to a game every week, that's for sure. We're talking £12 for a club like Raith up to £25 for Ibrox, Parkhead and Easter Road. That's bordering on the obscene.

OK, so the Old Firm can charge what they like and they'll still get full houses most of the time. But everywhere else, teams are running out to banks of empty seats that could be filled with just a little simple marketing. Put it this way: wouldn't it be better to drag in 10,000 fans at £5 a skull than 5,000 at £10?

Football's moving away from the working man. It's getting to the stage where you need to have a lot of money to follow your team everywhere and buy all the merchandise that comes with your obsession. That's wrong – because one day, the new fans with the money will get fed up and move on to something else, and then who'll go along?

Next for the chop? The ridiculous new offside rule. If ever there was a change brought in because some pen-pushers were bored one day, this is it. All that second-phase, active–passive stuff is rubbish. You're either offside or not, there are either two defenders between you and the line or there aren't. It was never easy for refs and linesmen when it was as basic as that, but now it's simply impossible.

Then there's the stupidity of making players go off the park after treatment for injuries – and even worse, the schoolboy practice of being expected to kick the ball out of the park when an opponent hits the deck. Listen, we're professionals. We know when someone's hurt and when they're at it. We don't need to be told, so let us get on with the game. And if someone is genuinely injured and someone else doesn't have the decency to stop the game, *then* the ref should step in.

But that's the problem with the game, the true physical element has been stripped away so far that no one seems to know what's a tackle and what's a foul, who's down there for a reason and who's at it.

Ask yourself, how many times have you cursed that a move's been stopped in mid-flow for the sake of someone 60 yards away who then gets up and walks away like nothing's happened? We need to keep the game moving, take it away from the spoilers and give it back to those who want to create entertainment.

Anyway, injuries are part of the game, so the game has to carry on around them where possible – just as the game has to carry on instead of being stopped every two minutes for spy-in-the-stand decisions. People keep whining about using cameras to get referees off the hook on big decisions, but there are two reasons why I'd be against that.

One, unless you can put the technology in at every ground and not just the ones where TV goes, it's not fair. The rules must apply to everyone.

And two, human error's one of the biggest factors in football. Players don't get to go back and re-do things we get wrong, so why should referees?

Arguments are great. They make the world go round.

FOURTEEN

WHAT HAPPENS NEXT?

As I get out of the car in Strathclyde Park, there's a boy playing keepy-uppy just behind the Holiday Inn.

He's pretty good, a great touch, nice and relaxed. I've seen him there plenty of times, away in his own wee world, dreaming that he's bamboozling defenders at Hampden or Ibrox or Parkhead.

Though I call him a boy, he must be 80, if he's a day.

He always makes me smile.

He always makes me imagine myself doing the same when I'm that age.

Fingers, toes and cruciates crossed that I'm still able to.

I know that look on his face, that expression of concentration that's both focused in on the job in hand and at the same time ever so far away.

When your eye's on the ball, nothing else matters. And that goes whether you're knocking it around on your own in a park or fighting for it in front of 50,000 screaming fans in an Old Firm showdown.

That's the reason so many guys like me only wake up to the outside world once we've kicked that ball for the last time.

There's been one at my feet from before I could walk. When I got shouted in for dinner, I picked it up and shoved it under my arm. When I went to bed, it went with me the way other kids clung onto a favourite teddy.

Football came before exams, girlfriends, drinking, discos. Nothing and nobody was going to come between me and my dream.

Down all the years I've written of in the previous chapters, that dream drove me; not towards a pot of gold, but the opposition goal. To a life of training, playing, training, playing. Sure, injuries set me back plenty of times, but they were never, ever going to beat me.

I'm not stupid, though. Always knew it would have to end sometime. Just didn't want to think too much about it.

Even remember the first time reality pinged me behind the ear.

It was a coaching course for South Lanarkshire Council a couple of years back. We'd set up this drill that involved dribbling round cones and back to pass the ball on to the next guy.

Halfway through it, this middle-aged bloke caught my eye. Great control, great movement, head bobbing, feet dancing. A natural.

I gave him a nickname.

'Go on, Snakehips – show them how it's done!'

He must have played before, and you wondered if he'd had dreams of making it, where and when it had all changed for him, what held him back.

Watching him made me think of all the boys I'd played with who'd been far better than me as youngsters but who hadn't had the application or the determination or even just the luck to go all the way. Snakehips could have made it, no doubt about that.

Then the drill's finished and one of the others says: 'Well done, Willie.'

And it hits me right between the eyes.

He's not one of the ones who slipped through the net.

He's one of the few who've thrilled the many by *hitting* the net.

He's Willie Pettigrew.

I felt about six inches tall. He hadn't said who he was, and I hadn't clicked.

When I was a kid, he was already a legend. Scored for fun with Motherwell, was linked with all the big clubs and should really have been a superstar.

He won three more caps for Scotland than I did, and had he been with Rangers or Celtic it would have been ten times more.

Someone told me he was working at Asda, and that really rocked me back on my heels.

Lanarkshire's a huge football area that has produced a stack of top players down the decades, but not many better than Willie. Yet he ends up stacking shelves or pushing trolleys or whatever they had him doing.

He didn't do it because he'd hit the skids, nor because he was lazy, but because that's the way football is. It chews men up and spits them out again in bits.

It hit me right there that one day soon, if the phone stopped ringing and the offers dried up, it could be me stacking shelves. The prospect didn't frighten me. But it sure as hell made my mind work overtime.

Which is more than the rest of me has ever done.

I've never worked a proper day in my life. Sure, we mump and moan when we're running in the rain and the wind, when we don't fancy a double session, when the hill's too steep or the ground too hard, but what hardship is it really? We're still being paid to be in football, and that's the dream come true.

Yes, I've had some bad breaks along the way these last 23 years or so, but how can I whinge about them to everyone else out there who never even got to play one single game for a living?

Still, from the moment I went part-time in the summer of 2002, the day when I'd need to follow Willie Pettigrew and so many other dreamers into the job market was coming. Nearer and nearer, faster and faster.

Wonder if Willie thinks of himself as a success or a failure? If it eats away at him that he's doing manual labour when other players with less talent ended up as bigger stars?

If he's like me, it won't. If he's a normal working boy who simply made the most of the chance he was given for as long as he could, he'll have accepted from an early age that one day he'd have to go out and graft.

That was always my mindset. I was never obsessed with making fortunes, having the big mansion or the fleet of cars. I've got my dad's work ethic and that'll never leave me.

I've asked him to show me the ropes of the roofing game, but he's not having it. For a start, I don't think he thinks I could hack it. But I also don't think *he* could hack having people look at me like: 'What's happened to him?'

That wouldn't bother me, though, no more than signing on did. Hard graft wouldn't embarrass me. If it's been good enough for my dad all these years, it's good enough for me.

So, if it's not roofing, what'll it be?

Every day I look around me and try to picture myself in the shoes of posties, van drivers, barmen, you name it. I think to myself: 'I can see you in that uniform . . .'

A binman's life even looks good to me – no kidding. They're out in the fresh air, doing physical work, and the patter between them must be brilliant. I watch them and know I could live with that.

Or, if the shop finally takes off, Carol can be out at the front smiling and making the sales, and I could be through the back humping boxes around. And I think I'd be a really good school janny.

Though I know for sure that some people will be reading this and wondering who I'm kidding. Rangers? Scotland? Big moves to Hearts and Sunderland? And he's talking about lugging bins around?

Everyone thinks you're cruising. I met my old Falkirk mate Scott McKenzie in the Accies gym a while back, and he was talking about going into the taxi game. I said that sounded interesting and could he get me some info.

He laughed and went: 'Aye, sure – as if you need a taxi job when you're onto your second million . . .'

I'm used to that, to this perception that either I'm loaded or my multimillionaire brother keeps me in Gucci. It used to bother me, but not any more. Water off a duck's back now.

Money's something I've never had that much of – and I don't mean that I've been skint, because that's never been the case. I just mean there's never physically been a lot in my pocket.

I'm like my dad: the wages go to my wife, and I get anything I need for petrol or a beer. Don't have a cash card, won't sign for anything in shops. Either pay for it or don't get it.

Carol and I have been comfortable in as much as we've never gone short, we've always had nice things and bought nice things for the kids.

I've never saved – but then, how many people from normal working families do? The wages come in, you pay the bills and you take whatever's left over and you enjoy it.

These days, though, we have to be more careful than ever about what we enjoy. We appreciate our holidays more because it's been harder to pay for them. We scour the Internet or Teletext for deals.

But I'm a great believer that there's always something around the corner, and while it's not a theory that would win me any Go-Getter of the Year awards, it's one that's rarely let me down.

One avenue that has opened up is a little bit of media work, and I've enjoyed that. Rangers TV gave me a shout to go on their phone-in show one Monday night and it became a regular slot, working with presenter Ali Douglas and guys like Andy Goram, Craig Paterson and Robert Prytz.

Talking about football's easy, and once you're comfortable with the studio and the cameras, it's no bother. I was even brave enough to go on screen in a pink shirt one night.

You soon learn, though, that, even though it's live and there's absolutely no doubt about what you've said during the show, your words can be turned round to give them a whole different meaning.

One morning, right in the middle of the crisis Rangers were having in the last few months of big Alex's reign, I woke up to a back-page headline in the *Daily Record* screaming that I'd demanded he drop Barry.

It was while *Celebrity Big Brother* was on the box, and the reporter Keith Jackson's line was that I'd voted my wee brother out of the Ibrox team.

What I'd actually said was that Barry was carrying a couple of niggling injuries and that for his own good and the good of the team he could maybe be rested now and again.

Barry was fine about it. He'd seen the show, and he agreed with what I was saying. Even Alex came out a week or two later and admitted he'd have left him out if he could have afforded to.

But then again, sometimes you can even surprise yourself with your own words.

The show gave me a DVD of an hour-long interview I'd done in November that was shown on Hogmanay, but which I hadn't seen.

I sat down to watch it with Dad just after New Year, when I was still down in the dumps about the final knee op, and didn't realise until we were sitting there how much I'd spoken about him.

Almost everything Ali asked about my career ended up coming back to Dad's influence: how he was always there for me, the advice he gave me, how much his opinions meant to me.

It's awkward, two men's men sitting next to each other on the couch, the son listening to himself tell the world how highly he rates his dad.

But the bit about the interview that had completely slipped my mind was all the stuff about my playing career.

There I was, on the screen, telling the world how much I still loved it, how great the lower leagues were, how honest the people were, how it was no different from the Old Firm once you crossed that white line.

Then there I was, a few days later, with a surgeon putting me to sleep and giving me a wake-up call in the space of a couple of hours.

And now here I was, on the couch, feeling like it was a different lifetime. Like they were interviewing some other, optimistic guy who'd be pulling his boots on for a long time to come.

Dad and I were both silent for a while when the show finished. Then he said: 'You're welling up, son.'

It was only the macho thing that kicked in then and stopped me crying for real, because I sure as hell felt like it.

Then he poured me a half and started talking the mickey out of me.

He's brilliant, a carbon copy of every dad who grew up round about the war, devoted to his family and his work and uncomfortable with anything and anyone he thinks is above him.

Even if they couldn't lace his boots.

When I was at Rangers, the comps I left for him got him into one of the lounges at half-time, but he wouldn't go. It was only a sausage roll and a bit of cake, yet to him it seemed to represent much more than that.

He thought the other people in that room would be better than him – the same reason why he won't go into a bank or a nice restaurant or take time off and travel to see Barry play in Europe.

One Sunday he was late getting Ross to training with Hearts, but instead of going over to the coach and explaining what was what, he got embarrassed and just turned the car round and took the wee man home.

We fell out about that one, because Ross suffered for a grown-up's inability to communicate with other grown-ups.

But you know what? I'm not much different. If I need to make an important phone call, I'll ask Carol to do it or it won't get done. I'm uneasy around people with money, with inflated ideas of themselves. Yet, like my dad, I'm very proud of who I am and where I come from. It's an odd contradiction.

I keep telling Dad to give up his Saturday morning half-shifts so he can watch the boys play football, but he's too set in his ways. He's a worker.

It doesn't look like he'll ever give up the roofs, but he always had a hankering to run a sweetie shop. That one baffles me.

I mean, this is the guy whose nickname on building sites used to be Schizo because of the trigger-switch temper he had. I once saw him punch his foreman out for messing him about. Social workers would have a field day with that one, but Dad has a finely tuned sense of injustice that I've always understood and shared.

Somehow I just can't picture him putting on a grin and serving kids with quarters of Kola Kubes.

Carol's the opposite – she's brilliant with people, which is one of the main reasons I wanted our shop to succeed and still hope it does.

My mum? She grafts her fingers to the bone as a home help for the council and will do anything for her family. She's always on the go.

These are the people who influence me, people who know the value of what they have and don't get hung up about what they don't have. Unfortunately, there are too many people in football these days who merely know the price of stuff.

The game's full of greed, of those who put money before the game itself. And yes, I hear you coming back at me with the old favourite that modern football's all about finance.

But save your breath. Because, for me, that'll never be the case.

You know what I hate? Strikers getting bonuses for scoring goals. Isn't that their job? And if they demand extra money for doing it properly, shouldn't they take a drop in wages when they miss sitters?

Midfielders don't get bonuses for the killer pass that lets the centre-forward tap one in. Defenders don't get bonuses for throwing themselves into last-ditch tackles. Goalkeepers get the same money even if they save three penalties in a cup final. Strikers should not be any different.

Winning is the real bonus, a buzz worth more than any money in the bank. When I was young, it would set me off on a right good night out with the boys. Now, as an old git, it's the cue for *X Factor*, a Chinese takeaway and a nice glass of red.

Surroundings change. Ambitions change. But winning remains the greatest feeling on earth.

And if you think real fans are impressed by how much big-timers earn every week, think again. If you think the true diehard looks at the Footsie results before the footie results, you're off your head.

Punters will never turn up on a Saturday to watch piles of £20 notes lined up on either side of the halfway line. But they will always come and see the team they love, whether it's filled with millionaires or paupers, if that team is honest and gives its best.

I've played in teams from both ends of the financial scale, and plenty in between, and they're basically all the same. The English superstars Souness brought to Ibrox had the same insecurities as the frees and kids Gordon Dalziel cobbled together in my abortive season with Raith.

Even the money I've earned has gone full circle. If only my body could do the same.

I started out at Rangers on £150 a week, got a hike to £300, then another to £700. Went to Hearts on the same wage, then peaked at £1,200 with Sunderland.

Took a drop to £1,000 at Falkirk, then £500 at Dunfermline and Ross County. At Clydebank, it was £450. At Alloa £300. At Hamilton £210. And at Raith, all the way back to £150.

The going rate as a kid at a big club turned out to be the same as the going rate for a veteran in the part-time world.

For me, that's a neat and tidy way to wrap it all up.

Somehow, the less I've earned, the more it's meant. It's a Peter Pan thing, time's catching up on me, so every training session, every game, every bus journey back, they've all been an adventure to be enjoyed to the full.

And if you think I look at young guys starting out and wish I was that young again, you'd be wrong.

The ones who make me green are Teddy Sheringham and Davie Irons, guys who've made it into their 40s unscathed. I know how hard it is to make it through your 30s that fit and that focused. Their desire must be incredible.

Their legs? They must be made of the same stuff as aeroplane black boxes.

Once upon a time, they were like I was, like Barry once was, like my three boys are now. Desperate to get their big chance.

Darren, Ross and Lewis will settle down with me to watch a match on the box and after ten minutes they'll get fed up with the theory and get stuck in to the practical. They can manage an hour of pretending our street's hosting the World Cup final before they start winding each other up.

Come homework time, it doesn't take much threatening to get them to knuckle down. Just tell them they won't be getting football and their pencils are a blur. They live for it. Though, of course, that means a military operation to get them to train and play with their teams.

Darren's out Mondays, Tuesdays and Fridays with Hearts at Heriot-Watt – we drop him at Strathy Park and he gets picked up by bus – and plays on Saturdays. Ross trains with Hearts on Mondays at Dalziel Park in Motherwell and has started playing for Mill United. Lewis goes on Tuesdays to the Power League astroturf pitches in Hamilton for training with South Lanarkshire Council.

Getting them all where they need to be – and back – as often as we do leaves your head spinning, but we wouldn't change it for the world. A parent's support means so much.

When I was a kid, I used to ask my dad every week if he was coming to see me play. I knew he would be, but I wanted to hear him say 'Yes.'

It was always such a thrill when he did.

Thing is, once your kids are 16 they'll pretty soon be leaving home or, at the very least, won't want you hanging about them, so you have to put the time in when you can. Mum and Dad went everywhere with me, and I hope they know how much I appreciate it.

I don't like the way kids are assessed by their teams these days. Instead of being signed up on schoolboy forms at 12 then given until they're 16 to develop, they're assessed almost constantly.

That's wrong. You can't put pressure on boys that young to know what they want or expect them to be as strong or tall as they're going to be. All you know at that age is that you want to play football, so if you find somewhere to play that's also fun, you're made up.

Instead, these days you're constantly on a knife-edge about whether or not they'll be kept on from month to month. A while back, Carol and I went to a sort of parents' night for Darren's team at Heriot-Watt.

We thought it was to give us a progress report. Instead, when we got there, youngsters were being told they were no longer wanted.

My old Falkirk teammate Stevie Fulton takes that age group, and he was the one left to do the dirty work. You could tell it was killing him – he could hardly look the mums and dads in the eye.

When it came to us, he sort of stammered: 'Er . . . we've looked at who should stay and who should go, and we've . . . well . . . had a look at Darren and . . .'

We prepared ourselves for the worst.

'. . . he's being kept on.'

He looked totally relieved just to have got the words out. It was a rotten situation for him, a rotten situation for the kids and for their folks.

But I suppose that, no matter how often they assess you, there's always a thin line between success and failure in this game, right from those young days when scouts first come to watch you.

You might have been brilliant all season, but that morning you wake up feeling lousy and you have a stinker, and the guy goes away and reports back that you're not as good as they thought you were.

And your chance is gone.

Or you might not impress the scout from the club you hoped

to but one from hundreds of miles from your family home, and when you get there, you might not settle and they might cut their losses and let you go.

It's not just about how much talent you have. It's not even about your strength of character. So much about success in football is down to being in the right place at the right time.

In my case, Ibrox under Graeme Souness was the right place at the wrong time.

With Barry, it was Dick Advocaat appearing at exactly the right moment to give him the platform to become the player I always knew he could be. From fringe player to club captain inside a couple of years, then international captain and financially independent husband and father pretty soon after.

Today, he has all I ever wanted for him when he was crawling around dodging darts in our bedroom in Little Earnock.

You just hope that he and every other player lucky enough to be as well sorted appreciate what they've got. That they never take a second of their privileged existence for granted.

That they think about a guy like Ted McMinn once in a while.

Ted was a teammate of mine who came up through the ranks with Queen of the South and made himself a cult hero with the Ibrox fans. He was a top man who lived the dream and lived it to the absolute maximum.

Yet there he is now, minus a foot after contracting gangrene. Life can be bloody cruel sometimes.

Stories like these shouldn't make Barry feel guilty, just thankful – and I think they do. He's definitely more money-orientated than I am, but as he's grown up he's spoken less about money than he used to.

Now that he has it all and needn't worry about his future, he seems to enjoy the game more. He's comfortable, but he's not in the comfort zone.

I don't blame him for having a material streak, because it's a far more material world he's come up in – and with the amount of money he and his teammates earn, it'd be hard *not* to become obsessed by cash.

Barry knows every penny that comes in and where it goes. He understands business, too – when I told him Carol and I were in partnership at the shop, he shook his head and said: 'You should have set up a limited company.'

Plus, he's always had an agent, and these guys are all about money – making it, investing it, multiplying it.

I'd be lying if I said I'd never thought about what life would be like with his kind of dough stashed under the bed.

For a start, I'd burn my chest hair on the light bulb.

But what would I do with all that cash? What would my luxuries be?

That's easy. People.

All I'd want is to make everyone around me happy, to help improve their lives as much as I could. Sound schmaltzy? Well, tough, it's how it is.

We've all had that late-night conversation about what we'd do if the lottery came up, and the truth is that if I hit the jackpot one Saturday night, every penny's already accounted for.

No yacht moored in Monte Carlo. No country estate. No Ferraris. Not even the 50 Armani suits hanging in a wardrobe the size of a small village.

None of that would fit me right, I know that for sure. So I'd stick to paying the mortgage off, getting decent cars for me and Carol, putting enough cash away for a couple of decent holidays a year and a bit more to make sure we could buy what we needed when we wanted.

I've got this notion that if I really am finished playing, I'll go on a tour of all the clubs who've signed me. If the six numbers did come up, I could even include Adelaide on the farewell tour itinerary.

But even after all that, there would still be a stack left over. So here's the deal. After salting plenty away to give the kids a secure future, I'd spread the rest around everyone who means the most to me, be that family or friends.

For instance, here's something I've always had a notion for. Taking all those closest to me out as often as possible – book out a nice restaurant every couple of Sundays and invite the lot of them for a good meal and a few drinks. There's nothing like getting together with the people you're closest to, sitting round a table and having a laugh. That's my idea of value for money.

When I was at Rangers and earning a good bit more than my mates, I really hope I never flashed it around. I certainly don't think I did. All I tried to do was maybe buy an extra round or two in the pub, stick a bit more in the kitty for nights out than the others could afford.

Same went when I moved up to the first-team squad at Rangers but was still going out with my pals from the reserves. I'd bung in a wee bit more than my share, but only because I could. They'd have done the same if the roles were reversed.

A guy I really admire for his attitude to money is the Gretna chief executive Brooks Mileson. That man would win gold for Britain if selfless good deeds became an Olympic sport. He's spent fortunes on taking his club up the divisions, and he's forever handing out wedges to sportspeople and other deserving causes all over the country.

Why does he do it? Simply because he can.

And that's the best reason of all.

He's worked his balls off all his life, then he's looked at his bulging bank balance and realised that you can't take it with you, so you might as well use it to bring as much happiness as possible to the world around you.

I read somewhere that he is now richer than Elton John. Well, it's said that Elton spends hundreds of thousands of pounds every year on fresh flowers for around the house. Brooks spread a little colour by helping others make the most of their talents. Each to his own, that's my motto.

All I know is, football could do with another dozen like Brooks – and the world in general could do with thousands.

Question is, if you've spent a lifetime in football and it hasn't filled up your bank book, what has it given you?

Again, easy.

Friends. Memories. And, if you're lucky, a few medals.

The friendships are the best thing. Make a pal in this game and he's a pal for life. I'm lucky to have been close to guys from right across the dressing-room spectrum, from sophisticated gentlemen like Ray Wilkins to rough-and-ready lower-league legends like Paul Kinnaird.

Razor I've already talked about. A one-off as a footballer and a man. Then you get someone like PK, who ducked and dived his way through the lower leagues and picked up five championship medals in five years with five different clubs. He's also unique.

Then there's big KB, the man who's shuddering tackle knackered my knee at Falkirk all those years back. There are three reasons why I never held a grudge about that:

1. He didn't mean it.

2. Injuries are part of football, and

3. Anyone who pulls the Big Man up is probably the kind of thrillseeker who flicks lions on the wedding tackle with wet towels.

The Big Man. He even calls himself that.

'Carol? It's the Big Man. Is the Wee Man there?'

Just a great guy, like so many I've mentioned in these pages and so many more I probably should have. Teammates, dressing-room buddies, room-mates. We can go our separate ways then meet up again years later and it's like we've just popped out for ten minutes.

At Tynecastle, I shared with George Wright on trips. He always wanted to do something outside football and got his way, as an agent and on a soft-porn TV show with nude model Jo Guest.

Like they said about another Georgie: where did it all go wrong?

He's just one of a dozen and more I've shared a billet with, but whoever's in the other bed, the patter's always the same.

Durranty was funny, Wrighty was funny, Gary Bennett at Sunderland was funny, Brian Hamilton at Falkirk was funny.

When I signed for Raith, we went to Ireland for a few days in the pre-season, and I roomed with Scott Crabbe. I used to bring him a cup of tea to wake him up, then bring him breakfast in bed.

He wasn't a morning person, loved his kip, but I kept on at him like a nagging wife until he got himself into gear.

With Scotland Under-18s, I roomed with the Hibs full-back Kevin McKee. I liked him, but he scared me. He looked like Jesus and sat reading for hours. He really freaked me out.

Of course, maybe if you asked them all about rooming with me, they might not be so complimentary. I'm sure they certainly wouldn't fall about recalling all the jokes I told them, because that's not my scene.

I'm not a storyteller; I'm a listener. But everyone needs a party trick in this game, so I became the stuntman. I'd dive over couches. Bars. Tables loaded with drinks. Brain-of-Britain stuff like that.

Once I met Carol, of course, I had a room-mate for life. And as I've got older and brought up a family, I've been quite happy that the overnights and the training camps have become fewer and fewer.

Down the leagues, there isn't the money for hotels, so your relationships are forged in cars or minibuses going to training or on the bus to games.

But it's still great crack, still the same bonding exercise. It's still a mad mix of daft boys and posers and grumpy old-stagers, of card players and music lovers and non-stop talkers.

It's 23 years since I got to know my first busload, and 23 years from now they'll still be my pals.

The memories and the medals? They kind of dovetail with each other.

I sometimes wonder what happened to that loser's badge Souness threw away in the Hampden dressing room back in 1989.

Did it get swept up, unnoticed, and end up in the rubbish?

Did a cleaner take it and put it in their display cabinet, inventing some story about how his favourite player gave them it?

Souness thought it meant nothing, but he was wrong. We might have lost, but that runners-up prize was still a reward for getting there – and very, very few players who set out in the game *do* get there.

Then again, many other players have realised that, in the long run, the financial value of their medals is their real worth.

I was talking to Bobby Russell not long ago, and he told me he'd had his three from the 1978 Treble season set in a little case and sold them at auction for £10,000.

He wasn't upset about letting them go, and the money had come in handy. When I told Carol, though, she didn't approve. For her, medals are too important to be flogged to the highest bidder – and an awful lot of people not directly involved in the game might agree.

To the onlooker, it's the pieces of silverwear and the little golden badges that represent triumph. For those of us down on the pitch, the actual winning and losing means more.

And no one can buy your experiences from you.

Some businessman might throw a few grand about at a dinner to get his hands on a signed shirt from some big match. He'll go home and put it on the wall of his lounge or his office and it'll be a tremendous conversation piece when he has guests or clients in. He'll also feel good that his cash has gone to a good cause, be it a charity or a hard-up player's bank account.

But at the end of the day, the shirt didn't win the game. The guy who wore it did. And long after the mementos have been shifted up into the loft because the wife wants to redecorate, the memories of the culmination of all the hard work put in over a season or even an entire career will still be fresh as this morning's milk.

I have two Championship medals and two from the League Cup, and they're no doubt worth a few bob. Would I flog them? Don't tell Carol, but maybe I would. If it meant I could take the kids for a few weeks in Florida or pay off some more of the mortgage, why not?

It would mean I'd grafted hard to win them and they in turn would have done something important for me. Don't the experts say your investment should work for you?

Though here's a little story of selflessness that a lovely guy kept quiet from me for a long, long time. On Rangers TV one night, they showed a behind-the-scenes documentary, and the legendary Tiny – who looked after the boys day in, day out – told how Durranty had come in one day and given her a Reserve League medal he'd won.

What a superb gesture. He knew how much a souvenir like that would mean to someone behind the scenes at the club, someone who was never given awards despite all her priceless work. And even better, he handed it over in private, with no fuss. Yet people still call him a bad boy.

Durranty says our medals from the Dubai Cup are worth about £25,000, but I reckon he's at it. If I took mine to a dealer, it'd just about sum up my luck with money if he bit it and found chocolate inside.

I don't have any trophies in the house. In fact, there's only even one photo from my career on show – a shot from the Hearts days that's up in the utility room because Carol says it made me look like Bobby Ewing.

When we first won the league under Souness in 1987, the chairman David Holmes – an absolute gem of a man – ordered little replicas of the trophy for all of us, which was a great gesture.

The medal from that league's the one that means most, especially to Mum and Dad. They were so proud and that was worth nearly as much to me as the team's achievement.

They have two display cabinets full of medals and assorted Player of the Year prizes Barry and I have won. Barry himself has a little museum to his achievements in the pool room at Fergie Towers.

One other big plus the game's given me is the joy of being at home for big chunks of the day to spend time with Carol and the kids. When I start a proper job, that'll be really hard to give up.

I'd feel really guilty about being out of the house 12, 14 hours a day, not seeing the boys from breakfast till past their bedtime. Especially when my favourite bit of the day is seeing them coming hammering in from school at lunchtime.

It reminds me of being wee and charging across the road from Barlanark Primary to my Granny Fergie's to get fed. Not that it's a time when I get to catch up with much of what they've being doing. They'll settle down to their beans on toast or sandwiches or sausage rolls or whatever, and it goes like this:

Me: '*So, what was happening at school this morning?*'
Them: *Shrug. Munch. Grunt.*

Then, the second they've finished, they want to get back round the road to join in the football. And quite right, too.

Their school's just round the corner, not even five minutes away. So off they go again, haring away in case they miss anything. It's just such a buzz for me, and I'm aware that not many dads get to share that kind of stuff with their kids. Lewis is the cheeky one. He's been here before, we're sure of it. Ross has the temper, the little fiery bit in him the same as his dad. Darren's quieter, a lot more shy, more like Barry.

They're close, though, probably thanks to the close spread of ages. If there's one thing I'd have changed about me and Barry it's the age gap. It would be nice to have a brother nearer my own age.

So, yes, I get a wee pang of jealousy when I think of the boys growing up as pals as well as brothers, going out together for a beer one day. I just hope they still like their old dad enough to let him tag along for half an hour. They could leave me in some pensioner's pub with a Guinness and a set of dominoes while they go off and do their thing.

Which only leaves one question unanswered.

What *does* happen next?

When I originally wrote this chapter, it looked like being the taxis or the bins or wherever they needed a willing pair of hands. But remember that thing I reckoned was always around the corner? Turned out it was.

The day before I drove up to sign my release papers from Raith, the phone went. It was Albion Rovers manager Jim Chapman, asking me if I could go in and help him out.

Money? Forget it.

Glamour? You're having a laugh.

Excitement? *Bucketloads.*

The chance to get back into a dressing-room, to be among the boys, to get out there on the training pitch and shape a team, to turn up on matchday and feel that thrill: all of it was too good to turn down. I couldn't have been happier had Real Madrid offered me a place in the dugout – and that's no lie.

Because football's football.

So, come the Saturday, there I was, on the touchline at Cliftonhill in the pouring rain, watching this bunch of raw kids going 1–0 up on Third Division promotion-chasers Cowdenbeath, and life was magnificent.

Somehow I doubt my brother would understand that sentiment – though I don't mean that as a dig. He's just never been there, never been round the rough edges of life. Didn't grow up in the tenements, didn't call a halt to the street kickabouts to flee sword-wielding gangs.

While I've been writing this book, some Rangers fans have gone back to the way they used to be with Barry. The team's not been good enough, he's taken the brunt of the stick, and I can see that it bothers him.

Sometimes I wish he'd step it up a bit, take the game by the scruff of the neck the way he did that day he dragged his team back into the Scottish Cup Final in 2002, or when he led them to the Treble the following season.

He's capable of carrying the fight to the opposition, beating men, playing one–twos, getting himself into shooting positions. He needs to be more selfish instead of always wanting to make others look good.

I watched him in Roy Keane's first Old Firm game, and even though it was at Ibrox, the Irishman imposed himself on the midfield far too much for my liking. I wanted our Barry to rattle his cage, but it never happened.

Then he came up against Villarreal in the Champions League, and the boy Riquelme gave a magnificent display of one-touch football. He didn't run about daft, but he made every pass count. He didn't cross balls into dangerous areas; he drilled them, like he was taking a shot. Barry could do that. He could do what Keane did for Celtic. He's got it all in his locker. I just hope against hope that he hasn't settled for his lot, that going to England then coming back so soon hasn't kicked the ambition out of him. I want him to look across that line at the Riquelmes and Keanes and tell them: 'This is *my* stage.'

But then, this is the crux of the problem with the modern game:

How do you make a rich man work?

Can you grab him and shake him and remind him what really matters? Or take all the money and possessions away and send him to live up a close in Barlanark for a fortnight?

It's not his fault that he's never run down to the corner shop for his £1 sandshoes, that he's never really had to do anything on the cheap. You can't hold someone's background against them.

Certainly the nation hasn't. It made my heart burst with pride when the news broke during the World Cup in Germany that my wee brother had been awarded an MBE, not just for his achievements on the football pitch but for his charity work off it.

A Ferguson. At the Palace. What a wonderful feeling for our entire family. What a reward for all the graft he's put in down the years, all the kicks and the criticism – and, yes, all the earache he's taken from me.

But early in the book I wrote about how I hoped that one day he'd take the decision to give it a go down the divisions – and, gong or no gong, I still dream of him doing it. Though that's a major difference between us. For me, there *was* no decision. It was no dream. It was reality. It just happened.

If I wanted to stay in the game, I had to go where I was wanted. That won't be the case for Barry. He won't have to worry about the real world. Once his days at the top are done, he'll be able to do pretty much whatever he fancies. It'd just be nice if he fancied a spell with the Accies or Alloa or some other club from a town where they stand and watch the Old Firm supporters' buses roll out every week. Call it giving something back, call it what you want. I just call it wanting to play on and on as long as you can. And that's the one downer about going into battle with the Rovers, the fact that I can't play, can't even demo drills in training.

It's never got any easier being around the boys when you can't take part, but you can't just disappear. That's why I started going back into training with Raith as soon as the crutches got thrown away. One night, wee Frank Connor appeared from nowhere. Now, I've already written how much I love the guy, but some of the younger boys didn't have a clue who he was. But in he ploughed, slaughtering them in the dressing-room. And they're going: 'Who's this auld fud?'

He was having a real go about players who pull fancy tricks and get nowhere. He said: 'In my day, you went up to the full-back, you dropped the shoulder and you gave it zimmy, zimmy, zimmy.'

I think he made the zimmy, zimmy, zimmy bit up. But you got the drift of what he meant. I like seeing Darren pull some of the stuff he sees Ronaldinho and Henry doing on the telly, but there's a time and a place. Nothing drives you dafter in a game than working your backside off to win possession and then finding that one of your mates tries to meg a guy for the sake of it and gives it away again.

Though who am I to talk? Rangers tried to slap that kind of stuff out of me from the age of 12, and I was still getting into bother for it under Souness. If I was fit now, I'd still be doing it, too. The fact that I can't is frustrating as hell. But one step at a time, eh?

We didn't end up beating Cowdenbeath that day. They were stronger and fitter and just that little bit savvier. They got level then pushed ahead and won 3–1. But I came off knowing what we could work on at training on Tuesday and Thursday for the following Saturday at Montrose. And after we drew 2–2 there, there was more to work on. There's always more.

Cliftonhill was the first rung on the coaching ladder for me as a former player. The chance to step up the second came right out of the blue.

I'd been doing the schools coaching with Gerry Britton for a while when he said one day: 'If I got a manager's job, would you come and work with me?'

'Sure,' I said, 'speak to me when it happens.'

So the end of the season comes with the Rovers, a lifetime's education in the politics of a complicated wee club crammed into a couple of months, and I'm working out ways of keeping the boys in training during the summer. Then the phone goes and it's a mate saying well done on the Stranraer job.

I've gone: 'What Stranraer job?'

And he says: 'It's all round the shop, you're going there as Gerry's No. 2.'

The football grapevine's incredible. Neil Watt had only just announced he was leaving, Gerry was still a signed player at Brechin City, and I was organising pre-season with Chappy, but the world seemed to know before me that I was on the move.

So I spoke to Gerry and he said, yes, he was talking to them, but nothing was sorted as he was still trying to arrange a pay-off from Brechin. If that didn't happen, he was going nowhere.

When I came back from a week away in Portugal with Carol, though, there it was in the papers: Gerry Britton is the new manager of Stranraer with Derek Ferguson as his No. 2.

First thought: 'Chappy. He'll be raging.'

As far as I was concerned, there had been nothing to tell him, because it was all just gossip. But now that it was in print, he'd have every right to think I'd been sneaking around behind his back. Thankfully, when I spoke to him there was no problem. He knew it was a chance for me to build on what I'd learned from him at Cliftonhill, and he wished me all the best.

So I phoned Gerry and told him we were on. Then I went down with him to meet the committee at Stair Park and another adventure began. As I write this, we're working like dogs to sign a whole new team, because they ended last season with only *one* player – striker Michael Moore – still under contract.

Stranraer have gone from Third to Second to First and now back to Second in the past three seasons, and they have established themselves as one of the strongest part-time clubs in the business. But a squad turnover that big in a matter of weeks means a whole new start for everyone.

It's as exciting as it is challenging as it is scary. But that's football – no, that's life. You never know what's around that next corner, but, whatever it is, you face it head on and see where you go next.

That's the way I am, and I'm willing to bet it's also the way dozens, even hundreds, of other career footballers have lived their lives through the years.

Has being that way made me a success or a failure? I'll leave other people to decide that. Do I care if they decide I am a failure? Not one bit.

On the very first page, I wrote about a life of two halves. I had a ball in the first, then it all went a bit black, but once things settled down I started having a ball again. Just in a different way.

And all I'm sure of is today is that I'm a man who's been lucky enough not to have to go out and work for a living until he was heading for middle age.

Life begins at 40?

Well, real life does . . .

ACKNOWLEDGEMENTS

There are so many people I need to thank, it's hard to know where to start. But here goes.

From my life in football, I owe so much to John Greig, to the late Stan Anderson, to all the staff at Ibrox – but particularly Tiny and Irene – to Alex Macdonald, Joe Jordan and Frank Connor, to John Lambie and to Roy McGregor.

Plus a special mention to Paul McStay, for being the first to let me coach kids, probably my first real job.

And in real life?

To my boys, Darren, Ross and Lewis, great sons who have brought so much joy into our lives.

To precious Lauren, taken so soon but always in our hearts.

To my mum Maureen and dad Archie, for always being there. They worked so hard to provide a decent life for Barry and me, and we couldn't have better role models.

To Millie and Danny, the best in-laws a man could have. They give us love and support, they help with the boys almost every day and Millie keeps me well fed.

To Barry, for being my wee brother and achieving all I ever dreamed he would. I love him, even when he's a crabbit so-and-so. And to Margaret and Kyle, Conor and Cara, all our love.

To my aunt Angela, her husband Brian Murphy and their son Kevin, just for being there and being who they are.

To Caroline, for being a great cousin and an invaluable support to Carol.

To Johnny and Tracy Bayne, trusted friends through thick and thin.

To Louise Bell, the best ITU nurse in the world, who loved our baby girl and has been so good to our boys.

To Robert McGregor, Mark Paterson and Jim Gillespie, terrific and trusted pals over so many years.

To Jenny Mudie, our neighbour who feeds the boys so many lunchtimes and looks after them at home time when we're not around.

To Granny Fergie, Gran and Granda Buchanan. God bless.

But most of all, to my darling Carol, my first girlfriend and my last. Without her, I would be nothing. With her, anything and everything is possible. I love you.